Real-Resumes for
Media, Newspaper, Broadcasting & Public Affairs Jobs...
including real resumes used to change careers
and transfer skills to other industries

Anne McKinney, Editor

PREP PUBLISHING

FAYETTEVILLE, NC

PREP Publishing
1110½ Hay Street
Fayetteville, NC 28305
(910) 483-6611

Library of Congress Cataloging-in-Publication Data

Real-resumes for media, newspaper, broadcasting & public affairs jobs : including
real resumes used to change careers and transfer skills to other industries / Anne
McKinney, editor.
   p. cm. -- (Real-resumes series)
  ISBN 978-1475093681; 1475093683
   1. Résumés (Employment) 2. Mass media. 3. Newspapers. 4. Broadcasting. 5. Career changes. I. McKinney, Anne, 1948- II. Series.

 HF5383 .R395873 2002
 650.14'2--dc21   2002027096
                           CIP

Printed in the United States of America

By PREP Publishing

Business and Career Series:

RESUMES AND COVER LETTERS THAT HAVE WORKED

RESUMES AND COVER LETTERS THAT HAVE WORKED FOR MILITARY PROFESSIONALS

GOVERNMENT JOB APPLICATIONS AND FEDERAL RESUMES

COVER LETTERS THAT BLOW DOORS OPEN

LETTERS FOR SPECIAL SITUATIONS

RESUMES AND COVER LETTERS FOR MANAGERS

REAL-RESUMES FOR COMPUTER JOBS

REAL-RESUMES FOR MEDICAL JOBS

REAL-RESUMES FOR FINANCIAL JOBS

REAL-RESUMES FOR TEACHERS

REAL-RESUMES FOR STUDENTS

REAL-RESUMES FOR CAREER CHANGERS

REAL-RESUMES FOR SALES

REAL ESSAYS FOR COLLEGE & GRADUATE SCHOOL

REAL-RESUMES FOR AVIATION & TRAVEL JOBS

REAL-RESUMES FOR POLICE, LAW ENFORCEMENT & SECURITY JOBS

REAL-RESUMES FOR SOCIAL WORK & COUNSELING JOBS

REAL-RESUMES FOR CONSTRUCTION JOBS

REAL-RESUMES FOR MANUFACTURING JOBS

REAL-RESUMES FOR RESTAURANT, FOOD SERVICE & HOTEL JOBS

REAL-RESUMES FOR MEDIA, NEWSPAPER, BROADCASTING & PUBLIC AFFAIRS JOBS

REAL-RESUMES FOR RETAILING, MODELING, FASHION & BEAUTY JOBS

REAL-RESUMES FOR HUMAN RESOURCES & PERSONNEL JOBS

Judeo-Christian Ethics Series:

SECOND TIME AROUND

BACK IN TIME

WHAT THE BIBLE SAYS ABOUT...Words that can lead to success and happiness

A GENTLE BREEZE FROM GOSSAMER WINGS

BIBLE STORIES FROM THE OLD TESTAMENT

Table of Contents

A WORD FROM THE EDITOR:
ABOUT THE REAL-RESUMES SERIES

Welcome to the Real-Resumes Series. The Real-Resumes Series is a series of books which have been developed based on the experiences of real job hunters and which target specialized fields or types of resumes. As the editor of the series, I have carefully selected resumes and cover letters (with names and other key data disguised, of course) which have been used successfully in real job hunts. That's what we mean by "Real-Resumes." What you see in this book are *real* resumes and cover letters which helped real people get ahead in their careers.

The Real-Resumes Series is based on the work of the country's oldest resume-preparation company known as PREP Resumes. If you would like a free information packet describing the company's resume preparation services, call 910-483-6611 or write to PREP at 1110½ Hay Street, Fayetteville, NC 28305. If you have a job hunting experience you would like to share with our staff at the Real-Resumes Series, please contact us at preppub@aol.com or visit our website at http://www.prep-pub.com.

We hope the superior samples will help you manage your current job campaign and your career so that you will find work aligned to your career interests.

The resumes and cover letters in this book are designed to be of most value to people already in a job hunt or contemplating a career change. If we could give you one word of advice about your career, here's what we would say: Manage your career and don't stumble from job to job in an incoherent pattern. Try to find work that interests you, and then identify prosperous industries which need work performed of the type you want to do. Learn early in your working life that a great resume and cover letter can blow doors open for you and help you maximize your salary.

Real-Resumes for
Media, Newspaper, Broadcasting & Public Affairs Jobs...
including real resumes used to change careers
and transfer skills to other industries

Anne McKinney, Editor

As the editor of this book, I would like to give you some tips on how to make the best use of the information you will find here. Because you are considering a career change, you already understand the concept of managing your career for maximum enjoyment and self-fulfillment. The purpose of this book is to provide expert tools and advice so that you *can* manage your career. Inside these pages you will find resumes and cover letters that will help you find not just a job but the type of work you want to do.

Introduction:
The Art of
Changing
Jobs...
and Finding
New Careers

Overview of the Book

Every resume and cover letter in this book actually worked. And most of the resumes and cover letters have common features: most are one-page, most are in the chronological format, and most resumes are accompanied by a companion cover letter. In this section you will find helpful advice about job hunting. Step One begins with a discussion of why employers prefer the one-page, chronological resume. In Step Two you are introduced to the direct approach and to the proper format for a cover letter. In Step Three you learn the 14 main reasons why job hunters are not offered the jobs they want, and you learn the six key areas employers focus on when they interview you. Step Four gives nuts-and-bolts advice on how to handle the interview, send a follow-up letter after an interview, and negotiate your salary.

The cover letter plays such a critical role in a career change. You will learn from the experts how to format your cover letters and you will see suggested language to use in particular career-change situations. It has been said that "A picture is worth a thousand words" and, for that reason, you will see numerous examples of effective cover letters used by real individuals to change fields, functions, and industries.

The most important part of the book is the Real-Resumes section. Some of the individuals whose resumes and cover letters you see spent a lengthy career in an industry they loved. Then there are resumes and cover letters of people who wanted a change but who probably wanted to remain in their industry. Many of you will be especially interested by the resumes and cover letters of individuals who knew they definitely wanted a career change but had no idea what they wanted to do next. Other resumes and cover letters show individuals who knew they wanted to change fields and had a pretty good idea of what they wanted to do next.

Whatever your field, and whatever your circumstances, you'll find resumes and cover letters that will "show you the ropes" in terms of successfully changing jobs and switching careers.

Before you proceed further, think about why you picked up this book.
- Are you dissatisfied with the type of work you are now doing?
- Would you like to change careers, change companies, or change industries?
- Are you satisfied with your industry but not with your niche or function within it?
- Do you want to transfer your skills to a new product or service?
- Even if you have excelled in your field, have you "had enough"? Would you like the stimulation of a new challenge?
- Are you aware of the importance of a great cover letter but unsure of how to write one?
- Are you preparing to launch a second career after retirement?
- Have you been downsized, or do you anticipate becoming a victim of downsizing?
- Do you need expert advice on how to plan and implement a job campaign that will open the maximum number of doors?
- Do you want to make sure you handle an interview to your maximum advantage?

- Would you like to master the techniques of negotiating salary and benefits?
- Do you want to learn the secrets and shortcuts of professional resume writers?

Using the Direct Approach

As you consider the possibility of a job hunt or career change, you need to be aware that most people end up having at least three distinctly different careers in their working lifetimes, and often those careers are different from each other. Yet people usually stumble through each job campaign, unsure of what they should be doing. Whether you find yourself voluntarily or unexpectedly in a job hunt, the direct approach is the job hunting strategy most likely to yield a full-time permanent job. The direct approach is an active, take-the-initiative style of job hunting in which you choose your next employer rather than relying on responding to ads, using employment agencies, or depending on other methods of finding jobs. You will learn how to use the direct approach in this book, and you will see that an effective cover letter is a critical ingredient in using the direct approach.

The "direct approach" is the style of job hunting most likely to yield the maximum number of job interviews.

Lack of Industry Experience Not a Major Barrier to Entering New Field

"Lack of experience" is often the last reason people are not offered jobs, according to the companies who do the hiring. If you are changing careers, you will be glad to learn that experienced professionals often are selling "potential" rather than experience in a job hunt. Companies look for personal qualities that they know tend to be present in their most effective professionals, such as communication skills, initiative, persistence, organizational and time management skills, and creativity. Frequently companies are trying to discover "personality type," "talent," "ability," "aptitude," and "potential" rather than seeking actual hands-on experience, so your resume should be designed to aggressively present your accomplishments. Attitude, enthusiasm, personality, and a track record of achievements in any type of work are the primary "indicators of success" which employers are seeking, and you will see numerous examples in this book of resumes written in an all-purpose fashion so that the professional can approach various industries and companies.

Using references in a skillful fashion in your job hunt will inspire confidence in prospective employers and help you "close the sale" after interviews.

The Art of Using References in a Job Hunt

You probably already know that you need to provide references during a job hunt, but you may not be sure of how and when to use references for maximum advantage. You can use references very creatively during a job hunt to call attention to your strengths and make yourself "stand out." Your references will rarely get you a job, no matter how impressive the names, but the way you use references can boost the employer's confidence in you and lead to a job offer in the least time.

You should ask from three to five people, including people who have supervised you, if you can use them as a reference during your job hunt. You may not be able to ask your current boss since your job hunt is probably confidential.

A common question in resume preparation is: "Do I need to put my references on my resume?" No, you don't. Even if you create a references page at the same time you prepare your resume, you don't need to mail, e-mail, or fax your references page with the resume and cover letter. Usually the potential employer is not interested in references until he meets you, so the earliest you need to have references ready is at the first interview. Obviously there are exceptions to this standard rule of thumb; sometimes an ad will ask you to send references with your first response. Wait until the employer requests references before providing them.

An excellent attention-getting technique is to take to the first interview not just a page of references (giving names, addresses, and telephone numbers) but an actual letter of reference written by someone who knows you well and who preferably has supervised or employed you. A professional way to close the first interview is to thank the interviewer, shake his or her hand, and then say you'd like to give him or her a copy of a letter of reference from a previous employer. Hopefully you already made a good impression during the interview, but you'll "close the sale" in a dynamic fashion if you leave a letter praising you and your accomplishments. For that reason, it's a good idea to ask supervisors during your final weeks in a job if they will provide you with a written letter of recommendation which you can use in future job hunts. Most employers will oblige, and you will have a letter that has a useful "shelf life" of many years. Such a letter often gives the prospective employer enough confidence in his opinion of you that he may forego checking out other references and decide to offer you the job on the spot or in the next few days.

With regard to references, it's best to provide the names and addresses of people who have supervised you or observed you in a work situation.

Whom should you ask to serve as references? References should be people who have known or supervised you in a professional, academic, or work situation. References with big titles, like school superintendent or congressman, are fine, but remind busy people when you get to the interview stage that they may be contacted soon. Make sure the busy official recognizes your name and has instant positive recall of you! If you're asked to provide references on a formal company application, you can simply transcribe names from your references list. In summary, follow this rule in using references: If you've got them, flaunt them! If you've obtained well-written letters of reference, make sure you find a polite way to push those references under the nose of the interviewer so he or she can hear someone other than you describing your strengths. Your references probably won't ever get you a job, but glowing letters of reference can give you credibility and visibility that can make you stand out among candidates with similar credentials and potential!

The approach taken by this book is to (1) help you master the proven best techniques of conducting a job hunt and (2) show you how to stand out in a job hunt through your resume, cover letter, interviewing skills, as well as the way in which you present your references and follow up on interviews. Now, the best way to "get in the mood" for writing your own resume and cover letter is to select samples from the Table of Contents that interest you and then read them. A great resume is a "photograph," usually on one page, of an individual. If you wish to seek professional advice in preparing your resume, you may contact one of the professional writers at Professional Resume & Employment Publishing (PREP) for a brief free consultation by calling 1-910-483-6611.

Part One: Some Advice About Your Job Hunt

What if you don't know what you want to do?

Your job hunt will be more comfortable if you can figure out what type of work you want to do. But you are not alone if you have no idea what you want to do next! You may have knowledge and skills in certain areas but want to get into another type of work. What *The Wall Street Journal* has discovered in its research on careers is that most of us end up having at least three distinctly different careers in our working lives; it seems that, even if we really like a particular kind of activity, twenty years of doing it is enough for most of us and we want to move on to something else!

That's why we strongly believe that you need to spend some time figuring out *what interests you* rather than taking an inventory of the skills you have. You may have skills that you simply don't want to use, but if you can build your career on the things that interest you, you will be more likely to be happy and satisfied in your job. Realize, too, that interests can change over time; the activities that interest you now may not be the ones that interested you years ago. For example, some professionals may decide that they've had enough of retail sales and want a job selling another product or service, even though they have earned a reputation for being an excellent retail manager. We strongly believe that interests rather than skills should be the determining factor in deciding what types of jobs you want to apply for and what directions you explore in your job hunt. Obviously one cannot be a lawyer without a law degree or a secretary without secretarial skills; but a professional can embark on a next career as a financial consultant, property manager, plant manager, production supervisor, retail manager, or other occupation if he/she has a strong interest in that type of work and can provide a resume that clearly demonstrates past excellent performance in *any* field and *potential* to excel in another field. As you will see later in this book, "lack of exact experience" is the last reason why people are turned down for the jobs they apply for.

How can you have a resume prepared if you don't know what you want to do?

You may be wondering how you can have a resume prepared if you don't know what you want to do next. The approach to resume writing which PREP, the country's oldest resume-preparation company, has used successfully for many years is to develop an "all-purpose" resume that translates your skills, experience, and accomplishments into language employers can understand. What most people need in a job hunt is a versatile resume that will allow them to apply for numerous types of jobs. For example, you may want to apply for a job in pharmaceutical sales but you may also want to have a resume that will be versatile enough for you to apply for jobs in the construction, financial services, or automotive industries.

Based on more than 20 years of serving job hunters, we at PREP have found that your best approach to job hunting is **an all-purpose resume** and **specific cover letters tailored to specific fields** rather than using the approach of trying to create different resumes for every job. If you are remaining in your field, you may not even need more than one "all-purpose" cover letter, although the cover letter rather than the resume is the place to communicate your interest in a narrow or specific field. An all-purpose resume and cover letter that translate your experience and accomplishments into plain English are the tools that will maximize the number of doors which open for you while permitting you to "fish" in the widest range of job areas.

Figure out what interests you and you will hold the key to a successful job hunt and working career. (And be prepared for your interests to change over time!)

"Lack of exact experience" is the last reason people are turned down for the jobs for which they apply.

Your resume will provide the script for your job interview.
When you get down to it, your resume has a simple job to do: Its purpose is to blow as many doors open as possible and to make as many people as possible want to meet you. So a well-written resume that really "sells" you is a key that will create opportunities for you in a job hunt.

This statistic explains why: The typical newspaper advertisement for a job opening receives more than 245 replies. And normally only 10 or 12 will be invited to an interview.

But here's another purpose of the resume: it provides the "script" the employer uses when he interviews you. If your resume has been written in such a way that your strengths and achievements are revealed, that's what you'll end up talking about at the job interview. Since the resume will govern what you get asked about at your interviews, you can't overestimate the importance of making sure your resume makes you look and sound as good as you are.

Your resume is the "script" for your job interviews. Make sure you put on your resume what you want to talk about or be asked about at the job interview.

So what is a "good" resume?
Very literally, your resume should motivate the person reading it to dial the phone number or e-mail the screen name you have put on the resume. When you are relocating, you should put a local phone number on your resume if your physical address is several states away; employers are more likely to dial a local telephone number than a long-distance number when they're looking for potential employees.

If you have a resume already, look at it objectively. Is it a limp, colorless "laundry list" of your job titles and duties? Or does it "paint a picture" of your skills, abilities, and accomplishments in a way that would make someone want to meet you? Can people understand what you're saying? If you are attempting to change fields or industries, can potential employers see that your skills and knowledge are transferable to other environments? For example, have you described accomplishments which reveal your problem-solving abilities or communication skills?

The one-page resume in chronological format is the format preferred by most employers.

How long should your resume be?
One page, maybe two. Usually only people in the academic community have a resume (which they usually call a *curriculum vitae*) longer than one or two pages. Remember that your resume is almost always accompanied by a cover letter, and a potential employer does not want to read more than two or three pages about a total stranger in order to decide if he wants to meet that person! Besides, don't forget that the more you tell someone about yourself, the more opportunity you are providing for the employer to screen you out at the "first-cut" stage. A resume should be concise and exciting and designed to make the reader want to meet you in person!

Should resumes be functional or chronological?
Employers almost always prefer a chronological resume; in other words, an employer will find a resume easier to read if it is immediately apparent what your current or most recent job is, what you did before that, and so forth, in reverse chronological order. A resume that goes back in detail for the last ten years of employment will generally satisfy the employer's curiosity about your background. Employment more than ten years old can be shown even more briefly in an "Other Experience" section at the end of your "Experience" section. Remember that your intention is not to tell everything you've done but to "hit the high points" and especially impress the employer with what you learned, contributed, or accomplished in each job you describe.

Once you get your resume, what do you do with it?

You will be using your resume to answer ads, as a tool to use in talking with friends and relatives about your job search, and, most importantly, in using the "direct approach" described in this book.

When you mail your resume, always send a "cover letter."

Never mail or fax your resume without a cover letter.

A "cover letter," sometimes called a "resume letter" or "letter of interest," is a letter that accompanies and introduces your resume. Your cover letter is a way of personalizing the resume by sending it to the specific person you think you might want to work for at each company. Your cover letter should contain a few highlights from your resume—just enough to make someone want to meet you. Cover letters should always be typed or word processed on a computer—never handwritten.

1. Learn the art of answering ads.

There is an "art," part of which can be learned, in using your "bestselling" resume to reply to advertisements.

Sometimes an exciting job lurks behind a boring ad that someone dictated in a hurry, so reply to any ad that interests you. Don't worry that you aren't "25 years old with an MBA" like the ad asks for. Employers will always make compromises in their requirements if they think you're the "best fit" overall.

What about ads that ask for "salary requirements?"

What if the ad you're answering asks for "salary requirements?" The first rule is to avoid committing yourself in writing at that point to a specific salary. You don't want to "lock yourself in."

There are two ways to handle the ad that asks for "salary requirements."

What if the ad asks for your "salary requirements?"

First, you can ignore that part of the ad and accompany your resume with a cover letter that focuses on "selling" you, your abilities, and even some of your philosophy about work or your field. You may include a sentence in your cover letter like this: "I can provide excellent personal and professional references at your request, and I would be delighted to share the private details of my salary history with you in person."

Second, if you feel you must give some kind of number, just state a range in your cover letter that includes your medical, dental, other benefits, and expected bonuses. You might state, for example, "My current compensation, including benefits and bonuses, is in the range of $30,000-$40,000."

Analyze the ad and "tailor" yourself to it.

When you're replying to ads, a finely tailored cover letter is an important tool in getting your resume noticed and read. On the next page is a cover letter which has been "tailored to fit" a specific ad. Notice the "art" used by PREP writers of analyzing the ad's main requirements and then writing the letter so that the person's background, work habits, and interests seem "tailor-made" to the company's needs. Use this cover letter as a model when you prepare your own reply to ads.

Date

Exact Name of Person
Exact Title
Exact Name of Company
Address
City, State, Zip

Dear Exact Name of Person: (or Dear Sir or Madam if answering a blind ad)

With the enclosed resume, I would like to express my interest in exploring employment opportunities with your organization. I am an experienced newspaper industry professional with an extensive management background.

I was recruited for my current position by Washington's oldest continuously owned newspaper. As Classified Manager, I took over a department which had lacked a manager for more than a year, and I have made numerous contributions to profitability and efficiency while managing 17 people. While training and motivating the staff, I provided leadership in selecting and then installing a new front-end system which replaced a nonWindows, nonmouse system and interfaced it with the billing system. I managed our simultaneous transition to a 50-inch web and new press installation..

In a previous position with *Spokane News*, I was promoted from Classified Director to Publisher by one of the nation's largest weekly alternative newspaper publishers, which owned eight publications in major U.S. cities. As the Publisher of *Summit Classifieds,* I managed 50 people while producing a weekly shopper in the Spokane area. Through my leadership, we revamped rates, increased revenues, and cut costs. As a result of the upgrades, 60% of the subsidiary was sold for the largest amount ever paid at that time for a product of its type in the U.S. Prior to my promotion to Publisher, I performed with distinction as Classified Director and, in that capacity, I managed 12 inside and outside sales professionals while upgrading the front-end and generating an additional $415,000 yearly by establishing a voice personals audiotext system.

Although I am held in the highest regard by my current employer and can provide outstanding references at the appropriate time, I have decided to selectively explore opportunities. In every community in which I have worked, in my spare time I have assumed leadership roles in local, state, and national organizations and have been a highly visible representative of the newspaper. In Seattle, I have been active in the United Way and other organizations. In Tacoma, I was chairman of numerous fund drives, membership drives, and professional organizations. In Spokane, I received numerous awards for my leadership in the Kidney Foundation.

If you can use a results-oriented and technologically knowledgeable newspaper person with a proven ability to translate new concepts into operating realities that positively impact the bottom line, I hope you will contact me to suggest a time when we might discuss your needs.

Sincerely,

Geraldine T. Epstein

Employers are trying to identify the individual who wants the job they are filling. Don't be afraid to express your enthusiasm in the cover letter!

2. Talk to friends and relatives.

Don't be shy about telling your friends and relatives the kind of job you're looking for. Looking for the job you want involves using your network of contacts, so tell people what you're looking for. They may be able to make introductions and help set up interviews.

About 25% of all interviews are set up through "who you know," so don't ignore this approach.

3. Finally, and most importantly, use the "direct approach."

More than 50% of all job interviews are set up by the "direct approach." That means you actually mail, e-mail, or fax a resume and a cover letter to a company you think might be interesting to work for.

The "direct approach" is a strategy in which you choose your next employer.

To whom do you write?

In general, you should write directly to the *exact name* of the person who would be hiring you: say, the vice-president of marketing or data processing. If you're in doubt about to whom to address the letter, address it to the president by name and he or she will make sure it gets forwarded to the right person within the company who has hiring authority in your area.

How do you find the names of potential employers?

You're not alone if you feel that the biggest problem in your job search is finding the right names at the companies you want to contact. But you can usually figure out the names of companies you want to approach by deciding first if your job hunt is primarily geography-driven or industry-driven.

In a **geography-driven job hunt,** you could select a list of, say, 50 companies you want to contact **by location** from the lists that the U.S. Chambers of Commerce publish yearly of their "major area employers." There are hundreds of local Chambers of Commerce across America, and most of them will have an 800 number which you can find through 1-800-555-1212. If you and your family think Atlanta, Dallas, Ft. Lauderdale, and Virginia Beach might be nice places to live, for example, you could contact the Chamber of Commerce in those cities and ask how you can obtain a copy of their list of major employers. Your nearest library will have the book which lists the addresses of all chambers.

In an **industry-driven job hunt,** and if you are willing to relocate, you will be identifying the companies which you find most attractive in the industry in which you want to work. When you select a list of companies to contact **by industry,** you can find the right person to write and the address of firms by industrial category in *Standard and Poor's, Moody's,* and other excellent books in public libraries. Many Web sites also provide contact information.

Many people feel it's a good investment to actually call the company to either find out or double-check the name of the person to whom they want to send a resume and cover letter. It's important to do as much as you feasibly can to assure that the letter gets to the right person in the company.

On-line research will be the best way for many people to locate organizations to which they wish to send their resume. It is outside the scope of this book to teach Internet research skills, but librarians are often useful in this area.

What's the correct way to follow up on a resume you send?

There is a polite way to be aggressively interested in a company during your job hunt. It is ideal to end the cover letter accompanying your resume by saying, "I hope you'll welcome my call next week when I try to arrange a brief meeting at your convenience to discuss your current and future needs and how I might serve them." Keep it low key, and just ask for a "brief meeting," not an interview. Employers want people who show a determined interest in working with them, so don't be shy about following up on the resume and cover letter you've mailed.

STEP THREE: Preparing for Interviews

But a resume and cover letter by themselves can't get you the job you want. You need to "prep" yourself before the interview. Step Three in your job campaign is "Preparing for Interviews." First, let's look at interviewing from the hiring organization's point of view.

What are the biggest "turnoffs" for potential employers?

One of the ways to help yourself perform well at an interview is to look at the main reasons why organizations *don't* hire the people they interview, according to those who do the interviewing.

Notice that "lack of appropriate background" (or lack of experience) is the *last* reason for not being offered the job.

The 14 Most Common Reasons Job Hunters Are Not Offered Jobs (according to the companies who do the interviewing and hiring):

1. Low level of accomplishment
2. Poor attitude, lack of self-confidence
3. Lack of goals/objectives
4. Lack of enthusiasm
5. Lack of interest in the company's business
6. Inability to sell or express yourself
7. Unrealistic salary demands
8. Poor appearance
9. Lack of maturity, no leadership potential
10. Lack of extracurricular activities
11. Lack of preparation for the interview, no knowledge about company
12. Objecting to travel
13. Excessive interest in security and benefits
14. Inappropriate background

It pays to be aware of the 14 most common pitfalls for job hunters.

Department of Labor studies have proven that smart, "prepared" job hunters can increase their beginning salary while getting a job in *half* the time it normally takes. (4½ months is the average national length of a job search.) Here, from PREP, are some questions that can prepare you to find a job faster.

Are you in the "right" frame of mind?

It seems unfair that we have to look for a job just when we're lowest in morale. Don't worry *too* much if you're nervous before interviews. You're supposed to be a little nervous, especially if the job means a lot to you. But the best way to kill unnecessary fears about job hunting is through 1) making sure you have a great resume and 2) preparing yourself for the interview. Here are three main areas you need to think about before each interview.

Do you know what the company does?

Don't walk into an interview giving the impression that, "If this is Tuesday, this must be General Motors."

Research the company before you go to interviews.

Find out before the interview what the company's main product or service is. Where is the company heading? Is it in a "growth" or declining industry? (Answers to these questions may influence whether or not you want to work there!)

Information about what the company does is in annual reports, in newspaper and magazine articles, and on the Internet. If you're not yet skilled at Internet research, just visit your nearest library and ask the reference librarian to guide you to printed materials on the company.

Do you know what you want to do for the company?

Before the interview, try to decide how you see yourself fitting into the company. Remember, "lack of exact background" the company wants is usually the last reason people are not offered jobs.

Understand before you go to each interview that the burden will be on you to "sell" the interviewer on why you're the best person for the job and the company.

How will you answer the critical interview questions?

Anticipate the questions you will be asked at the interview, and prepare your responses in advance.

Put yourself in the interviewer's position and think about the questions you're most likely to be asked. Here are some of the most commonly asked interview questions:

Q: *"What are your greatest strengths?"*

A: Don't say you've never thought about it! Go into an interview knowing the three main impressions you want to leave about yourself, such as "I'm hard-working, loyal, and an imaginative cost-cutter."

Q: *"What are your greatest weaknesses?"*

A: Don't confess that you're lazy or have trouble meeting deadlines! Confessing that you tend to be a "workaholic" or "tend to be a perfectionist and sometimes get frustrated when others don't share my high standards" will make your prospective employer see a "weakness" that he likes. Name a weakness that your interviewer will perceive as a strength.

Q: *"What are your long-range goals?"*

A: If you're interviewing with Microsoft, don't say you want to work for IBM in five years! Say your long-range goal is to be *with* the company, contributing to its goals and success.

Q: *"What motivates you to do your best work?"*

A: Don't get dollar signs in your eyes here! "A challenge" is not a bad answer, but it's a little cliched. Saying something like "troubleshooting" or "solving a tough problem" is more interesting and specific. Give an example if you can.

Q: "What do you know about this organization?"

A: Don't say you never heard of it until they asked you to the interview! Name an interesting, positive thing you learned about the company recently from your research. Remember, company executives can sometimes feel rather "maternal" about the company they serve. Don't get onto a negative area of the company if you can think of positive facts you can bring up. Of course, if you learned in your research that the company's sales seem to be taking a nose-dive, or that the company president is being prosecuted for taking bribes, you might politely ask your interviewer to tell you something that could help you better understand what you've been reading. Those are the kinds of company facts that can help you determine whether or not you want to work there.

Go to an interview prepared to tell the company why it should hire you.

Q: "Why should I hire you?"

A: "I'm unemployed and available" is the wrong answer here! Get back to your strengths and say that you believe the organization could benefit by a loyal, hard-working cost-cutter like yourself.

In conclusion, you should decide in advance, before you go to the interview, how you will answer each of these commonly asked questions. Have some practice interviews with a friend to role-play and build your confidence.

STEP FOUR: Handling the Interview and Negotiating Salary

Now you're ready for Step Four: actually handling the interview successfully and effectively. Remember, the purpose of an interview is to get a job offer.

A smile at an interview makes the employer perceive of you as intelligent!

Eight "do's" for the interview

According to leading U.S. companies, there are eight key areas in interviewing success. You can fail at an interview if you mishandle just one area.

1. **Do wear appropriate clothes.**

You can never go wrong by wearing a suit to an interview.

2. **Do be well groomed.**

Don't overlook the obvious things like having clean hair, clothes, and fingernails for the interview.

3. **Do give a firm handshake.**

You'll have to shake hands twice in most interviews: first, before you sit down, and second, when you leave the interview. Limp handshakes turn most people off.

4. **Do smile and show a sense of humor.**

Interviewers are looking for people who would be nice to work with, so don't be so somber that you don't smile. In fact, research shows that people who smile at interviews are perceived as more intelligent. So, smile!

5. **Do be enthusiastic.**

Employers say they are "turned off" by lifeless, unenthusiastic job hunters who show no special interest in that company. The best way to show some enthusiasm for the employer's operation is to find out about the business beforehand.

6. Do show you are flexible and adaptable.

An employer is looking for someone who can contribute to his organization in a flexible, adaptable way. No matter what skills and training you have, employers know every new employee must go through initiation and training on the company's turf. Certainly show pride in your past accomplishments in a specific, factual way ("I saved my last employer $50.00 a week by a new cost-cutting measure I developed"). But don't come across as though there's nothing about the job you couldn't easily handle.

7. Do ask intelligent questions about the employer's business.

An employer is hiring someone because of certain business needs. Show interest in those needs. Asking questions to get a better idea of the employer's needs will help you "stand out" from other candidates interviewing for the job.

8. Do "take charge" when the interviewer "falls down" on the job.

Go into every interview knowing the three or four points about yourself you want the interviewer to remember. And be prepared to take an active part in leading the discussion if the interviewer's "canned approach" does not permit you to display your "strong suit." You can't always depend on the interviewer's asking you the "right" questions so you can stress your strengths and accomplishments.

Employers are seeking people with good attitudes whom they can train and coach to do things their way.

An important "don't": Don't ask questions about salary or benefits at the first interview. Employers don't take warmly to people who look at their organization as just a place to satisfy salary and benefit needs. Don't risk making a negative impression by appearing greedy or self-serving. The place to discuss salary and benefits is normally at the second interview, and the employer will bring it up. Then you can ask questions without appearing excessively interested in what the organization can do for you.

Now...negotiating your salary

Even if an ad requests that you communicate your "salary requirement" or "salary history," you should avoid providing those numbers in your initial cover letter. You can usually say something like this: "I would be delighted to discuss the private details of my salary history with you in person."

Once you're at the interview, you must avoid even appearing *interested* in salary before you are offered the job. Make sure you've "sold" yourself before talking salary. First show you're the "best fit" for the employer and then you'll be in a stronger position from which to negotiate salary. **Never** bring up the subject of salary yourself. Employers say there's no way you can avoid looking greedy if you bring up the issue of salary and benefits before the company has identified you as its "best fit."

Don't appear excessively interested in salary and benefits at the interview.

Interviewers sometimes throw out a salary figure at the first interview to see if you'll accept it. You may not want to commit yourself if you think you will be able to negotiate a better deal later on. Get back to finding out more about the job. This lets the interviewer know you're interested primarily in the job and not the salary.

When the organization brings up salary, it may say something like this: "Well, Mary, we think you'd make a good candidate for this job. What kind of salary are we talking about?" You may not want to name a number here, either. Give the ball back to the interviewer. Act as though you hadn't given the subject of salary much thought and respond something like this: "Ah, Mr. Jones, I wonder if you'd be kind enough to tell me what salary you had in mind when you advertised the job?" Or ... "What is the range you have in mind?"

Don't worry, if the interviewer names a figure that you think is too low, you can say so without turning down the job or locking yourself into a rigid position. The point here is to negotiate for yourself as well as you can. You might reply to a number named by the interviewer that you think is low by saying something like this: "Well, Mr. Lee, the job interests me very much, and I think I'd certainly enjoy working with you. But, frankly, I was thinking of something a little higher than that." That leaves the ball in your interviewer's court again, and you haven't turned down the job either, in case it turns out that the interviewer can't increase the offer and you still want the job.

Salary negotiation can be tricky.

Last, send a follow-up letter.
Mail, e-mail, or fax a letter right after the interview telling your interviewer you enjoyed the meeting and are certain (if you are) that you are the "best fit" for the job. The people interviewing you will probably have an attitude described as either "professionally loyal" to their companies, or "maternal and proprietary" if the interviewer also owns the company. In either case, they are looking for people who want to work for *that* company in particular. The follow-up letter you send might be just the deciding factor in your favor if the employer is trying to choose between you and someone else. You will see an example of a follow-up letter on page 16.

A follow-up letter can help the employer choose between you and another qualified candidate.

A cover letter is an essential part of a career change.

A cover letter is an essential part of a job hunt or career change.
Many people are aware of the importance of having a great resume, but most people in a job hunt don't realize just how important a cover letter can be. The purpose of the cover letter, sometimes called a **"letter of interest,"** is to introduce your resume to prospective employers. The cover letter is often the critical ingredient in a job hunt because the cover letter allows you to say a lot of things that just don't "fit" on the resume. For example, you can emphasize your commitment to a new field and stress your related talents. The cover letter also gives you a chance to stress outstanding character and personal values. On the next two pages you will see examples of very effective cover letters.

Please do not attempt to implement a career change without a cover letter such as the ones you see in Part Two of this book. A cover letter is the first impression of you, and you can influence the way an employer views you by the language and style of your letter.

Special help for those in career change
We want to emphasize again that, especially in a career change, the cover letter is very important and can help you "build a bridge" to a new career. A creative and appealing cover letter can begin the process of encouraging the potential employer to imagine you in an industry other than the one in which you have worked.

As a special help to those in career change, there are resumes and cover letters included in this book which show valuable techniques and tips you should use when changing fields or industries. The resumes and cover letters of career changers are identified in the table of contents as "Career Change" and you will see the "Career Change" label on cover letters in Part Two where the individuals are changing careers.

Date

**Addressing the Cover
Letter:** Get the exact
name of the person to
whom you are writing. This
makes your approach
personal.

Exact Name of Person
Exact Title of Person
Company Name
Address
City, State Zip

Dear Sir or Madam:

First Paragraph: This
explains why you are
writing.

    With the enclosed resume, I would like to make you aware of my strong desire to become a part of your organization.

Second Paragraph: You
have a chance to talk
about whatever you feel is
your most distinguishing
feature.

    As you will see from my resume, I recently earned my Bachelor of Science in Journalism degree at the University of North Carolina at Chapel Hill. Since it has always been my childhood dream to become a newspaper reporter, my college graduation was an especially meaningful event in my life. And I was thrilled to get my degree from the university that schooled Charles Kuralt and other great writers.

Third Paragraph: You
bring up your next most
distinguishing qualities and
try to
sell yourself.

    While earning my college degree, I completed internships with major newspapers and magazines, and for four years I successfully assumed all the duties of a photojournalist for my college newspaper "The Daily Tar Heel." During those internships, under the guidance of experienced newspaper and magazine reporters, I wrote stories about local sports, politics, and current events.

Fourth Paragraph: Here
you have another
opportunity to reveal
qualities or achievements
which will impress your
future employer.

    In summer jobs during high school and while earning my college degree, I worked in all aspects of the newspaper business. Even as a youth, I became one of my hometown newspaper's youngest-ever carriers, and I handled the responsibilities of delivering papers to a newspaper route with absolute reliability. It was during my youth that I decided that I one day wanted to handle the responsibility for the writing of the newspaper columns inside the papers I delivered.

Final Paragraph: She
asks the employer to
contact her. Make sure
your reader knows what
the "next step" is.

    If you can use a highly motivated young professional with unlimited personal initiative as well as strong personal qualities of dependability and trustworthiness, I hope you will contact me to suggest a time when we might meet to discuss your needs. I can provide excellent personal and professional references, and I am eager to apply my natural creativity and skills in journalism to benefit your publication.

Sincerely,

**Alternate Final
Paragraph:** It's more
aggressive (but not too
aggressive) to let the
employer know that you
will be calling him or her.
Don't be afraid to be
persistent. Employers are
looking for people who
know what they want to
do.

Melanie Thompson

Alternate final paragraph:
    I hope you will welcome my call soon when I contact you to try to arrange a brief meeting to discuss your needs and how my talents might help you. I appreciate whatever time you could give me in the process of exploring your needs.

Date

Exact Name of Person
Title or Position
Name of Company
Address (number and street)
Address (city, state, and zip)

Dear Exact Name of Person: (or Dear Sir or Madam if answering a blind ad)

I would appreciate an opportunity to talk with you soon about how I could contribute to your organization through my skills as a Broadcasting Sales Manager.

You will see from my resume that I began working when I was 16 years old while in high school. I became a skilled sales person while working for numerous retailers during the summer, and then in my senior year of high school I had an opportunity to become involved in commissioned sales for radio advertising. I had an opportunity to learn from veteran professionals, and with their help I sold the most radio advertising during the month of July of any single sales professional ever. That summer cemented my desire to make a career out of broadcast sales.

Most recently I have worked as a Broadcast Sales Manager for WKFT-86.5 FM. I am well known for my ability to establish effective working relationships, and my customers know that I treat their business needs as though their needs were my own. I am held in the highest regard by my current employer and can provide outstanding references at the appropriate time. I have become skilled at hiring, training, and supervising others, and I have developed numerous novices into award-winning sales professionals.

I have, however, decided to explore career opportunities in a larger market. I am single and can relocate and travel as extensively as your needs require.

If you can use a self-starter who could rapidly become a valuable part of your organization, I hope you will contact me to suggest a time when we might meet to discuss your needs and how I might serve them. I can provide outstanding references.

Sincerely,

Lonnie Patton

cc: Thomas Crane

Date

Exact Name of Person
Title or Position
Name of Company
Address (number and street)
Address (city, state, and zip)

Follow-up Letter

Dear Exact Name:

A great follow-up letter can motivate the employer to make the job offer, and the salary offer may be influenced by the style and tone of your follow-up letter, too!

    I am writing to express my appreciation for the time you spent with me on 9 December, and I want to let you know that I am sincerely interested in the position of Controller which you described.

    I feel confident that I could skillfully interact with your 60-person work force in order to obtain the information we need to assure expert controllership of your diversified interests, and I would cheerfully travel as your needs require. I want you to know, too, that I would not consider relocating to Salt Lake City to be a hardship! It is certainly one of the most beautiful areas I have ever seen.

    As you described to me what you are looking for in a controller, I had a sense of "déjà vu" because my current boss was in a similar position when I went to work for him. He needed someone to come in and be his "right arm" and take on an increasing amount of his management responsibilities so that he could be freed up to do other things. I have played a key role in the growth and profitability of his multi-unit business, and he has come to depend on my sound financial and business advice as much as my day-to-day management skills. Since Christmas is the busiest time of the year in the restaurant business, I feel that I could not leave him during that time. I could certainly make myself available by mid-January.

    It would be a pleasure to work for a successful individual such as yourself, and I feel I could contribute significantly to your construction business not only through my accounting and business background but also through my strong qualities of loyalty, reliability, and trustworthiness. I am confident that I could learn Quick Books rapidly, and I would welcome being trained to do things your way.

Yours sincerely,

Jacob Evangelisto

In this section, you will find resumes and cover letters of media, newspaper, broadcasting, and public affairs professionals—and of people who want to work in those fields. How do they differ from other job hunters? Why should there be a book dedicated to people seeking jobs in these areas? Based on more than 20 years of experience in working with job hunters, this editor is convinced that resumes and cover letters which "speak the lingo" of the field you wish to enter will communicate more effectively than language which is not industry specific. This book is designed to help people (1) who are seeking to prepare their own resumes and (2) who wish to use as models "real" resumes of individuals who have successfully launched careers in the media, newspaper, broadcasting, and public affairs fields or who have advanced in the field. You will see a wide range of experience levels reflected in the resumes in this book. Some of the resumes and cover letters were used by individuals seeking to enter the field; others were used successfully by senior professionals to advance in the field.

Newcomers to an industry sometimes have advantages over more experienced professionals. In a job hunt, junior professionals can have an advantage over their more experienced counterparts. Prospective employers often view the less experienced workers as "more trainable" and "more coachable" than their seniors. This means that the mature professional who has already excelled in a first career can, with credibility, "change careers" and transfer skills to other industries.

Newcomers to the field may have disadvantages compared to their seniors. Almost by definition, the inexperienced professional—the young person who has recently earned a college degree, or the individual who has recently received certifications respected by the industry—is less tested and less experienced than senior managers, so the resume and cover letter of the inexperienced professional may often have to "sell" his or her potential to do something he or she has never done before. Lack of experience in the field she wants to enter can be a stumbling block to the junior manager, but remember that many employers believe that someone who has excelled in anything— academics, for example—can excel in many other fields.

Some advice to inexperienced professionals...
If senior professionals could give junior professionals a piece of advice about careers, here's what they would say: Manage your career and don't stumble from job to job in an incoherent pattern. Try to find work that interests you, and then identify prosperous industries which need work performed of the type you want to do. Learn early in your working life that a great resume and cover letter can blow doors open for you and help you maximize your salary.

Media, newspaper, broadcasting, and public affairs folks might be said to "talk funny." They talk in lingo specific to their field, and you will find helpful examples throughout this book.

Date

Exact Name of Person
Exact Title
Exact Name of Company
Address
City, State, Zip

ACCOUNT EXECUTIVE

for an advertising agency. This individual is seeking her first "real" job in the media field.

Dear Exact Name of Person: (or Dear Sir or Madam if answering a blind ad):

With the enclosed resume, I would like to make you aware of my background of excellence in advertising sales, marketing, management, and customer service, as well as of the strong communication, planning, and organizational skills that I could put to work for your organization.

While completing my Bachelor of Science in Communications with a concentration in Advertising, I played a key role in the creation of a complete advertising campaign for one of the largest consumer electronics corporations in the world. In the process of completing this project, our team conducted market research, created focus groups, developed creative strategies, and produced positioning and market statements for the product.

During my advertising internship, I assisted in the creation, development, and implementation of an effective fund-raising event for a nonprofit organization. I performed outside sales of advertising space in the event's promotional material while soliciting donations for the charity auction. In my first job after graduating from college, I met or exceeded all sales and production goals while calling on established accounts to renew their commitment to purchase ad space in a direct mail brochure.

Although I have excelled in my current position, I am in the process of seeking other employment because the company is going out of business due to the weak economy. It is my strong desire to find a position with a public relations or advertising agency where my education and outgoing personality can be of value.

If you can use an articulate young professional whose abilities have been proven in a variety of challenging sales and customer service environments, I hope you will welcome my call soon so that we may arrange a brief meeting to discuss your goals and how my background might serve your needs. I can provide outstanding references at the appropriate time.

Sincerely,

Jodi Madeline Harding

JODI MADELINE HARDING

1110½ Hay Street, Fayetteville, NC 28305 • preppub@aol.com • (910) 483-6611

OBJECTIVE
To benefit an organization that can use an articulate young professional with exceptional communication, organizational, and planning skills who offers a versatile background in sales, management, public relations, customer service, and training.

EDUCATION
Bachelor of Science in **Communication**, with a minor in **Psychology** and a concentration in **Advertising**, San Diego State University, San Diego, CA, 2003.
Project: Was a key member of a team that developed a complete advertising campaign for the Sony X-Box video game console.
- Conducted market research, created focus groups, and produced product positioning and marketing statements.
- Prepared a detailed media plan and produced an effective slide show presentation using Microsoft PowerPoint.

Completed one year of college studies in Liberal Arts at the Heartland Community College in Bloomington, IN before transferring to San Diego State University.

AFFILIATIONS
Member, Public Relations Student Society of America (PRSSA), 2002.
- Served on the Agency Committee and organized Internship Interview Week 2002; attended and was invited to speak at the PRSSA National Conference in Los Angeles, CA, October, 2002.
- Honored for achieving the highest advertising sales for the Society's *"Previews"* magazine.

COMPUTERS
Familiar with many of the most popular computer operating systems and software, including Windows; Microsoft Word, PowerPoint, and Excel; Adobe Pagemaker and Photoshop; QuarkXpress; electronic mail; and the Internet.

EXPERIENCE
ACCOUNT EXECUTIVE. Hayward Designs, Chicago, IL (2003-present). In my first job out of college, personally contacted established accounts via telephone to obtain renewals of existing advertisements in a brochure produced by this local advertising sales agency.
- Met or exceeded all sales and production goals while working under tight deadlines; honed my ability to persuasively present products and overcome customer objectives.
- I am seeking other employment because the company is going out of business due to the weak economy and poor cash flow. I can provide outstanding references.

ACCOUNT EXECUTIVE. Shoreline Help Center, San Diego, CA (2002). In an Advertising Sales internship with this local nonprofit organization, sold advertising space in a brochure for a charity fund-raising event sponsored by the Help Center that eventually reached 14,000 people.
- Assisted in the creation and implementation of the Southern California Bed Race fund-raiser from concept development, through the planning and organization stages, to completion.
- Performed outside sales, soliciting local business and private individuals both over the phone and in person to acquire items for the fund-raiser's auction.

TRAINER and **HOSTESS.** Robertson's Inn, San Diego, CA (1999-02). While completing my Bachelor's degree, applied my organizational skills and restaurant expertise, assisting an inexperienced management staff in all aspects of operating this busy local establishment.

PERSONAL
Excellent personal and professional references upon request, as is a portfolio of my work.

Date

Exact Name of Person
Title or Position
Name of Company
Address (no., street)
Address (city, state, zip)

ACCOUNT EXECUTIVE
for an FM radio station

Dear Exact Name of Person: (or Dear Sir or Madam if answering a blind ad)

I am sending the enclosed resume to make you aware of my interest in exploring opportunities with your organization. I am a creative young professional with well-developed written and oral communication skills, a proven ability to handle high-pressure environments, and a flair for public relations, along with plenty of energy and enthusiasm.

Currently, I am an Account Executive with WXLZ 99.9 FM in Tacoma, Washington. In this position I have discovered how much I enjoy developing creative and informative advertising copy while also planning promotional events and selling advertising air time to direct and agency accounts. I took over a "dead" account list upon starting and have surpassed all sales goals set monthly by the general and sales managers. I also successfully adapted to the shifting client base when the station transitioned from an oldies format to CHR (contemporary hits radio).

While working in a variety of retail sales positions to finance my B.A. degree, I learned skills that, coupled with my education, groomed me for my first job out of college with a high-end interior design corporation based in Los Angeles. I dealt with major corporate accounts in the fabric division which maintained annual sales of $2,000,000. I communicated with a variety of people in this position ranging from the company president, to major corporate clients such as Polo/Ralph Lauren, to well-known celebrities including Elizabeth Taylor.

Through my combined experience and education, as well as proven corporate success, I feel that I would be a valuable asset to your organization.

I hope you will welcome my call soon to arrange a brief meeting at your convenience to discuss your current and future needs and how I might serve them. Thank you in advance for your time.

Sincerely yours,

Brooke L. Smith

Alternate last paragraph:
I hope you will call or write soon to suggest a time convenient for us to meet and discuss your current and future needs and how I might serve them. Thank you in advance for your time.

BROOKE LYNN SMITH

1110½ Hay Street, Fayetteville, NC 28305 • preppub@aol.com • (910) 483-6611

OBJECTIVE
To benefit an organization that can use a creative young professional with well-developed written and oral communication skills, a proven ability to handle high-pressure environments, and a flair for public relations, along with energy and enthusiasm.

EDUCATION
Bachelor of Arts degree, Western Washington University, Bellingham, WA, 2001.
- Majored in Political Science with a concentration in History; completed coursework in:
  Advanced Expository Writing   Business Law   Creative Writing
  Public Speaking   Economics   Public Finance

EXPERIENCE
ACCOUNT EXECUTIVE. WXLZ 99.9 FM, Standard Media, Tacoma, WA (2003-present). Sell advertising air time to direct and agency accounts while writing creative copy, developing advertising materials, and planning promotional events.
- Took over a "dead" account list with only two active accounts and aggressively developed new business; now service a large customer base and have surpassed all sales goals set monthly by the general manager and sales manager.
- Compile media statistical reports on the local listening audience.
- Successfully adapted to the shifting client base as the station changed from an oldies format to CHR (contemporary hits radio).
- Coordinate with station executives and other personnel such as programmers, traffic managers, disk jockeys, and engineers on a daily basis.
- Discovered my "knack" for developing creative and informative advertising copy.

CUSTOMER SERVICE REPRESENTATIVE. Exclusive Interiors, Los Angeles, CA (2001-02). Provided customer service while expediting purchase orders and sales transactions involving fabric, wall coverings, furniture, and accessories for this major corporation with 15 showrooms, 17 fabric companies, two mills, and one printing plant nationwide.
- Communicated with the company president, showroom manager, corporate clients such as Polo/Ralph Lauren, Macy's, and Nordstroms', and well-known celebrities including Elizabeth Taylor, Cameron Diaz, and Meg Ryan.
- For the fabric division, maintained support operations for annual sales of $2,000,000.
- Facilitated the release of fabric for *The Wedding Planner* motion picture account; sold over $60,000 worth of material. Satisfied one disappointed client by replacing $5,000 in flawed imported Indian fabric with fabric from the company's own line.

Financed my college education through the following often simultaneous positions:
SALES ASSOCIATE. University Pride, Bellingham, WA (2000-2001). Refine my knowledge of merchandising and marketing techniques and day-to-day retail operations in this shop selling clothing and college memorabilia.
- Monitored inventory and product flow to ensure proper stock levels.
- Performed accounting duties and checked creditworthiness of customers.

SALES REPRESENTATIVE. Express International, Bellingham, WA (1999-00). For this store selling women's clothing and accessories, averaged $2,000 in daily sales.
- Ranked as the "number two" sales representative during a special promotion.

PERSONAL
Am a highly-motivated and well-organized professional who enjoys interacting with a variety of individuals. Relish the opportunity to transform new ideas into working realities. Have knowledge of Windows, Microsoft operating systems, and Word software. Am a member of the Tacoma Ad Club and the local Chamber of Commerce.

Date

Exact Name of Person
Title or Position
Name of Company
Address (no., street)
Address (city, state, zip)

ACCOUNT EXECUTIVE
for a major market radio
station

Dear Exact Name of Person: (or Dear Sir or Madam if answering a blind ad)

Can you use a high-energy sales professional with a proven "track record" of success along with the drive and determination to always do her best?

In my current position, I have excelled in a dual role of motivating and managing account executives and maintaining a high level of personal sales at a regional radio station. Previously, as an account executive, I was "Top Sales Professional of the Month" almost every month. My skills and drive have allowed me to exceed goals while becoming the company's first account executive to surpass ever-increasing sales goals of $20,000, followed by $25,000, and the current $30,000 level.

As a very "people-oriented" individual, I have been described as performing with "the professionalism of someone many years her senior" and as possessing a degree of "empathy which gives her the edge" when dealing with staff members as well as clients and potential clients.

Through my experience in a radio station which has survived the stress of making two complete format changes and undergoing a change in ownership, all within a three-and-a-half year period, I feel that I have proven my adaptability and flexibility.

I hope you will welcome my call soon to arrange a brief meeting at your convenience to discuss your current and future needs and how I might serve them. Thank you in advance for your time.

Sincerely yours,

Linda L. Miller

Alternate last paragraph:
I hope you will call or write soon to suggest a time convenient for us to meet and discuss your current and future needs and how I might serve them. Thank you in advance for your time.

LINDA LOUISE MILLER

1110½ Hay Street, Fayetteville, NC 28305   •   preppub@aol.com   •   (910) 483-6611

OBJECTIVE

To apply my proven "track record" of success in sales and marketing to an organization that can use a creative professional with strong communication and motivational skills and the ability to get the job done under tight deadlines and rapidly changing circumstances.

EXPERIENCE

Earned the respect of upper-level management while producing excellent results during a period which included an ownership change and two format changes, Jones Media Group and Pennsylvania Broadcasting Corp., Pittsburgh, Villanova, and Johnstown, PA:

2003-present: ACCOUNT EXECUTIVE. WMAX 100 FM, Pittsburgh. Transferred to a larger market to maintain account base and recruit new business.

2002-03: LOCAL SALES MANAGER. WJMF 99.3 FM, Villanova. Was promoted to oversee a staff of four account executives and a traffic manager, motivating and leading this team to reach corporate sales goals while maintaining my own high level of sales.
- Consistently maintained a minimum of 30% of total station revenue on my own.
- Applied my creativity and marketing talents to prepare sales packages and materials while working closely with community leaders and preparing public service events.
- Handled the General Sales Manager's job during an extended period when the position was vacant, thereby justifying upper management's faith in my decision-making and managerial skills.
- Interviewed prospective employees and made hiring decisions.
- Worked closely with home office personnel to coordinate the details of an early 2003 promotion tied in with a change from an "hot adult contemporary" to "oldies" format.
- Analyzed data and participated in making decisions on revenue and expense changes caused by the shift in audience due to the new format.

Experience with the Pennsylvania Broadcasting Corp:
2000-02: ACCOUNT EXECUTIVE. WJMF 99.3 FM, Villanova. Further refined my sales and promotion planning techniques while creating retail store and service business advertising campaigns and promotions.
- Took over an unproductive account list and quickly transformed it into the station's highest producer as well as the source of the station's largest amount of new business.
- Exceeded corporate goals and budgets during a period of turmoil caused by the uncertainty of working under changing ownership.
- Was honored as **"Top Sales Professional of the Month"** at least every other month.

1999-00: ACCOUNT EXECUTIVE. WSML 97.7 FM, Johnstown. Was hired to assist in developing sales and promotions during a period of transition caused by format change.
- Learned to maintain my concentration on the job at hand during stressful transition periods as the station changed from a "gospel" to an "hot adult contemporary" format.
- Became an asset by "pitching in" during peak work loads.

EDUCATION

B.S., Business Management, The University of Scranton, Scranton, PA, 1999.
- Excelled in specialized course work including the following:

  | human resource management | commercial law | marketing |
  | organizational behavior | industrial relations | effective sales techniques |

PERSONAL

Am a highly creative quick thinker. Can contribute a positive attitude and a true concern for others. Offer knowledge of computer operations; use Word software. Will relocate.

Date

Exact Name of Person
Title or Position
Name of Company
Address (no., street)
Address (city, state, zip)

ACCOUNT EXECUTIVE

for a New Mexico radio
station

Dear Exact Name of Person: (or Dear Sir or Madam if answering a blind ad)

Can you use an experienced sales/marketing professional with proven leadership abilities along with a "track record" of accomplishments related to developing new business, servicing existing accounts, and identifying new market opportunities?

Currently, I am Senior Account Executive with WMRD-FM in Albuquerque, New Mexico. I have found my drive and skills to be highly suited to the position and have enjoyed consistent success with the station. In one year I generated a **600%** increase in revenue and was named Salesperson of the Year. I have completed qualifications for and was awarded the title of Certified Radio Marketing Consultant, an honor given to only 5% of people in the radio industry.

Previously, I was employed with the Federal Communications Commission in Washington, D.C., a position I applied for even though I had less formal training than the usual applicant. I was hired based on my success in telecommunications courses and my natural adeptness with setting up communications systems. I enjoyed a large amount of success during the time that I was employed with the FCC but ultimately left to pursue my interest in the sales and marketing aspect of the radio business.

While working full time in my current job I have also earned a Bachelor of Science degree in Business Administration by attending school at night. It is this sort of hard work and dedication coupled with my impressive track record and proven leadership abilities that I can offer your organization.

I hope you will welcome my call soon to arrange a brief meeting at your convenience to discuss your current and future needs and how I might serve them. Thank you in advance for your time.

Sincerely yours,

Martin A. Padmos

Alternate last paragraph:
I hope you will call or write soon to suggest a time convenient for us to meet and discuss your current and future needs and how I might serve them. Thank you in advance for your time.

MARTIN ANDREW PADMOS

1110½ Hay Street, Fayetteville, NC 28305   •   preppub@aol.com   •   (910) 483-6611

OBJECTIVE   To benefit an organization that can use an experienced sales/marketing professional with proven leadership abilities along with a "track record" of accomplishments related to developing new business, servicing accounts, and identifying new market opportunities.

EDUCATION   **Bachelor of Science B.S.** degree in Business Administration, University of New Mexico, Albuquerque, NM, 2003.
- Completed this degree at night while excelling in a full-time job.
- Was elected to numerous leadership positions in the Student Government Association.

COMPUTERS   Skilled with Windows, Word, Excel; Adobe Illustrator, Quark Xpress, Calendar Creator Plus.

EXPERIENCE   **SENIOR ACCOUNT EXECUTIVE.** WMRD 105.5 FM, Albuquerque, NM (2001-present). Am continually developing new business to increase the station's revenue while servicing existing accounts and recommending solutions for "problem" accounts.
- Began with WMRD-FM as an entry-level Account Executive, and was promoted to Senior Account Executive based on my exceptional attitude and superior results.
- Generated a 600% increase in revenue in one year! Was named **Salesperson of the Year**, 2002.
- Was responsible for $132,000 in billings in my first year and for $432,000 in 2003!
- Completed qualifications for and was awarded the title of Certified Radio Marketing Consultant; was selected for this honor given to only 5% of people in the radio industry.
- Am the General Sales Manager's "right arm" in developing the sales marketing plan.
- Developed a Corporate Training Guide now used by the company's new employees.

In four years, rapidly climbed the promotions ladder with the Federal Communications Commissions (FCC) department, Washington, D.C.:
1999-01: COMMUNICATIONS DIRECTOR. Led my department to be named best in the agency for two consecutive years and personally received consistent commendations; managed 15 people and multimillion-dollar assets while analyzing requirements, planning projects, and coordinating team activities in the establishment of communications networks.
- Was handpicked for this job normally held by those with much more formal experience.

1998-99: COMMUNICATIONS SUPERVISOR. Was officially commended and, as a result, promoted to the above position, for my achievements in planning, coordinating, and managing projects to construct communications facilities and to install area networks and related equipment; analyzed illustrative graphs and overlays for project requirements.

1997-98: COMMUNICATIONS SPECIALIST. (Received numerous letters of appreciation from top executives for my exceptional performance in installing and validating communications networks as well as making sure all FCC guidelines were strictly followed.

SALES REPRESENTATIVE. Black Hills Jewelers, Brookings, SD (1990-97). Began working in this job when I was 15 years old.
- *Advertising*: Learned to develop advertisements and sales campaigns.
- *Finance*: Conducted investigations into accounts receivable, and examined reports from financial institutions on current contracts; prepared contracts to establish new accounts.

PERSONAL   Have a talent, which has been refined by experience, for motivating others and inspiring them to work as a team in achieving high goals. Believe in "leadership by example."

Date

Exact Name of Person
Title or Position
Name of Company
Address (no., street)
Address (city, state, zip)

ACCOUNT EXECUTIVE
for a radio broadcast group

Dear Exact Name of Person: (or Dear Sir or Madam if answering a blind ad)

With the enclosed resume I'd like to make you aware of my interest in exploring employment opportunities with your organization. I am an experienced and creative radio account executive with strong communication skills that have been refined in a variety of previous positions in teaching, coaching, sales, and management.

I have enjoyed exceptional success with the Matthews Broadcast Group as an Account Executive, including being named the President Club winner for 18 straight months in a row, an award based on the percentage above quota, the unit rate, number of new clients, and profitability factors. In addition to my responsibilities as Account Executive, I also function as the Website Administrator for two separate station affiliate websites.

Prior to joining the communications industry, I excelled as a teacher and coach in the Golden County School System. I honed my leadership and communications skills as well as establishing a reputation of success in feats such as increasing the track team membership by over 500% in 2 years, and also leading the team from last place to second place. In my substitute teaching positions, I taught all grades from K-12 and virtually every subject ranging from World History, to Band, to P.E.

With this kind of "track record" in versatility and my strong leadership skills and enthusiasm, I feel I would be an ideal choice for your organization. I hope you will welcome my call soon to arrange a brief meeting at your convenience to discuss your current and future needs and how I might serve them. Thank you in advance for your time.

Sincerely yours,

Cameron R. Lemaster

Alternate last paragraph:
I hope you will call or write soon to suggest a time convenient for us to meet and discuss your current and future needs and how I might serve them. Thank you in advance for your time.

CAMERON ROBERT LEMASTER

1110½ Hay Street, Fayetteville, NC 28305 • preppub@aol.com • (910) 483-6611

OBJECTIVE

To contribute to an organization that can use an experienced and creative radio account executive with strong communication skills that have been refined in previous positions in teaching, coaching, sales, and management.

COMPUTERS

Experienced with Windows, Word, Publisher, Outlook, PowerPoint, Pagemaker, Dreamweaver, Illustrator, PhotoShop, and many other programs/software.

CERTIFICATION

Certified Radio Marketing Consultant (CRMC).

EDUCATION

Earned **Bachelor of Science in History**, University of Colorado at Boulder, 1999.
Completed **Associate of Arts in General Studies**, University of Colorado at Boulder, 1997.
Effective Teacher Training, Pikes Peak Community College, Colorado Springs, CO, 1999.

EXPERIENCE

ACCOUNT EXECUTIVE. Matthews Broadcast Group, Inc., Boulder, CO (2002-present). Have excelled through applying my strong communication and problem-solving skills.

- Was the Matthews Broadcast President Club winner for 18 straight months in a row.
- Was the WZFC overall **President Club winner** in 2003 and was ranked second overall in the entire company; this award is based on the percentage above quota, the unit rate, number of new clients, and profitability factors.
- In addition to my responsibilities as Account Executive, function as the **Website Administrator** for two separate websites: the WHLY (1035FM.com) and WSLY (FOX977.com).
- Provide profit-making insights into advertising strategy as an Advertising Consultant.

Prior to changing careers into radio sales and advertising, excelled as a teacher and coach in the Golden County School System, Boulder, CO:
2000-02: HEAD TRACK COACH, Boulder Middle School. Through aggressive recruiting and because of my popularity with students, increased students involved in track from eight to 45 within two years!

- Hard work, relentless training, and persistent discipline took the team from last to second place! On my own initiative, established and implemented a track team and became their first track coach.

1999-2002: **ASSISTANT TRACK COACH, Boulder High School.** Coached both boys and girls, jumpers and sprinters, and officiated track meets for High School and College level students.

- Provided team leadership as well as individual attention to large groups of 50 students and more. Organized numerous track meets, and chaperoned groups of students on trips.

1998-2002: **SUBSTITUTE TEACHER.** In popular demand as a Substitute Teacher, substituted in every grade from K-12 and taught nearly every subject ranging from World History, to Band, to PE.

- Learned the inner workings of a school system, from classroom to district-level operations.
- Was featured in *Mountain City Press*, a weekly Boulder publication, 1999, for my historical research paper.

PERSONAL

Can provide outstanding references. Highly refined ability to deal with people in a gracious way. In my spare time, compete in track events and in mountain bike racing.

Date

Exact Name of Person
Title or Position
Name of Company
Address (no., street)
Address (city, state, zip)

Dear Exact Name of Person: (or Dear Sir or Madam if answering a blind ad)

Can you use a mature marketing, sales, and advertising professional who offers a background including management and finance as well as excellent problem-solving, research, and written and verbal communication skills?

In my current position as Account Executive for a radio station, I have excelled as the station's representative to nine advertising agencies and two in-house organizations. I took over existing accounts when other Account Executives left the station and now maintain these with a high level of customer satisfaction. I earned certification as a Radio Marketing Master after completing an extensive course in advanced sales training specifically for those specializing in radio sales. My exceptional performance in this position has resulted in the station's adding 30 new local clients in just one year.

In a previous position with the international advertising firm Leo Burnett, I built an impressive track record in the research department where I applied my analytical and demographics skills. Because of my keen ability for learning languages and fluency in several, as well as my success in extensive research on Southeastern European markets, I was transferred to the firm's Italian office. During this time, I developed my supervisory skills as Senior Research Analyst as well as serving as a Translator. While working with the firm, through frequent presentations to large groups including my superiors and high-profile clients, I also honed my public speaking skills.

Through my experience in a variety of different fields and environments, I feel that I have proven my adaptability and flexibility as a truly well-rounded individual. These qualities combined with my exceptional skills would make me a valuable asset to your organization.

I hope you will welcome my call soon to arrange a brief meeting at your convenience to discuss your current and future needs and how I might serve them. Thank you in advance for your time.

Sincerely yours,

Janie M. Vickers

Alternate last paragraph:
I hope you will call or write soon to suggest a time convenient for us to meet and discuss your current and future needs and how I might serve them. Thank you in advance for your time.

JANIE MEGAN VICKERS

1110½ Hay Street, Fayetteville, NC 28305   •   preppub@aol.com   •   (910) 483-6611

OBJECTIVE

To offer experience in marketing, sales, and advertising to an organization that can use a mature professional who offers a background which includes management and finance as well as excellent problem-solving, research, and written and verbal communication skills.

EXPERIENCE

ACCOUNT EXECUTIVE. WSTR/Z103, Abilene, TX (2003-present). As the radio station's representative to nine advertising agencies and two in-house agencies, personally produce a monthly average of $20,000 in billed commercial time while servicing direct local as well as advertising agency accounts and prospecting for clients.

- Utilize cold calling, referrals, and personal research into prospective advertisers which has resulted in adding 30 new local clients in just one year.
- Took over existing accounts when other account executives left the station and now maintain these accounts with a high level of customer satisfaction.
- Earned certification as a **Radio Marketing Master (RMM)** after completing an 80-hour course in advanced sales training for those specializing in radio sales, 2003.
- Serve as the treasurer of the Abilene Area Advertising Federation.

Refined my management, sales, and merchandising skills while excelling in positions of increasing responsibility with Goldfarb's Jewelers in Abilene, TX:
2002: ASSISTANT MANAGER. As assistant store manager, opened and closed the store, managed merchandise; controlled inventory, and directed credit-handling procedures.

2000-01: CREDIT MANAGER/SALES ASSOCIATE. As a part of the store management team, managed in-house installment charge accounts; approved/disapproved customer credit lines based on credit information; collected on and resolved delinquent accounts; reported charged-off accounts; and initiated legal actions.

Developed supervisory, research, and analytical skills with Leo Burnett, an international advertising firm based in Chicago, IL:
1999-00: SUPERVISORY RESEARCH ANALYST. Chicago, IL Presented briefings to audiences averaging 200 people, comprised of anyone from head firm supervisors up to executive contract clients, while also polishing managerial and supervisory abilities. Supervised all other Research Analysts and Assistants in the organization.

1996-99: SENIOR RESEARCH ANALYST and **TRANSLATOR.** Rome, Italy. Contributed my writing and analytical skills as an editorial assistant involved in verifying facts, rewriting/modifying reports, reading drafts, and conferring with Italian authors; applied my Italian language skills editing translated reports.

SPECIAL KNOWLEDGE

Computers: operate computer systems including PC and Macintosh, including European versions, using software including Word, dBase III, and Windows.
Instruction and public speaking: have tutored college athletes and Italian adults in English, taught CPR certification courses, instructed coworkers in research subjects, and conducted formal and informal briefings for high-profile clients.

EDUCATION & TRAINING

B.A. in Advertising with a minor in Spanish, University of Illinois at Chicago, 1990. Completed 10 semester hours towards a Master of Public Administration (M.P.A.) degree. Excelled in the intensive 36-week Italian language course at the University of Chicago.

PERSONAL

Have a talent for languages: in addition to Italian, know Spanish, German, and Russian.

Date

Exact Name of Person
Exact Title
Exact Name of Company
Exact Address
City, State zip

ACCOUNT EXECUTIVE

for a television network
affiliate

Dear Exact Name: (or Dear Sir or Madam if answering a blind ad)

I am writing to express my strong interest in the position of Account Executive which your company advertised in the Macon Herald News on Sunday, April 11. With the enclosed resume, I would like to make you aware of my background as an articulate communicator and experienced sales professional who offers a track record of accomplishments in media advertising sales and management.

As you will see from my resume, I have been aggressively recruited for my last two positions, both of which involved building an operation "from scratch." As a Director of Sales and Marketing for Sevier Media, I hit the ground running, and within six months, I had developed a new station into a desirable acquisition candidate which was quickly sold for a handsome profit. Once this one-year contract was completed, I was recruited by Wilson Communications and relocated to the Dalton area.

More recently WGSH-TV, the up-and-coming children's affiliate for the new FOXK network, selected me to open up the Dalton market as their first account executive, developing new business for the station. In earlier positions in the advertising sales field, I built a reputation as a creative, results-oriented professional who could be counted on to turn around troubled operations and motivate the existing sales force, forging a powerful team of effective professionals and making strong contributions to profitability.

Although I have made as much as $60,000 in my earlier positions, I understand that an account executive position will start at a lower rate of compensation. I am accustomed to working on the basis of a salary plus commission, and I am confident that my contributions to your bottom-line sales and the increases in advertising revenues that I generate will quickly prove my worth to your company.

If you can use a persuasive professional whose sales ability has been proven in a variety of challenging positions, I hope you will welcome my call soon when I try to arrange a brief meeting to discuss your goals and how my background might serve your needs. I can provide outstanding references at the appropriate time.

Sincerely,

Tobias J. Wright

TOBIAS J. WRIGHT

1110½ Hay Street, Fayetteville, NC 28305   •   preppub@aol.com   •   (910) 483-6611

OBJECTIVE

To benefit an organization that can use an articulate sales professional with exceptional communication, organizational and supervisory skills who offers an extensive background in advertising sales and sales management, as well as training and motivating sales forces.

EDUCATION

Bachelor of Science in **Business Administration**, University of Georgia, Athens, 1983.

EXPERIENCE

ACCOUNT EXECUTIVE. WGSH-TV, FOXK-17 (Wilson Communications), Dalton, GA (2003-present). Recruited by Wilson Communications to open up the Dalton territory for FOXK-17, a new FOX affiliate channel targeted towards 18-hr FoxKids programming; develop new accounts "from scratch," calling on local businesses to sell television advertising.

DIRECTOR OF SALES & MARKETING. Sevier Media, Dothan, AL (2001-02). Aggressively recruited by this former employer and chosen to coordinate and implement all phases of the start-up operation for a new radio station in Dothan, AL.
- Oversaw all marketing of this new station, including advertising and promotions.
- Hired and trained personnel, building a motivated sales team to effectively capture market share in radio advertising against competition from more established stations.
- Developed the station's web site, directing layout and design as well as training a web marketing sales staff of five employees. Worked with a web designer to develop web sites for three counties of southern Alabama; coordinated web site sales and marketing.

ACCOUNT EXECUTIVE. Tyler Group Communications (WKQQ-FM, Double-Q 98.1), Waxahachie, TX (2000-01). Serviced existing accounts and developed new business accounts. Worked with the Programming department, assisting with copywriting and ad production.

With Sevier Media, was selected for my ability to "turn around" troubled operations; provided training to the sales force in the following positions, 1998-00:
2000: GENERAL SALES MANAGER. WJSP AM & FM, Charleston, SC. Supervised up to 10 employees, providing motivation and training to the existing sales force, as well as interviewing, hiring, and training new personnel for the sales department.
- Oversaw servicing of and maintained contact with local and regional accounts; directly oversaw all national sales for the station; formulated budgets for sales department.

1999: GENERAL SALES MANAGER. WMML-FM & WCOM-FM, Macon, GA. Managed the sales forces at two separate locations, supervising a local sales manager and six account executives; developed budgets and prepared revenue forecasts for the stations.
- Worked directly with Star Radio, the national representation firm.

1998: GENERAL SALES MANAGER. WDJR-FM, Oldies 94.5, Rome, GA. Directed a sales department with six account executives and an annual net budget of $1.3 million dollars; managed all aspects of the department, including supervision of the sales force, personnel matters, budgeting, and forecasting revenues.
- Planned, coordinated, and implemented innovative and effective sales programs.

Highlights of earlier experience: Excelled in earlier sales positions as an **ACCOUNT EXECUTIVE** for Turner Outdoor Advertising (1992-1998), consistently exceeding monthly and annual sales quotas, and as **ASSISTANT MANAGER** at the Macon County Civic Center (1984-1991). Directed the in-house advertising agency, which coordinated all media advertising, promotions, and sponsorships.

Date

Exact Name of Person
Exact Title
Exact Name of Company
Exact Address
City, State zip

ACCOUNT EXECUTIVE
for a television station
specializing in outside sales

Dear Exact Name: (or Dear Sir or Madam if answering a blind ad)

With the enclosed resume, I would like to make you aware of my background as an enthusiastic and goal-oriented sales professional with exceptional communication skills who offers the proven ability to develop new accounts while increasing the profitability of existing accounts. Although I am held in high regard by my current employer and can provide excellent references, I am selectively exploring other opportunities and would appreciate your holding my interest in your company in confidence at this time.

I was recruited for my current job as an Outside Sales Representative because of my outstanding personal and professional reputation. I have been highly effective in generating new business while providing quality service to existing accounts. In a previous position with WROK-FM, I served as an Account Executive in the advertising sales department. Within two years on the job, I had quadrupled my monthly sales average, from $15,000 per month when I took the position to almost $60,000 per month. Due to my exceptional salesmanship, I was able to acquire or was given the responsibility for 60 additional accounts. On the phone or in person, I quickly built a strong rapport with clients. I established a reputation as an articulate communicator with the ability to close even the toughest accounts by effectively presenting innovative solutions to the client's marketing challenges.

Earlier with Lancome cosmetics/McAlpin's stores, I supervised three Beauty Advisors at the Sugartree Mall location while making purchasing and inventory control decisions for an exclusive product line;. By planning and implementing innovative and effective marketing strategies, promotions, and other events, I boosted sales and increase market share for all products in the line.

If you can use an energetic, articulate sales professional with the proven ability to present ideas effectively and initiate creative marketing strategies, I hope you will contact me. I can assure you in advance that I have an outstanding reputation, and I would quickly become a valuable asset to your organization.

Sincerely,

Chloe Christiansen

CHLOE CHRISTIANSEN

1110½ Hay Street, Fayetteville, NC 28305 • preppub@aol.com • (910) 483-6611

OBJECTIVE
To contribute to an organization that can use an experienced sales professional with exceptional communication, customer service, and time-management skills.

EXPERIENCE
ACCOUNT EXECUTIVE. WKMT (TV-27), Magnolia, AR (2003-present). Because of my outstanding professional reputation, was recruited for this position as an Outside Sales Representative for television advertising; call on local businesses and negotiate contracts.
- Assess company needs and create advertising campaigns to boost image and sales.
- Serve existing clients and cultivate new accounts.

ACCOUNT REPRESENTATIVE. WJYT Radio, Magnolia, AR (2002-03). For this popular music station, developed new accounts while serving existing customers.

ACCOUNT EXECUTIVE. WROK Radio (Lerner Communications), Magnolia, AR (1999-2002). Serviced existing accounts and developed new clients, presenting the benefits and services of radio advertising and promotional events to businesses in our listening area; I resigned from my position when the station changed ownership.
- In two years, increased monthly sales from an average of $15,000 per month to nearly $60,000 per month; acquired or was given responsibility for 60 additional accounts.
- Created and developed radio ads and promotional campaigns designed to strongly present the client's products and services to local consumers.
- Quickly built a rapport with clients, determining their goals and expectations in order to develop marketing and promotional strategies to satisfy their needs.
- Determined the reasons for customer resistance, then tactfully overcame objections by presenting solutions in a positive, client-focused manner.

BUSINESS MANAGER. Lancome Cosmetics-McAlpin's, Magnolia, AR (1984-1999). Managed all aspects of marketing and sales for this major cosmetics company's operations in McAlpin's retail locations throughout the area.
- Supervised three Beauty Advisors at Sugartree Mall and one at Shadywood Shopping Plaza, providing customer service and sales activities for the Lancome line of cosmetics.
- Collaborated with the Account Coordinator; planned and implemented marketing strategies and promotional events to increase market share.
- Maintained thorough records and conducted regular inventories to optimize ordering and ensure strong in-stock position.
- Assisted customers in the selection, use, and purchase of cosmetics.

EDUCATION
Attended the Regional Supervisory Program training course, sponsored by McAlpin's Department Stores, 1995.
Graduated from Tates Creek High School, Lexington, KY, 1981.

PERSONAL
Excellent personal and professional references are available upon request.

Date

Exact Name of Person
Title or Position
Name of Company
Address (no., street)
Address (city, state, zip)

ACCOUNTING MANAGER
with sales and collections
experience

Dear Exact Name of Person: (or Dear Sir or Madam if answering a blind ad)

Can you use an experienced professional who offers outstanding abilities related to managing business operations, maximizing human resources, and handling accounting procedures?

I offer a reputation for adaptability, the ability to quickly learn new ideas and procedures, and a talent for finding ways to guide employees to increased productivity. In a "track record" of performance with WCRT-TV 48 in Cedar Rapids, IA, I applied my abilities in the areas of sales, accounting, personnel recruiting, and office administration. I succeeded in reducing costs and increasing sales related to both local and national account activities.

As you will see by my resume, I studied Business Administration with a concentration in Accounting. I have extensive experience in accounting at the television station where I currently work as well as in earlier jobs.

I hope you will welcome my call soon to arrange a brief meeting at your convenience to discuss your current and future needs and how I might serve them. Thank you in advance for your time.

Sincerely yours,

Annmarie L. Rodrigue

Alternate last paragraph:
I hope you will call or write soon to suggest a time convenient for us to meet and discuss your current and future needs and how I might serve them. Thank you in advance for your time.

ANNMARIE L. RODRIGUE

1110½ Hay Street, Fayetteville, NC 28305   •   preppub@aol.com   •   (910) 483-6611

OBJECTIVE

To apply my knowledge related to business management and office procedures as well as my education and experience in accounting to an organization that can use a proven communicator, planner, and organizer.

EXPERIENCE

ACCOUNTING MANAGER. WCDR-TV, Cedar Rapids, IA (2003-present). Work part time providing accounting support; prepare a variety of financial statements including general ledgers, profit and loss statements, and balance sheets in addition to maintaining accounts payable/receivable and payroll.

BUSINESS MANAGER. WLRQ-FM, Cedar Rapids, IA (2002-03). Performed a wide range of administrative functions including ensuring the station complied with Equal Opportunity Laws, maintaining files, billing clients, and providing personnel administration.
- Earned recognition for accuracy, reliability, and motivation.
- Oversaw administrative functions for three radio stations.
- Managed and compiled data gathered by telemarketing department.

Earned a reputation as an adaptable, dynamic quick learner with a track record of accomplishments while at WCRT-TV 48, Cedar Rapids, IA:
2000-02: BUSINESS MANAGER and **HUMAN RESOURCES MANAGER.** Supervised operations and accounting personnel while also managing personnel recruiting and financial statement preparation. Implemented new accounting procedures, decreasing bad debt rate by 35%. Reorganized office operations for increased productivity.

1999-00: SALES REPRESENTATIVE. Sold television advertising time to area businesses and designed advertising campaigns to meet client needs.
- Refined my communication and public relations skills working with people from all types and sizes of businesses.

1998-99: ADMINISTRATIVE ASSISTANT FOR SALES AND MARKETING. Was promoted from accounting technician to coordinate sales personnel working on local accounts and to prepare national sales contracts.
- Established a program which eliminated the "middle man" and made national sales through direct contacts; increased sales 30% and reduced costs 15%.
- Designed sales packages and made presentations to clients.

1997-98: ACCOUNTING TECHNICIAN. Gained experience in numerous areas of accounting, including accounts payable/receivable, monthly billings, disbursements, payroll accounting, and weekly cash flow reporting.
- Provided assistance in the preparation of logs, schedules, and formats. Processed credit applications and maintained accurate balances on payroll and operating accounts.

EDUCATION

Studied **Business Administration** with a concentration in **Accounting**, Kirkwood Community College, Cedar Rapids, IA.

COMPUTER SKILLS

Offer experience in using computers and a variety of software including: Word, Windows, Lotus, Media Management Systems, Quickbooks, and Property Management Systems.

PERSONAL

Am known for my organization skills and efficiency. Insist on high performance standards for myself and my employees.

Date

Exact Name of Person
Title or Position
Name of Company
Address (no., street)
Address (city, state, zip)

**ADVERTISING &
MARKETING DIRECTOR**

for a leading advertising
agency

Dear Exact Name of Person: (or Dear Sir or Madam if answering a blind ad.)

I would appreciate an opportunity to talk with you soon about how I could contribute to your organization through my proven communication and sales skills as well as my background related to consumer accounts management, advertising, and marketing/ sales.

As you will see from my resume, I have excelled in a variety of roles related to advertising and marketing. Most recently, I developed and implemented marketing plans for one of the largest shopping mall in Arkansas. While handling all media purchases and electronic print production, I became known for creating exciting marketing promotions and creating innovative advertising materials. As the advertising/marketing director for an ad agency, I received an award from a television station for coordinating a promotion which attracted over 30,000 people.

In previous jobs within a fast-paced advertising and marketing firm, I was evaluated as a "natural salesperson" while earning rapid promotions from editor of the agency's newsletter to account coordinator and production manager. I was praised by the agency's creative Vice-President as being "the best" he'd ever seen at being able to "see all sides" of complex problems.

I hope you will welcome my call soon to arrange a brief meeting at your convenience to discuss your current and future needs and how I might serve them. Thank you in advance for your time.

Sincerely Yours,

Carla N. Dumar

Alternate last paragraph:
I hope you will call or write me soon to suggest a time convenient for us to meet and discuss your current and future needs and how I might serve them. Thank you in advance for your time.

CARLA N. DUMAR

1110½ Hay Street, Fayetteville, NC 28305 • preppub@aol.com • (910) 483-6611

OBJECTIVE
To contribute to an organization that can use a talented young communicator regarded as a "natural salesperson" who offers versatile skills related to consumer accounts management, advertising, and marketing/sales.

HONORS & AWARDS
Known as someone who gives 100%, have received these and other honors:
- Was named Runner-up in the "Student of the Year" Competition, Jonesboro Community College, Jonesboro, AR, 1993.
- Was named an Outstanding Young Woman nationally, 1996.
- Received an award for "outstanding leadership, character, and community service" by the City of Jonesboro, 2000.

EXPERIENCE
Established a "track record of rapid promotion based on talents and contributions, Spaulding Direct Marketing, Jonesboro, AR:
2003-present: **ADVERTISING & MARKETING DIRECTOR.** Formally evaluated as a "natural salesperson" by one of the state capitol's leading advertising agencies, was promoted rapidly in this "track record:"

2002-03: **DIRECTOR OF CORPORATE COMMUNICATION.** With this promotion, became the highest ranking woman after only 18 months with the company.
- Developed and conducted presentations to new businesses/clients.
- Managed the agency's "image" to the outside world.
- Handled extensive external public relations; Consulted with all forms of electronic media.
- Was offered another promotion and praised as a gifted communicator.

1999-02: **ACCOUNT EXECUTIVE** and **PUBLIC RELATIONS COORDINATOR.** After being promoted to handle several key accounts, established outstanding rapport with clients. Coordinated communication between the client and agency.
- Learned how to sell a creative product. Was complimented by the creative Vice-President as being "the best" he'd ever seen at being able to "see all sides" of a complex problem.

1998-99: **ACCOUNT EXECUTIVE** and **EDITOR/PRODUCTION MANAGER.** As Editor of the agency's newsletter, managed the newsletter through all stages, including layout and mechanicals.
- Wrote production schedules and the time line; arranged photography.
- Performed liaison with clients regarding factual data.
- Acted as the newsletter's final proofreader.

Other experience:
DEPUTY CLERK OF SUPERIOR CLERK. Arkansas Judicial Department, Jonesboro, AR (1995-1997). Learned the internal workings of all phases of Small Claims Court.
- Excelled in a job which expanded my tolerance and taught me to deal patiently with people from all walks of life.

EDUCATION
Studied Business Administration in the Bachelor of Science Program, Arkansas State University, 1999. Previously studied nursing, Jonesboro Technical College, AR, 1993.

PERSONAL
Have an extraordinary ability to relate to and establish rapport with people. Am a planner by instinct and am able to see and resolve little problems before they become big ones. Have authored/published several articles.

Exact Name of Person
Exact Title of Person
Exact Name of Company
Address
City, State zip

ART DIRECTOR
for national consumer
product accounts

Dear Exact Name of Person: (Dear Sir or Madam if answering a blind ad)

I would appreciate an opportunity to talk with you soon about my interest in contributing to your organization through my expertise in art direction, publications coordination, and graphic design including computer graphics.

With a B.S. degree in Art Education and years of Macintosh experience including PageMaker, Freehand, PhotoShop, Microsoft Word, and MacWrite, I have excelled in jobs as a corporate art director, advertising agency art director, mechanical artist, and layout artist/illustrator.

In one job I set up and organized a corporation's first in-house art department, and single-handedly I handled the duties of account executive, creative director, art director, media buyer, production manager, copywriter, and mechanical artist. In every job I have ever held, I have helped to reduce costs and increase efficiency through my creativity, technical know-how, and hard work.

I offer the proven ability to excel under the pressure of tight deadlines, and I would be delighted to provide outstanding personal and professional references.

I hope you will welcome my call soon when I try to arrange a brief meeting at your convenience to discuss your current and future needs and how I might serve them. Thank you in advance for your time.

Yours sincerely,

Michelle A. McArthur

Alternate last paragraph:
I hope you will call or write me soon to suggest a time when we might meet to discuss your current and future needs and how I might serve them. Thank you in advance for your time.

MICHELLE A. MCARTHUR

1110½ Hay Street, Fayetteville, NC 28305   •   preppub@aol.com   •   (910) 483-6611

OBJECTIVE
I want to offer my expertise in all areas of advertising and graphic design, including extensive computer graphics experience, along with my exceptionally strong planning, organizational, and production management skills.

EDUCATION
Earned **B.S. degree in Art Education**, Oregon State University, Corvallis, OR, 1986.
Studied **Computer Graphics**, Rogue Community College (RCC), Grant's Pass, OR, 2001.

HONORS
Invited to serve on Advisory Board, RCC Design Department, 2001-02.
Recipient of advertising's **Addy Award** for catalog design, 1998.
Recipient of Dillard's Stores' Advertising Award for **best newspaper advertisement,** 1987.

EXPERIENCE
SENIOR ART DIRECTOR. Sweeney Heard Advertising, Portland, OR (2003-present). For national accounts including Frito-Lays, Playtex, Hanes, and Nabisco, design and produce advertising materials including the following:

brochures	logos	point-of-sale materials
packaging	FSI's	trade advertisements

- Cut typesetting costs in half by formatting type in-house on Macintosh rather than using outside typesetters. Supervise photography shoots, attend press proofs at printers, and supervise a junior art director.

ART DIRECTOR. Technique Inc., Grant's Pass, OR (1999-03). Established an in-house, one-person advertising agency through my ability to handle multiple roles including these:

Account Executive	Creative/Art Director	Copywriter
Production Manager	Mechanical Artist	Media Buyer

- Reduced costs by eliminating outside design and production charges.
- Directed all phases of the production of sales literature including catalogs, brochures, flyers, and statement stuffers; designed and produced trade ads, newspaper ad builder kits, and logos. Supervised photography, wrote copy, placed media, supervised videotape production, and ordered/supervised color printing.

ART DIRECTOR. Gallatin Advertising, Salem, OR (1989-99). Was promoted to Art Director after excelling as Mechanical Artist from 1989-91 producing mechanical art, operating stat camera, setting headline type on phototypositor, specifying type, and executing composites from rough layouts.

- Supervised mechanical artists; prepared printing quotes/job estimates; and designed brochures, ads, logos, outdoor boards, and TV storyboards for various clients including the agency's largest account, Technique Inc. Became skilled in account executive duties.

Other experience: Grant's Pass and Salem, OR.
MECHANICAL ARTIST. For an advertising agency and a design studio, produced meticulous mechanical artwork with speed and accuracy.
LAYOUT ARTIST/ILLUSTRATOR. For the retailer JC Penney's, produced newspaper and radio advertising for a group of 12 regional stores, handling layout of newspaper ads and creating a variety of illustrations.

COMPUTER
Offer six years of Macintosh experience with PageMaker, Freehand, Photoshop, Microsoft Word, and MacWrite. Learned Aldus Freehand through private training.

PERSONAL
Can provide outstanding personal/professional references.

Date

Exact Name of Person
Exact Title
Exact Name of Company
Address
City, State, Zip

BOOK EDITOR
for specialized travel titles
distributed through normal
bookstore channels

Dear Exact Name of Person: (or Dear Sir or Madam if answering a blind ad)

With the enclosed resume, I would like to express my interest in exploring employment opportunities with your organization. As you will see from my resume, I am an experienced book editor with experience in managing a profitable imprint and I offer a proven history of developing innovative and profitable new titles.

Currently as a book editor at Global Travel Publishing in Atlanta, GA, I am considered an expert in creating books that bring whole continents and destinations to life. I have worked with travel authors worldwide.

My experience in the book publishing industry came after previous experience as a College Instructor, Career Advisor/Business Instructor, and Vice President for a trade association in Washington, DC. I was that trade association's youngest and first woman vice president.

While I am highly regarded by my present employer and am being groomed for positions of further responsibility, I am selective exploring opportunities in other publishing companies. I hope you will contact me soon to suggest a time convenient for us to meet and discuss your current and future needs and how I might serve them. Thank you in advance for your time.

Sincerely,

Alice Bachus

Alternate last paragraph:
I hope you will welcome my call soon to arrange a brief meeting at your convenience to discuss your current and future needs and how I might serve them. Thank you in advance for your time.

ALICE BACHUS

1110½ Hay Street, Fayetteville, NC 28305   •   preppub@aol.com   •   (910) 483-6611

OBJECTIVE

To offer my expertise in publishing popular books that help people enjoy the human experience while working effectively with authors and helping my publisher identify and publish the most profitable and enduring titles.

EDUCATION

Master of Business Administration (M.B.A.) degree, Harvard Business School, 1994. Bachelor of Arts (B.A.) degree with concentrations in English and History, University of North Carolina at Chapel Hill, NC, 1985.

PUBLICATIONS

Have authored magazine and newspaper articles as well as booklets on travel:
* Editor of *TRAVEL ABROAD FOR LESS THAN $20 A DAY* published in Nov 1996 and reviewed by *Booklist* as "A guide that significantly enriches European travel."
* Editor of *DOING EUROPE IN STYLE*, published in April 1997 and designed to help experienced travelers find the choice spots.
* Contributor of several articles to *New Yorker and USA Today.*
* Author of two books under the name Caison Fough; currently completing two novels which depict the travel misadventures of a minister in the Caribbean.

AFFILIATIONS

Under the name Jennifer Scales, am currently Books in Print editor for national TV and Radio Producers Guild.

EXPERIENCE

BOOK EDITOR. Global Travel Publishing, Atlanta, GA (1997-present). For a company which publishes travel books, am involved in supervising production related to 10 titles annually.
* Am considered an expert in creating titles that bring whole continents and destinations to life. Oversee three junior editors, an art director, and report to the Publisher.

COLLEGE INSTRUCTOR. Tennessee State University, Dillwood, TN (1994-97). After earning my Harvard MBA, was a popular instructor of courses including production/operations management, finance, economics, management, and marketing.

VICE PRESIDENT OF CONSUMER AFFAIRS. National Television and Radio Producers Association, Washington, DC (1988-92). For a large trade association with 578 affiliated associations and a Washington staff of 500, was selected as its first Director of Consumer Affairs and eventually became the association's youngest and first woman vice president.
* Wrote the industry's first "Buyer's Guide."
* Dealt extensively with television/radio and with government consumer affairs officials.

BOOK EDITOR. Urban Land Institute, Washington, DC (1985-87). Handled the editing, rewriting, and layout of books and articles written by others.

INFORMATION OFFICER. National House Builders Council, London, England (1982-85). Directed communications and research activities for this national British organization which administers a 10-year warranty plan on homes throughout England, Ireland, and Wales.

PERSONAL

Extensively volunteer my time in the community, especially to child literacy programs. Am a cub scout den leader and cub master. Outstanding public speaking skills.

Exact Name of Person
Title or Position
Name of Company
Address (no., street)
Address (city, state, zip)

**BROADCASTING
ACCOUNT EXECUTIVE**

for a public radio station

Dear Exact Name of Person: (or Dear Sir or Madam if answering a blind ad.)

    I would appreciate an opportunity to talk with you soon about how I could contribute to your organization through my experience in the area of broadcast sales.

    As an Account Executive, I have earned recognition as a creative young professional who excels in designing effective advertising campaigns and ensuring that they are managed in the most beneficial way for the customer. In my most recent job, I handled as many as 100 regular accounts as well as prospected successfully for new accounts.

    While earning my degree in Speech Communications/Broadcast Performance, I also used my communication and strong interpersonal skills in jobs related to counseling and instructing college and high school students in stress management as well as personal safety and health.

    I hope you will welcome my call soon to arrange a brief meeting at your convenience to discuss your current and future needs and how I might serve them. Thank you in advance for your time.

Sincerely yours,

Candice M. Davidson

Alternate last paragraph:
    I hope you will call or write me soon to suggest a time convenient for us to meet and discuss your current and future needs and how I might serve them. Thank you in advance for your time.

CANDICE M. DAVIDSON

1110½ Hay Street, Fayetteville, NC 28305   •   preppub@aol.com   •   (910) 483-6611

OBJECTIVE   To benefit an organization in need of a persuasive young professional who offers experience in broadcast sales, along with excellent abilities in communicating verbally and in writing.

EDUCATION   Earned a **Bachelor of Arts (B.A.) degree in Speech Communications/Broadcast Performance,** University of Puget Sound, Tacoma, WA, 2000.

EXPERIENCE   **BROADCASTING ACCOUNT EXECUTIVE.** Tacoma Public Radio, Tacoma, WA (2003-present). Work closely with area businesses to develop radio advertising campaigns which would best familiarize listeners with their products or services.
- Service as many as 100 customers on a regular basis.
- Prospect for and develop new advertising accounts.
- Coordinate with traffic personnel to ensure advertising copy was correct and on time.
- Assist customers in broadcast scheduling, determining correct timing for their ads including time of day and frequency of their commercials.
- Have been recognized for my ability to effectively schedule air time for maximum exposure and targeting of listening audiences.
- Earned a reputation for creativity in designing campaigns and developing promotional ideas which were the most beneficial to the customer.

ACCOUNT EXECUTIVE. WHJC Talk Radio, Tacoma, WA (2000-2003). Developed new advertising accounts while servicing established accounts and designing and implementing numerous radio campaigns.
- Coordinated copy, announcers, and engineers to produce commercials.
- Played a key role in a major Kellogg's marketing campaign which resulted in a substantial increase in sales in the market area.

Refined my organizational and communication skills in these jobs while in college full-time, attending the University of Puget Sound, Tacoma, WA:
RESIDENT ASSISTANT. (1997-2000). For the University of Puget Sound's Department of Residence Life, enforced school regulations related to the living conditions and safety of 40 dormitory residents.
- Used my communication skills to design and teach seminars in subjects including stress management and personal safety/health. Was recognized for my ability to remain calm in handling crisis situations and medical emergencies.

COMMUNICATIONS DEPARTMENT ASSISTANT. (1992-1996). As the assistant to the department secretary, typed, filed, answered phones, and performed on-campus courier duties.
- Was known for my dependability and attention to detail.

Other experience: Seattle, WA
- As a Tutor/Counselor for the Academic Excellence Program, assisted young people in an orientation program designed to acquaint them with college life.
- As a Retail Sales Associate with the Rich's Department Store, was known for my professional, pleasant manner in dealing with customers.

TRAINING   Attended a seminar sponsored by WHJC in Tacoma on utilizing the Arbitron ratings as selling tools. Participated in stress and time management training programs.

PERSONAL   Outgoing and energetic individual. Can contribute to team efforts or can work independently.

CAREER CHANGE

Date

Exact Name of Person
Exact Title
Exact Name of Company
Address
City, State, Zip

Dear Exact Name of Person: (or Dear Sir or Madam if answering a blind ad)

I would appreciate an opportunity to talk with you soon about how I could contribute to Rowan University as the Assistant Director of Admissions through the application of my outstanding communication skills and reputation as a personable, persuasive, and articulate professional.

Throughout my years as a student at RU, I have been very active in a wide variety of campus activities and have contributed leadership to various student activities. The recipient of numerous honors and awards for my academic accomplishments, public speaking abilities, and contributions to the university community, I feel that I would be a strong representative for the university and able to relate effectively with incoming students. As you will see from my enclosed resume, I built a reputation as a talented speaker and scholar/athlete during my high school years and have continued to be known as a dedicated young professional who gives unselfishly of my time and talents.

I offer a reputation as an outstanding motivational speaker and have often been called on to make presentations to young people and encourage them to develop personal goals and strive to excel through strong morals and high personal standards. I am certain that I would be a productive and results-oriented admissions counselor who would motivate university students by setting an example for them to follow.

I hope you will call or write me soon to suggest a time convenient for us to meet and discuss your current and future needs and how I might serve them. Thank you in advance for your time.

Sincerely,

Vincent A. Parks

VINCENT ANDREW PARKS

1110½ Hay Street, Fayetteville, NC 28305   •   preppub@aol.com   •   (910) 483-6611

OBJECTIVE To offer my reputation as a persuasive and articulate speaker to an organization that can use a young professional who is known for drive and dedication as well as a high level of personal integrity and moral standards.

EDUCATION **B.A., Broadcast Journalism,** Rowan University, Glassboro, NJ, 2003.
- Refined communication and time management skills in activities which included:
  Student speaker for a "Right Now" reception in Trenton, 2002.
  Member of the Student Advisory Committee, 2002-03.
  Member of the Student Activity Fees Committee, 2002-03.
  President of the Glassboro Society Gospel Choir, 2001-present.

HONORS & AWARDS Was the recipient of numerous honors and awards including the following:
Glassboro Gospel Choir Anointed Spiritual Leader Award, 2001-02.
Department of Communication and Theater Outstanding Speaker Award, 2000.
RU Special Support Services Scholarship, 2000-01.
RU Special Support Services Certificate of Achievement in Academic Activities, 2000-01.
Our Generation Campus Ministries Integrity Award, 1999-2000.
Completed additional course work at Jersey City State College, NJ, and City College of CUNY, New York, NY, summers 2002 and 2001.

COMMUNITY INVOLVEMENT As a volunteer with the Glassboro Pregnancy Center, speak to high school students about the importance of setting high personal goals including in the matter of sexual abstinence. Served meals to the poor and homeless for the Glassboro Urban Ministries and received a Certificate of Appreciation from the Northeast NJ Radio Reading Service (1999).

EXPERIENCE *While attending college full time, learned the value of hard work in summer and holiday jobs which were often simultaneous and included the following:*
SALES ASSOCIATE. Structure, Trenton and Glassboro, NJ (summers and holidays 2001-2003). Excelled in providing quality customer service at two different locations of this fine men's clothing store: measured customers for alterations and proper fit.

BROADCASTING INTERN. WCNY 99.9-FM Radio Station, City College of CUNY, NY (summer 2002). Assisted the news director of this National Public Radio Station by rewriting local stories which had appeared in that day's *Village Voice* and acting as general assignment reporter for the "City Today" radio show.
- Covered political and entertainment activities throughout the region.
- Worked with equipment including reel-to-reel player/recorders, cartridge machines, tape and CD players, and computers. Played traditional and contemporary jazz music as well as announcing news which affected university students and residents of the region.

CAMP COUNSELOR. Camp Joseph, Trenton Youth Activities, Trenton, NJ (summers 1995-99). During two years as a Senior Camp Counselor and earlier years as a Junior Counselor, supervised as many as twelve 6 through 13-year-old day camp participants.

SPECIAL SKILLS Offer knowledge related to Windows and software including Word, PowerPoint, and Excel.

PERSONAL Earned awards as a high school scholar-athlete: placed on the Mid-North All Conference Academic All-American Team, lettered in football three years, and was named to Who's Who Among American High School Students for 1996-97.

Date

Exact Name of Person
Title or Position
Name of Company
Address (no., street)
Address (city, state, zip)

**COMMERCIAL ARTIST &
GRAPHIC ARTIST**

working freelance is
seeking advertising
agency work

Dear Exact Name of Person: (or Dear Sir or Madam if answering a blind ad.)

I would appreciate an opportunity to talk with you soon about how I could contribute to your advertising agency as a graphic designer/commercial artist.

As you will see from my resume, I recently earned my degree in Commercial Art and Design. In addition to my formal education I have had experience as a popular freelance artist, creating items ranging from logos to T-shirts.

Two floats I produced recently for an automobile dealership received "rave reviews" from the public and from my employer for their popular appeal and creativity. I am experienced at working within a budget to produce top-quality results.

You would find me to be a poised and hard-working young professional who could become a valuable asset to your business.

I hope you will welcome my call soon to arrange a brief meeting at your convenience to discuss your current and future needs and how I might serve them. Thank you in advance for your time.

Sincerely yours,

Tawanna L. Smith

Alternate last paragraph:
I hope you will call or write me soon to suggest a time convenient for us to meet and discuss your current and future needs and how I might serve them. Thank you in advance for your time.

TAWANNA L. SMITH

1110½ Hay Street, Fayetteville, NC 28305 • preppub@aol.com • (910) 483-6611

OBJECTIVE

I want to contribute to an organization that can use a creative and hard-working young professional who offers experience in office operations along with a formal education in commercial art and graphic design.

EDUCATION

Associate's degree in Commercial Art and Design, George Mason University, Fairfax, VA, 1999.
- Was named to the National Dean's List.
- Studied these and other areas:

graphic design	illustration	layout/design
drawing	commercial art	photography
computer graphics	typography/lettering	photostats

EXPERIENCE

COMMERCIAL ARTIST & GRAPHIC ARTIST (FREELANCE). Independent Contractor, Norfolk, VA (2003-present). While earning my Associate's Degree, have worked a popular freelance artist.
- Created a logo for a beauty shop.
- Produced posters for fraternities and sororities.
- Created hand-painted T-shirts.
- Refined my ability to use PageMaker and QuarkExpress in page layout.
- In my spare time after work, am taking a course related to Website Design.

TITLE CLERK, CASHIER and **RECEPTIONIST**. Gene Reed Chevrolet, Norfolk, VA (2002). In a summer job after earning my Associate's Degree, proved myself a valuable and versatile "Salesperson of Success" for this large, fast-paced automobile dealership.
- Operated the company's computer to input data, locate vehicles, and type rebates.
- Was sought out by management for my advertising ideas.
- Gained extensive "hands-on" experience in planning and organizing floats: created one float for a popcorn festival and another float expressing a Walt Disney theme.
- Used my imagination to find creative "short cuts" to bring the jobs in on time and within budget.
- Learned how to work within a restricted budget.
- Was praised by the automobile dealership for my flair in producing positive name recognition for the business.

SALES REPRESENTATIVE, DISPLAY MANAGER, and **MANAGER TRAINEE**. Linens and Things, Fairfax, VA (1999-2002). Worked full-time and part-time in this family business as time permitted while earning my Associate's degree.

Created displays.	Sold merchandise.
Handled drawing/painting.	Acted as cashier.
Performed bookkeeping.	Taught arts/crafts.

- Gained valuable insights into small business management.

COMPUTER SKILLS

Offer experience in using software including Illustrator, Microsoft Publisher, PageMaker, Media Management Systems; am experienced in creating PDF files for printers.

PERSONAL

Highly motivated in every project I undertake. Fast learner and overachiever who always persists until I get a job done in the best way.

CAREER CHANGE

Date

Exact Name of Person
Exact Title of Person
Exact Name of Company
Address
City, State, Zip

**COMMERCIAL
PHOTOGRAPHER**
for a high-quality studio

Dear Exact Name of Person: (Dear Sir or Madam if answering a blind ad)

I would appreciate an opportunity to talk with you soon about how I could contribute to your organization through my sincere desire to work as a dental assistant. At 25 years of age, I can show you in person that my natural drive, hard-working nature, and proven sales/customer service skills would enable me to rapidly master your requirements and become a valuable asset to you.

You will see from my resume that I have maintained a 4.0 GPA while attending the University of Cincinnati. I hope that will provide some glimpse into my highly dedicated personality as well as my natural intelligence.

Experienced in using computers and most standard office equipment, I have excelled in jobs in photographic sales, insurance sales, and optical sales. After considerable thought, I have decided that I want to work toward a career in dentistry, and I am hopeful that you will see my potential and offer me my first job in this field. I am a proven performer and you would not be taking a chance!

Please consider me for this position. I am confident that I could demonstrate during an interview that I am the person you are looking for and could count on. I hope I will hear from you soon so that we can set up a meeting at your convenience to discuss your current and future needs and how I might serve them. Thank you in advance for your time.

Sincerely yours,

Kevin Michael Chin

KEVIN MICHAEL CHIN

1110½ Hay Street, Fayetteville, NC 28305 • preppub@aol.com • (910) 483-6611

OBJECTIVE

To benefit an organization seeking an enthusiastic, energetic, and highly motivated professional skilled in sales and public relations who possesses sound bottom-line judgment along with excellent communication, time management, and planning abilities.

EXPERIENCE

COMMERCIAL PHOTOGRAPHER and SALES REPRESENTATIVE. First Choice Studios, Inc., Cincinnati, OH (2003-present). Consistently exceed the organization's performance and sales standards while ensuring customers are treated properly and receive the highest quality photographic products in this busy studio.
- Established new sales records and maintained a volume approximately 30% above corporate standards.
- Earned the distinction of being the first person in the company's history to receive "excellent" evaluations in all rated performance categories during my initial evaluation.
- Excel in dealing with customers no matter how tired and difficult they became by applying my talent for establishing rapport with people of all ages and cultures.
- Earned the respect of district executives and was soon entrusted with the sole responsibility for opening and closing the studio.
- Gained practical experience in using a digital point-of-sale computer system to ring up sales and receive payments from customers.

COLLEGE STUDENT. University of Cincinnati, Cincinnati, OH (2001-present). Completed college course work with honors while polishing my time management skills coordinating school and work.

INSURANCE SALES REPRESENTATIVE. State Farm Insurance Company, Toledo, OH (2000-01). Consistently led the district in sales as a licensed life and health insurance agent.
- Used my communication skills and ability to deal with others on their level while making cold calls on prospective clients and collecting premiums from existing clients.
- Was selected to attend a 48-hour training program on policy types and terminology for insurance sales.

OPTICIAN'S ASSISTANT and **SALES REPRESENTATIVE.** Lenscrafters, Toledo, OH (1997-99). Became highly aware of the importance of attending to details while making certain to take exact measurements so that customers' eyewear was made and fitted correctly.
- Cited for my rapport with others, worked independently while providing quality services.

Highlights of other experience: **OPTICIAN'S ASSISTANT** and **SALES REPRESENTATIVE.** Dawson Opticians, Toledo, OH. Became highly skilled in guaranteeing customer satisfaction with services and products while taking order requests, closing sales, and assisting customers in their selections in this part-time job while attending college.

EDUCATION

Completing course work toward a degree in Education, University of Cincinnati in Ohio.
- Placed on the National Dean's List with a 4.0 GPA.
Studied Business and Education, Owens Community College, Toledo, OH.

SPECIAL SKILLS

Am familiar with a wide range of computers and office equipment including:
PC platforms   typewriters — type 50 wpm   fax machines   copiers

PERSONAL

Enjoy working with children — was a volunteer teacher's assistant at an elementary school. Am a good listener and quick learner who adapts easily to new ideas and circumstances.

Date

Exact Name of Person
Title or Position
Name of Company
Address (no., street)
Address (city, state, zip)

**COMMUNICATIONS
DIRECTOR**

for a Fortune 500 company

Dear Exact Name of Person: (or Dear Sir or Madam if answering a blind ad.)

I would appreciate an opportunity to talk with you soon about how I could contribute to your organization through my outstanding abilities in professional communications and public/community relations, as well as through my experience in broadcast media and promotion.

My enclosed resume will "bring to life," I hope, the kinds of results I could produce for you.

- As Communications Director and Training/Activities Coordinator at Black and Decker Corporation, I have received numerous letters of commendation from corporate and division executives for exceptional work in publishing the plant magazines, newsletters, and promotional material.

- I have developed an outstanding community relations posture for Black and Decker Corporation while dealing with local colleges and businesses.

- In a previous job as a News Department Intern, I became familiar with media operations and gained extraordinary poise performing before the camera.

I hope you will welcome my call soon to arrange a brief meeting at your convenience to discuss your current and future needs and how I might serve them. Thank you in advance for your time.

Sincerely,

Tanya S. Samuels

(Alternate last paragraph:
I hope you will call or write me soon to suggest a time convenient for us to meet and discuss your current and future needs and how I might serve them. Thank you in advance for your time.)

TANYA S. SAMUELS

1110½ Hay Street, Fayetteville, NC 28305 • preppub@aol.com • (910) 483-6611

OBJECTIVE

To contribute to the success of an organization through my outstanding abilities in professional communications and public/community relations, as well as through my experience in broadcast media and promotion.

EDUCATION

Bachelor or Arts (B.A.) degree in both Journalism and Radio, TV, Motion Pictures, Lamar University, Beaumont, TX, 2000.
Associate of Arts degree, Beaumont Community College, Beaumont, TX, 1997.

EXPERIENCE

Black and Decker Corp., San Antonio, TX (2003-present). Excel in multiple roles performing public relations and communications for a 400-employee manufacturing site of this Fortune 500 corporation.
COMMUNICATIONS DIRECTOR. As Editor, write, edit, and lay out the plant's quarterly magazine, biweekly newsletter, and daily bulletin.

Public Relations & Communications

- Plan and administer a $30,000 budget.
- Direct a professional photographer and take photos.
- Wrote and edited five highly praised magazines and numerous newsletters which were distributed throughout the corporation.
- Received a letters of commendation from corporate and division management for exceptional work.
- Wrote news releases and promotional material praised for their creativity and clarity.

TRAINING/ACTIVITIES COORDINATOR. As Coordinator of all employee continuing education programs, managed meetings and activities. Managed $40,000 activities budget. Plan logistics for open houses, meetings, and parties. Interfaced with managers/college officials; set course guidelines.

- Consistently remained "under budget" for all programs and projects.
- Developed excellent working relationships in the business community while negotiating/ dealing with hotels, restaurants, rental agencies.

Community Relations

- Refined my leadership skills while supervising a 14-member committee.

Highlights of previous experience:
NEWSPAPER REPORTER. San Antonio Spectator, San Antonio, TX. (2001-2003). As the sole reporter for this weekly newspaper, conducted interviews and wrote informative, entertaining articles on a wide variety of subjects.

NEWS DEPARTMENT INTERN. WREK-TV, Beaumont, TX (1998-2001). Developed expertise in many areas of broadcasting and journalism including broadcast reporting, editing, shooting, and on-air work. Authored scripts; edited, shooting, and on-air work. Conducted interviews for on camera and off.

- Became skilled in using equipment including: studio cameras, "mini-cams," video tape recorder (VTR), editing machines.
- Gained poise and strengthened my public relations skills while extracting information from people in often hostile or strange situations.

PROMOTIONS AIDE. WJHZ-FM Radio, Beaumont, TX (summer 1998). Extensively polled people in order to analyze a programming change from "pop" to country music.

PERSONAL

Am a creative, energetic young professional who enjoys travel and meeting new people. Work well under the pressure of long hours and tight deadlines.

Date

Exact Name of Person
Exact Title
Exact Name of Company
Address
City, State, Zip

COMMUNICATIONS EDITOR

for the school board in Phoenix

Dear Exact Name of Person: (or Dear Sir or Madam if answering a blind ad)

With the enclosed resume, I would like to make you aware of my credentials and experience as a public relations professional and to express my interest in exploring employment opportunities with your organization. As you can see from my resume, I am a public relations professional who has earned national accreditation in General Public Relations (A.P.R.) and national accreditation in School Public Relations (A.S.P.R.) in addition to my B.A. in Mass Communication.

In my current position as Communications Editor for the Arizona School Boards Association, I act as the organization's "voice" and "face" while managing its vast communications and public relations efforts. While serving as editor of several publications, I serve as liaison to public officials, the media, and the community, directing the preparation of news releases, speeches, and a wide range of special written materials.

In my previous position as Community-Schools Relations Coordinator with Sun County Schools, I managed all communications efforts for a system of 23 schools. I am particularly proud of the fact that we increased the number of volunteers in our database from 200 to 800 while annual volunteer hours soared from 19,000 to 36,000. I was widely credited with significantly improving internal communications through tools which included a staff newsletter as well as staff round tables, and I was named Young Careerist of the Year by the Sun County Business and Professional Women's Association.

Highly regarded in my field, I am on the Board of Directors of the Arizona School Public Relations Association, and I am spearheading a project to develop a network of school public relations professionals to whom schools can turn in crisis situations. I have delivered presentations at national and state conferences on topics that included public relations for school board members, volunteerism in public schools, and the development of school/business partnerships. Prior to becoming an accredited public relations professional, I excelled as a Radio News Reporter and Anchor, so I offer expert knowledge of how media functions "behind the scenes."

While I can provide outstanding references at the appropriate time, I would appreciate your holding my expression of interest in your organization in confidence until after we have a chance to discuss your needs. I hope you will contact me soon to suggest a time when we might meet in person.

Sincerely,

Tanisha Dotson, A.G.P.R.

TANISHA DOTSON

1110½ Hay Street, Fayetteville, NC 28305   •   preppub@aol.com   •   (910) 483-6611

OBJECTIVE

To contribute to an organization that can use an accomplished public relations professional who offers expertise in speech writing, media relations, publication development, volunteer recruiting and management, special event planning, and all other areas of communication.

EDUCATION

B.A. in **Mass Communication,** minor in **Business Administration**, Arizona State University, Tempe, AZ, 1994.

ACCREDITATIONS

National accreditation in General Public Relations **(APR),** October 2002.
National accreditation in School Public Relations **(ASPR),** October 2002.

AFFILIATIONS

Member, Board of Directors, Arizona School Public Relations Association, 2001-present.
• Am spearheading a project to develop a network of school public relations professionals to whom schools can turn in crisis situations.
Member, Board of Directors, Sun County chapter of the American Heart Association, 2002-03.
Volunteer, United Way of Sun County, 2001-present.

HONORS

Selected as **"Young Careerist of the Year"** by the Sun County Business/Professional Women's Association, 2001; named first runner-up in the state "Young Careerist" program.

EXPERIENCE

COMMUNICATIONS EDITOR. Arizona School Boards Association, Phoenix, AZ (2003-present). Manage the preparation and distribution of all communications efforts, written and oral; serve as liaison to public officials and members of the print, radio, and tv media.
• **Communications and public relations management:** Oversee all communications and public relations to include speech writing, news releases, handling media relations, and acting as the organization's "voice" in problem situations.
• **Editing and publications management:** Am editor of publications which include the biannual magazine "SPEAK" as well as two monthly newsletters.
• **Subscription management:** Manage subscriptions to the association's monthly public relations packet for school public relations practitioners entitled "P.R. Today."
• **Professional presentations:** Delivered presentations at national conferences.
• **Website maintenance:** Am responsible for all content on our association website.
• **Desktop publishing:** Utilize Pagemaker and Microsoft Word.

COMMUNITY-SCHOOLS RELATIONS COORDINATOR. Sun County Schools, Mesa, AZ (1998-2003). Managed all communications efforts for a system of 23 schools.
• **Publications management:** Was responsible for publications that included a weekly newspaper column, employee newsletter, annual report, and community calendar.
• **Volunteer management:** Through my efforts, the number of volunteers in our database increased from 200 to 800, and volunteer hours soared from 19,000 to 36,000.

Internships: Excelled in these internships while completing bachelor's degree:
REPORTER. WTMP-TV 7, Tempe, AZ (June-Aug 1994). Handled news and feature stories.
PUBLIC RELATIONS INTERN. The Tempe Regional Theater, Tempe, AZ (Fall 1993). Created news releases and promotions for dinner theater productions.
Other experience:
RADIO NEWS REPORTER & ANCHOR. WAZM 107.3, Mesa, AZ (1994-97). Reported on educational, governmental, health, and social issues while writing features and reporting on special events. Presented live reports on elections and other events; anchored a daily 20-minute newscast.

Date

Exact Name of Person
Exact Title
Exact Name of Company
Address
City, State, Zip

Dear Exact Name of Person: (or Dear Sir or Madam if answering a blind ad)

I am writing to express my interest in seeking employment with your organization. My interests lie in public service, and I excel in providing effective and efficient communications, coordinating with the media, and providing consumer education through technology.

As you will see from my enclosed resume, I offer a track record of accomplishment based on my strong personal initiative and outstanding communication skills. As a Communications Technician for the City of Lafayette Communications Center, I create videos which are used for training purposes by the city. The training videos I have developed have been recognized for their role in reducing workplace accidents. In a prior position as a Public Safety Dispatcher II, I was part of a team responsible for implementing Computer Aided Dispatch operations (CAD), thus moving the department to new technology. I am a Certified Training Officer under the Associated Public Safety Communications Officers Inc. (APCO).

I hold a Bachelor of Science degree in Radio and Film and, in a previous position as a Journalist at a radio station, I wrote news stories from AP wire service, conducted telephone interviews, and recorded national public radio evening broadcasts. I also extensively interviewed public officials.

Based on my experience, education, and character, I am confident that I have the diversified skills and talents you need. I can provide excellent references at the appropriate time, and I hope you will contact me to suggest a time when we might meet in person to discuss the position and my strong qualifications for it.

Yours sincerely,

Angela P. Clevinstone

ANGELA P. CLEVINSTONE

1110½ Hay Street, Fayetteville, NC 28305 • preppub@aol.com • (910) 483-6611

OBJECTIVE
I want to contribute to an organization through my outstanding telecommunications skills, experience as a journalist, as well as my outgoing and enthusiastic personality.

EDUCATION
Bachelor of Science degree in Television and Film, Northwestern State University of Louisiana, Natchitoches, LA, 1993.
Graduated from Shreveport Arts High School as a Performing Arts Major, Shreveport, LA, 1988.
Completed numerous training programs and courses related to telecommunications, media relations, effective writing, and other areas sponsored by my employers.

EXPERIENCE
Excelled in the following track record of promotion with the City of Lafayette, LA:
2000-present: COMMUNICATIONS TECHNICIAN. Incorporate lesson plans, taped exercises, and provide hands-on training to employees through developing training videos.
- Created videos related to workplace safety which have helped to reduce accidents.

1994-2000: PUBLIC SAFETY DISPATCHER I/II. Dispatched public safety equipment and personnel in response to emergency requests for service; relayed information to fire, police, and rescue units as appropriate while maintaining safety of all parties.
- Simultaneously operated and monitored multichannel radio/telephone system and terminals utilizing computer-aided dispatch (CAD) as well as recording devices, including equipment for the hearing impaired.
- Certified to process police information through the National Crime Information Center (NCIC) and Department of Criminal Information (DCI).
- As PSD II, handled supervisory duties and trained new team members.

JOURNALIST. WSWL Radio, Northwestern State University of Louisiana, Natchitoches, LA (1990-1993). While earning my degree in Television and Film, wrote news stories from AP wire service, conducted telephone interviews, and recorded national public radio evening newscasts; interviewed police, fire, city hall, and board of education officials.

Other experience: Excelled in these jobs while pursuing my college degree, Natchitoches, LA:
Food Coordinator. Denny's Restaurant. Supervised several cooks and ensured quality of food and service.
Assistant Store Manager. The Cookie Company. Opened the store, baked and sold merchandise, and trained new employees. Served as Acting Manager for one month when the manager and crew resigned.
Sales Representative. The Gap, Magnolia Mall. Became skilled in merchandising and in creating eye-catching window displays.
Food Coordinator. International House of Pancakes, Northwestern State University of Louisiana. Coordinated and supervised six employees; trained 11 new employees.
Librarian's Assistant. Northwestern State University of Louisiana Science Library. Shelved books and assisted library patrons with materials and checkouts.

CERTIFICATIONS E.M.T. National Registry; State Bureau of Investigation Criminal Information Certification.

AFFILIATIONS
Associated Public Safety Communications Officers, Inc. (APCO); National Academy of Emergency Medical Dispatch of USA (EMD).

PERSONAL
Outstanding personal and professional references upon request. Strong work ethic.

Date

Exact Name of Person
Exact Title
Exact Name of Company
Address
City, State, Zip

Dear Exact Name of Person (or Dear Sir or Madam if answering a blind ad):

With the enclosed resume, I would like to express my interest in exploring employment opportunities with your organization.

As you will see from my resume, I offer more than 20 years of experience in highly technical formal and informal environments where I have become an acknowledged expert in the areas of digital imaging and archival photographic restoration. I offer a keen interest in scanning, color-balancing, and restoring archival photographic products as well as a broad base of experience as a photographer and photographic lab technician.

Currently with One World Photo Services, Inc., I perform as an Electronic Imaging Specialist with responsibility for still media in an electronics imaging center in New York City. I have been a key figure in several high-profile projects which include one commissioned by the Museum of American Architecture which resulted in the production of a book on the history of architecture in the U.S. Earlier as a Digital Scanner for Hudson Imaging in Springfield, VA, I worked independently on projects which provided discriminating clients such as the National Geographic Magazine and The National Archives with color-balanced and pleasing products.

I have built a reputation as a talented and quality conscious professional in a wide range of settings from self-employed commercial photographer and artist, to lab photographer for both medical and scientific research labs, to supervisor of photography and production teams. I have become proficient in using the full range of state-of-the-art computers, small and large format scanners, digital printers, aerial cameras, and still cameras as well as printers, processors, and test equipment.

If you can use a mature and technically skilled professional who can be counted on to produce results while ensuring the highest quality services and support, I hope you will call me soon to discuss how I could contribute to your organization. I will provide excellent professional and personal references at the appropriate time. Thank you for your time and consideration.

Sincerely,

Jeffrey J. Wince

JEFFREY JOEL WINCE

1110½ Hay Street, Fayetteville, NC 28305   •   preppub@aol.com   •   (910) 483-6611

OBJECTIVE

To offer strong technical skills in digital imaging and archival photographic restoration to an organization that can benefit from my attention to detail and emphasis on quality control gained through extensive experience as a photographer and lab technician.

EDUCATION & TRAINING

Completed 158 semester hours of course work emphasizing Architecture, Historic Preservation, Fine Arts, and Photography, Savannah College of Art and Design, Savannah, GA, and the University of Georgia, Athens, GA.
Earned certifications in photography, aerial photography, and archival historical photography.

EQUIPMENT EXPERTISE

Through experience and training, am skilled in using equipment including the following:
Computers: Macintosh with Adobe Photoshop software
Scanners: Kodak small format, Imacon Flextight large format, Umax flatbed, and Kodak high resolution models
Printers: Image Maker large format and Kodak and Hewlett Packard laser printers.
Minilabs: Fuji 720 and Noritsu 613 and 1201 color
Cameras: Agiflite 70mm and all formats of still cameras

EXPERIENCE

DIGITAL IMAGING SPECIALIST. One World Photo Services, Inc., New York, NY (2003-present). Utilize computers and computer-driven reproduction devices to produce still media in an electronics imaging center.
- Contributed to the success of several high-profile projects including one commissioned by the Museum of American Architecture, which produced a full color book on architecture.

DIGITAL SCANNING SPECIALIST. Hudson Images, Springfield, VA (1999-2000). Produced digital scans of 35mm color negatives as well as 35mm color slide images while working independently to determine proper techniques, procedures, and methods needed to produce pleasing photographic images for demanding professional clients.
- Emphasized quality control while manipulating and color balancing products for clients such as The National Geographic Magazine and The National Archives.

LOCATION AND LAB PHOTOGRAPHER. Savannah College of Art and Design (SCAD), Savannah, GA (1995-98). For SCAD, completed photo shoots at sites throughout the school's campus for use in catalog and promotional material for the school.
- Provided services which included documenting instrumentation techniques, lab experiments, specialized scientific photography, and exhibit photography.
- Processed black-and-white and color photographs; produced slides from negatives and flat art utilizing optical printers, camera stands, and other specialized piece of equipment.

Highlights of other experience:
Campus Photographer, University of Georgia. Supervised two other photographers while maintaining photo and video equipment.
Lab Photographer, University of Georgia Medical School, Athens, GA. Provided complete photographic services which included shooting negatives and slides of surgical procedures.
Commercial Photographer and Artist, Self-employed. Shot aerial film and used video equipment for commercial and real estate applications; did two-dimensional sketching.
Aerial Photographer, WDGA Channel 36 news, Athens, GA. Maintained video and photo equipment for aerial photography unit of the news station; handled unprocessed film.

PERSONAL

Speak, read, and write Spanish. Am single with no dependents. Available for relocation.

CAREER CHANGE

Date

Exact Name of Person
Title or Position
Name of Company
Address (no., street)
Address (city, state, zip)

DISC JOCKEY
for a successful talk
radio program

Dear Exact Name of Person: (or Dear Sir or Madam if answering a blind ad.)

Would you be interested in considering a new talented professional with extensive experience in radio announcing to join your broadcasting team?

As you will see from my resume, I am a professional radio disc jockey with talents that equip me for this opened position. I am proud of the fact that, at every station with which I have been associated, I have boosted ratings because of my effervescent personality and enthusiastic, likable style of relating to people. I have brought to broadcasting an understanding of people which I have acquired through versatile work experience which includes sales, retail management, fashion merchandising, and modeling.

At WBBM AM/FM, I was praised for my knowledge of all styles of music. I offer not only my ability to originate new ideas but also the practical skills to implement new concepts on the air. A true broadcasting professional with excellent interviewing skills as well as the ability to provide sensitive leadership to others when they are discussing sensitive or controversial subjects, I can provide outstanding personal and professional references.

Currently I am working on my B.A. degree in Media and Public Relations at DePaul University in Chicago while excelling in my current position. I am sharpening my public relation skills by gaining local celebrity status through dedicated community involvement. At KVXN, I am have successfully increased market share ratings by 38% in 2001 and 2002.

If you would like to talk in person about your needs, I would be delighted to make myself available at your convenience by phone or in person. I am certain you would find me to be someone who could become a valuable radio personality for your organization.

Yours sincerely,

Scott Rodney Wigle

SCOTT RODNEY WIGLE

1110½ Hay Street, Fayetteville, NC 28305   •   preppub@aol.com   •   (910) 483-6611

OBJECTIVE

To offer my outstanding communication, public relations, and computer skills along with my ability to reach people through the radio medium.

EDUCATION

B.A. in Media and Public Relations, DePaul University, Chicago, IL, degree anticipated in 2004.

EXPERIENCE

DISC JOCKEY. KVXN 79 FM, Chicago IL (2003-present). Refined my public speaking and communication skills in part-time positions at various area locations.
- Increased market share ratings by 38% in 2001 and 2002.
- Developed popularity within the local community because of involvement in community outreach programs.

RADIO ANNOUNCER INTERNSHIP. WBBM AM/FM, Chicago, IL (2002-2003). Developed many creative programming ideas which boosted station ratings; for example, provided leadership in developing a successful talk radio program.
- Utilized my expert knowledge of rhythm and blues and soul music.
- Handled day-time drives and acted as announcer for on-air contests.
- Participated in community activity promotions.
- Coordinated arrangements for various station gatherings which included parties, dinners, and award ceremonies.

BROADCASTING INTERN. WCIV 81 AM Radio, Chicago IL (2001-2002). Assisted the news director of this National Public Radio Station by rewriting local stories which had appeared in the published newsletter, *Radio Talk*.
- Covered political and entertainment activities throughout the city.
- Worked with equipment including reel-to-reel player/recorders, cartridge machines, tape and CD players, and computers.
- Played traditional and contemporary jazz music as well as announcing news which affected the residents of the Chicago.

DESKTOP PUBLISHING ASSISTANT. Quebecor Printing, Chicago, IL (1999-2001). Gained experience and proficiency in using PageMaker while engaged in developing layouts, editing, and proofreading materials for a variety of publications.
- Contributed my skills to ensure the quality of materials including: catalogs, brochures, public relations and sales materials, and displays.
- Learned the techniques for composing, editing, and proofreading specially needed for producing monthly newsletters.
- Was chosen to attend trade shows to introduce and sell products.
- Oversaw the details of ensuring bulk mailings were organized and sent out in a timely manner.

COMPUTER SKILLS

Am proficient in using Microsoft Word, PowerPoint, CorelDraw, PageMaker.

PERSONAL

Am exceptionally effective at researching, planning, and coordinating projects. Apply my problem-solving skills while displaying my effectiveness in crisis management.

Date

Exact Name of Person
Exact Title
Exact Name of Company
Address
City, State, Zip

Dear Exact Name of Person (or Dear Sir or Madam if answering a blind ad):

With the enclosed resume, I would like to express my interest in exploring employment opportunities with your organization. As you will see from my resume, I am an experienced distribution industry professional with a management background as well as a proven history of developing innovative new sales and marketing programs and solving problems.

Currently I am General Manager of Sandlin Press, a distributor of books and magazines based in Memphis. I advanced in a track record of promotion to General Manager after excelling in jobs as an Office Manager, Sales Manager, Buyer, and then Operations Manager. As Operations Manager, I transformed inefficient warehouse operations into a model of efficiency. In my current position, I manage a $10 million sales budget.

You will notice from my resume that Plath Press (my employer for 15 years) was recently acquired by Sandlin Press. I have been encouraged to remain with the new owners. However, I am selectively exploring opportunities with other industry firms.

I hope you will call or write me soon to suggest a time convenient for us to meet and discuss your current and future needs and how I might serve them. Thank you in advance for your time.

Sincerely,

Tonya L. Maggard

Alternate last paragraph:
I hope you will welcome my call soon to arrange a brief meeting at your convenience to discuss your current and future needs and how I might serve them. Thank you in advance for your time.

TONYA LORRAINE MAGGARD

1110½ Hay Street, Fayetteville, NC 28305　　•　　preppub@aol.com　　•　　(910) 483-6611

OBJECTIVE　　To apply my creativity in developing innovative new sales and marketing programs to an organization that can use a mature professional with expertise in dealing with people, solving complex distribution problems, improving market share, and satisfying customers.

EXPERIENCE　　*Provided a stable hands-on management style while excelling in a track record of advancement as a key figure in the continued growth of Sandlin Press (formerly Plath Press), a Memphis, TN, distributor of books and magazines:*

2003-present: GENERAL MANAGER. Sandlin Press. Control a $10 million sales budget while managing all phases of day-to-day operations.

- Plan routes so that approximately 75 employees could complete them and keep to scheduled delivery times. Manage sales account activities for two large grocery chains: met their needs by supplying 1,100 stores with all of their children's books as well as 330 stores with magazines and books of all types.
- Contribute valuable ideas as a member of a committee making decisions on computer applications and suggesting possible improvements in the existing system and to distribution procedures.
- Utilize my originality and creativity to develop informative and exciting ideas for publicity committees for national conventions.
- Sold representatives of grocery store chains on the idea of improving the type of display racks being used. Provide new corporate owners with my experience and knowledge of the news and magazine distribution process.

1999-2003: OPERATIONS MANAGER. Plath Press. Displayed a talent for handling complex simultaneous activities when I took over management of operations: oversaw warehouse operations, office administration, route scheduling and supervision, and merchandising.

- Founded and was elected as the first chairman of SPD, Inc., a group of 12 wholesale distributors from five states who organized to share resources and assistance.
- Elected as vice president of AFDNE and as chairman of a planning committee for a national convention, worked on numerous committees geared toward developing and maintaining relations with publishers as well as setting up round tables and conferences.
- On my own initiative, automated record keeping; researched options and directed the installation and conversion of records to a new system.

1993-99: SALES MANAGER and **BUYER.** Discovered a talent for sales and was effective in calling on potential buyers to sell and promote new products.

- Earned a reputation as a good listener who would take the time to understand what a customer needed and base my sales techniques on that knowledge.
- Applied my organizational skills and product knowledge to market and sell products with an emphasis on children's books to include participating in book fairs.
- Transferred to sales after six years (1987-93) as Office Manager handling accounts payable and receivable, payroll, and computer operations.

EDUCATION　　Completed a year of general studies at the University of Memphis, Memphis, TN, and 30 hours of Business Management course work at Shelby State Community College.

SPECIAL SKILLS　　Familiar with Word and PowerPoint with some exposure to Pagemaker.

PERSONAL　　Thrive on challenge and pressure. Highly self motivated with a talent for selling my ideas.

Date

Exact Name of Person
Title or Position
Name of Company
Address (no., street)
Address (city, state, zip)

Dear Exact Name of Person: (or Dear Sir or Madam if answering a blind ad.)

I would appreciate an opportunity to talk with you soon about how I could contribute to your organization through my management, marketing, and communication skills.

As you will see from my resume, I was selected editor of my college yearbook because of my well-known creativity as well as my ability to manage a fast-paced production operation.

In all the jobs I held while working my way through college, I became a valuable asset to my employers while refining my sales, marketing, and administrative skills. Those jobs helped me acquire insights into retailing, food service, and industrial operations. I have become convinced that hard work and excellent public relations skills are critical ingredients for success in any field.

You would find me to be a loyal and reliable young person who always gives 100% to my job. I hope you will welcome my call soon to arrange a brief meeting at your convenience to discuss your current and future needs and how I might serve them. Thank you in advance for your time.

Sincerely yours,

Mellissa O. Candelier

Alternate last paragraph:
I hope you will call or write me soon to suggest a time convenient for us to meet and discuss your current and future needs and how I might serve them. Thank you in advance for your time.

MELLISSA O. CANDELIER

1110½ Hay Street, Fayetteville, NC 28305　　•　　preppub@aol.com　　•　　(910) 483-6611

OBJECTIVE　　I want to contribute to an organization that can use a hard-working young professional with outstanding planning, organizing, and leadership skills.

EDUCATION　　Bachelor of Arts degree in Business Administration, Phoenix College, Phoenix, AZ, 2002.
- Was active in many community organizations including the Boys and Girls Club and the YMCA youth activities.

EXPERIENCE　　**EDITOR.** Phoenix College, Phoenix, AZ (2003-present). Because of my communication skills and management ability, was selected as editor of the college's yearbook "New Beginnings."
- Motivated and supervised the work of ten writers, production personnel, and others in conceiving and producing a top-quality publication which has received "rave reviews."

ADMINISTRATIVE AIDE. Phoenix College Admissions Office, Phoenix, AZ (2002-2003). Learned the skills involved in managing a busy office while orienting prospective new college students to college activities and marketing the unique qualities of this fine institution.
- Earned a reputation as an excellent "salesperson" with outstanding marketing and communication skills.

SALES REPRESENTATIVE. The Gap, Inc., Phoenix, AZ (2001-2002). Became known as a dynamic young professional who helped cement customer loyalty to this retailer through my strong desire to please the customer.
- Operated cash register; wrapped gifts.
- Assisted customers in making decisions.
- Participated in formal inventories; arranged displays.
- Refined my public relations skills while learning the "nuts and bolts" of successful retailing.

RECEPTIONIST. Drummond Industries, Phoenix, AZ (1999-2001). Worked in a large corporation employing hundreds of people, and was the customer's "first impression" of this business.
- Handled a busy switchboard; set up appointments.
- Participated in marketing projects.
- Performed typing and filing.
- Gained insights into effective business management practices.

ASSISTANT MANAGER. Pedro's Restaurant, Phoenix, AZ (1996-1999). Began working in this family-owned business as a hostess and cashier, and was promoted to handle increasing responsibilities related to managing the restaurant.
- Assured high standards of product quality and customer service.
- Trained and supervised waitresses and cooks.
- Learned about retail and wholesale activities in the food industry.

Other experience:
CAMPUS MINISTER. As a volunteer campus minister at Phoenix College, counseled students with serious problems.

PERSONAL　　Am bi-lingual: German and Spanish. Have computer and typing skills. Will relocate according to employer's needs.

Date

Exact Name of Person
Title or Position
Name of Company
Address (no., street)
Address (city, state, zip)

Dear Exact Name of Person: (or Dear Sir or Madam if answering a blind ad)

I would appreciate an opportunity to talk with you soon about how I could contribute to your organization through my creativity and technical expertise related to television and video editing, directing, and producing.

As you will see from my resume, I hold a B.S. degree in Broadcast Communication and have worked as a director, editor, cameraman, and producer at a production studio. Since I was usually working on limited budgets, I learned to be quite resourceful in turning ordinary gadgets into instruments that could be useful in the production process.

Most recently while working with the Occupational Safety and Health Review Commission in Springfield, VA, I have supervised technical writers and analysts in preparing videos and other material. I recently wrote and edited a nationally distributed Safety in the Workplace video for the Commission. As a manager, I have earned a reputation as an unflappable professional who knows how to instill enthusiasm and a spirit of teamwork in others. I enjoy helping my co-workers, and I have helped some of my colleagues earn distinctions and honors because of the mentoring and training I have provided.

You would find me in person to be a congenial fellow who prides myself on always striving for the best product. I am confident I could add value to your organization, as I have to all organizations of which I have been a part. I have worked with various editing systems, and I offer the proven ability to rapidly master new ones. Outstanding personal and professional references can be provided upon your request.

I hope you will call or write me soon to suggest a time convenient for us to meet and discuss your current and future needs and how I might serve them. Thank you in advance for your time.

Sincerely yours,

Orlando J. Perez

Alternate last paragraph:
I hope you will welcome my call soon to arrange a brief meeting at your convenience to discuss your current and future needs and how I might serve them. Thank you in advance for your time.

ORLANDO J. PEREZ

1110½ Hay Street, Fayetteville, NC 28305 • preppub@aol.com • (910) 483-6611

OBJECTIVE To contribute to an organization that can use a creative professional with technical expertise as a television cameraman, editor, director, and producer along with skills in preparing video and written products designed to advertise, market, and promote ideas.

EDUCATION **Bachelor of Science (B.S.)** degree, Broadcast Communication, Loyola College, Baltimore, MD, 1994; named to Dean's List and President's List (3.3 GPA).
A.A. degree *with honors*, Liberal Arts, Essex Community College, 1991.

LICENSE F.C.C. Radio Operators License

EXPERIENCE **Have progressed in the following track record of promotion with Occupational Safety and Health Review Commission, Springfield, VA:**
2002-present: EDITOR-IN-CHIEF & PRODUCER. Occupational Safety and Health Review Commission, Springfield, VA. Wrote and produced national Safety in the Workplace video for the OSHRC which was distributed to large organizations and plants all over the country to be shown during training sessions. Supervise six technical writers and analysts in the collection, analysis, and presentation of material.
- Developed written and video materials for a package which provided large companies with materials designed to reintroduce safety and health practices into workplaces which had received less than optimal ratings.
- Have become known for my professional style of meeting every deadline without getting flustered; always promote a cooperative team spirit.
- Was promoted to this job because of my excellent performance as OSHRC's Training Director.

2001-02: TRAINING DIRECTOR. Occupational Safety and Health Review Commission, Springfield, VA. Was hired to train writers and others producing audio/visual materials for the commission on the importance of safety in the workplace.
- Was chosen to manage technical and safety training for a 150-person organization; took over a program evaluated as average and increased its rating to "outstanding" as evaluated during a rigorous annual inspection.

Other experience:
DIRECTOR/EDITOR/CAMERAMAN/PRODUCER. Turnstile Productions, Rockville, MD (1998-00). For a daily show and three weekly programs aired by a local station in the Rockville and surrounding area, performed work on location and in the studio.
- Was responsible for pre-production, production, and post-production.
- Performed 90% of my work on a 3/4″ tape and editing system.
- Since all shoots were accomplished with minimal equipment, became very creative and resourceful in turning inexpensive gadgets into useful production equipment.

CAMERAMAN/EDITOR. Most Value Productions Media, Bel Air, MD (1996-98). Shot and edited commercials for local cable ad-insertion in a small market; wrote commercials.

PRODUCTION ASSISTANT. Dunston Media - Channel 18, Baltimore, MD (1993-95). Assisted on remote and in-studio segments for local shows and commercials as a cameraman, lighting technician, and technical director; this was a college internship.

PERSONAL Have worked with different editing systems and master new ones easily. Excellent references.

Date

Exact Name of Person
Title or Position
Name of Company
Address (no., street)
Address (city, state, zip)

Dear Exact Name of Person: (or Dear Sir or Madam if answering a blind ad.)

Can you use a creative and hard-working young professional who offers excellent communication skills as well as the ability to work well with others?

As you will see from my resume, I offer a "track record" of excelling in handling responsibility. Most recently I was promoted to Acting Editor-in-Chief of one of the country's oldest newspapers after proving myself as Managing Editor, Reporter, and Photographer. During college, I worked for *The Tennessee Herald* as a News Reporter and Photographer on a freelance basis, and I also worked for a radio station owned by the newspaper. Although the newspaper is conducting an active search nationally for its new Editor-in-Chief, I feel honored that I have been placed in this position, and I am the youngest person in the history of the newspaper ever to hold this responsibility. In jobs after college, I gained experience in preparing press releases for a politician, announcing television news, and operating a radio station.

I feel certain you would find me to be a self-motivated fast learner who would work hard to contribute to your goals.

I hope you will welcome my call soon to arrange a brief meeting at your convenience to discuss your current and future needs and how I might serve them. Thank you in advance for your time.

Sincerely yours,

Sheila V. McPherson

Alternate last paragraph:
I hope you will call or write me soon to suggest a time convenient for us to meet and discuss your current and future needs and how I might serve them. Thank you in advance for your time.

SHEILA V. MCPHERSON

1110½ Hay Street, Fayetteville, NC 28305 • preppub@aol.com • (910) 483-6611

OBJECTIVE   I want to contribute to an organization that can use a dependable and hard-working young professional who has excellent written and oral communication skills as well as strong public relations ability.

EXPERIENCE   *The Tennessee Herald,* **Chattanooga, TN. Advanced to this position in charge of overall newspaper operations by excelling in the following "track record:"**
2003-present: ACTING EDITOR-IN-CHIEF. Was recently promoted to supervise a staff of twelve while providing story assignments and deciding which stories/photos would be published. I was asked to assume this position when the previous editor resigned with no notice.
  * Write features and editorials. Continue to serve as one of the paper's photographers.
  * Monitor all aspects of newspaper distribution to 2,500 customers.
  * Dramatically improved the newspaper's physical look as well as its content.
  * Increased advertising sales 15% while also increasing distribution and consumer awareness of the product.

2002: MANAGING EDITOR, REPORTER, and **PHOTOGRAPHER.** Assisted the editor with editing and laying out copy while supervising a staff of five.
  * Reported/wrote stories; took photographs; assigned stories.
  * Used my public relations skills to develop excellent relationships with other organizations.

Highlights of other experience:
JUNIOR PRESS AGENT. "Gene Greenberg for State Senate" Campaign, Chattanooga, TN (2001). As a press intern for a successful senate race, released campaign information to the media and performed liaison with radio, television, and newspapers.
  * Wrote and distributed press releases. Attended press conferences and business meetings.

STUDIO ENGINEER. WAKM-AM Talk Radio, Chattanooga, TN (2000-2001). Assumed total responsibility for turning on and operating the radio transmitter.
  * Assisted the disc jockey in logging records.

NEWS REPORTER. WHEZ-FM Radio and *The Tennessee Herald,* Chattanooga, TN (1997-2000). Learned how to write and announce a radio newscast in a job that involved reporting the news and sports from my high school.
  * As a News Reporter for my high school paper, conducted interviews and refined my writing skills.

EDUCATION   **B.A. degree in Communications,** University of Tennessee at Chattanooga, 1998.
  * Was elected Secretary of my Senior class.
  * Received awards as a "Reporter of the Year" and for leadership.

PUBLICATIONS
  * Print: Have written features, news stories, and editorials published in college and local papers.
  * Television: Directed, produced, and edited a ten-minute television news feature; announced the five-minute news at midday for radio.

PERSONAL   Am a creative person who works well independently or as part of a team. Computer literate, have operated word processors. Will cheerfully relocate and travel as needed.

Date

Exact Name of Person
Exact Title
Exact Name of Company
Address
City, State, Zip

Dear Exact Name of Person: (or Dear Sir or Madam if answering a blind ad):

With the enclosed resume, I would like to express my interest in exploring employment opportunities with your organization.

As you will see from my resume, I have excelled in sales and sales management while working for my current employer. I have played a key role in the growth of my employer's business, and I have received numerous awards recognizing my accomplishments in establishing large accounts, achieving the status of top producer, and becoming recognized as the overall "staff person of the year." I take great pride in the fact that I have helped my customer accounts grow their businesses through the quality business advice and technical expertise I have provided. Putting my customer's needs first is the way I do business, and that philosophy has helped me gained the respect and loyalty of the accounts I serve.

In my spare time, I am active in my community, and I have served as President of the Board of Directors of My Sister's House, a respected "halfway house" for female substance abusers and alcoholics who wish to recover from that lifestyle. With a reputation as an effective and inspirational public speaker, I also donate much of my spare time to delivering motivational presentations at high schools, youth groups, colleges, as well as business and professional groups. I strongly believe that each of us has an obligation to help others in the community, and I aggressively seek to do my part. I am a member of the International Speakers Network, Inc.

Although I am held in high regard by my current employer, I have decided to selectively explore other opportunities in organizations that can use a highly motivated young person with unlimited personal initiative along with a talent for dealing effectively with others. If you can make use of my skills and experience, I hope you will contact me to suggest a time when we might meet to discuss your needs. At the appropriate time, I can provide excellent references, but I would appreciate your not contacting my current employer until after we speak.

Sincerely,

Thomas J. Catchpole, Jr.

THOMAS J. CATCHPOLE, JR.

1110½ Hay Street, Fayetteville, NC 28305　　·　　preppub@aol.com　　·　　(910) 483-6611

OBJECTIVE　　To benefit an organization that can use an accomplished young professional with strong sales and sales management skills along with a proven ability to work effectively with others in order to provide outstanding customer service and establish strong relationships.

PUBLIC　　Member, International Speakers Network, Inc.
SPEAKING　　Received letters of appreciation from these and other organizations for delivering effective
SKILLS　　motivational speeches which were praised for "mobilizing, inspiring, and empowering others."

COMMUNITY　　A committed community leader, and have provided leadership in the following organizations:
LEADERSHIP　　**President of the Board of Directors,** *My Sister's House,* 2002-present. Provide guidance to this organization funded by the Department of Mental Health. Recruited new people to the board of directors who have helped shape the vision of the organization. Initiated and implemented clothing and food programs. The organization provides assistance to women in recovery from substance abuse.
Public Speaker, *Shelby County Minority AIDS Speakers Bureau, Inc. and the City of Memphis Vocational Program.* Delivered motivational lectures on identifying and implementing personal and professional goals. Have been involved in youth outreach programs.
Past Member, *The Memphis Medical Employee Council and Activity Committee.* Presented to management the concerns of employees. Coordinated hospital contributions to My Sister's House clothing and food program.

EXPERIENCE　　**GENERAL SALES MANAGER.** Memphis Press, Memphis, TN (2003-present). Was promoted from Account Executive after excelling as the company's top producer; within one month tripled sales while developing new and servicing existing accounts.
- Have played a major role in the growth of this paper, which has expanded from two sections to three sections because of the growth of advertising revenue.
- Represent the publisher and the company at conferences, briefings, and interviews.
- Hire, train, and supervise all sales professionals; on my own initiative, regularly attend business workshops designed to increase motivation and raise production levels.
- As the top salesperson, earned numerous awards for consistently increasing my sales.
- Developed/solidified relationships in the Memphis market; landed important new large accounts. Was Top Sales Producer, 2003; Staff Person of the Year, 2001; and received a sales award, 2001.

DOOR-TO-DOOR SALES REPRESENTATIVE. Hoover, Memphis, TN (2002-03). Fine-tuned my customer service skills with prospective clients while conducting door-to-door sales.
- Sold Hoover cleaners via in-home demonstrations. Explained benefits to customers.

SALES REPRESENTATIVE. McClennan Distributor, Nashville, TN (2001-02). Through persistence, built a loyal client base through word-of-mouth; sold nutrition and health supplies.

FINANCIAL SALES REPRESENTATIVE. Citi Financial Services, Memphis, TN (1998-00). Refined my ability to sell an intangible product. Learned insurance and home equity products.

EDUCATION　　Extensive management and marketing training sponsored by Tallgrass, Inc. 2001.

PERSONAL　　Hard worker with a high energy level. Experienced in dealing with a broad range of people.

Date

Anne McKinney, Publisher
Prep Publishing
Box 66
Fayetteville, NC 28302

**GRAPHIC DESIGNER &
PROJECT COORDINATOR**

for a commercial printing
company

Dear Mrs. McKinney:

I would appreciate an opportunity to talk with you soon about how I could contribute to your publication through my experience in computer graphic design and layout in the field of desktop publishing.

My most recent job with Stillwater Printer has allowed me opportunities to develop proficiency in using PageMaker and Quark software while involved in the layout, proofreading, and editing of materials used in producing two monthly newsletters.

As a volunteer in the arts community, I have produced public relations materials while working as a project manager and chairman of art shows with full responsibility for developing all necessary publicity and public relations materials.

I hope you will call or write soon to suggest a time convenient for us to meet and discuss the current and future needs of your organization and how I might serve them. Thank you in advance for your time.

Sincerely yours,

Pandora L. Steigler

PANDORA L. STEIGLER

1110½ Hay Street, Fayetteville, NC 28305 • preppub@aol.com • (910) 483-6611

OBJECTIVE

I want to apply my creativity and experience related to graphics, the arts, and communications to an organization in need of a detail-oriented young professional who relates and works well with others.

SPECIAL SKILLS & AREAS OF EXPERTISE

- Offer skills in graphic design, layout, and desktop publishing.
- Am experienced in word processing, proofreading, and editing.
- Use Quark and PageMaker, Corel Draw, and Lotus.
- Have experience in directing video tape productions.
- Offer skills in office operations including typing, answering multiline phones, data/entry/keypunch, and bookkeeping.

EXPERIENCE

PROJECT COORDINATOR & GRAPHICS DESIGNER. Stillwater Printing, Lionville, PA (2003-present). Gained experience and proficiency in using PageMaker and Quark software while engaged in developing layouts, editing, and proofreading materials for a variety of publications.
- Contributed my skills to ensure the quality of materials including catalogs, brochures, public relations and sales materials, and displays.
- Learned the techniques for composing, editing, and proofreading specially needed for producing monthly newsletters.
- Was chosen to attend trade shows to introduce and sell products.
- Oversaw the details of ensuring bulk mailings were organized and sent out in a timely manner.

ADMINISTRATIVE ASSISTANT. Rebus, Inc., Pennsylvania, PA (2000-2002). Performed general office functions while completing correspondence, conducting research, and keeping the chief executive informed.
- Excelled in a 2000 internship and was asked to stay with the organization.
- Contributed to smooth running of the office by overseeing work in the president's absence, setting up a filing system, learning to research artists' biographical data, and updating mailing lists.

HIGHLIGHTS OF OTHER EXPERIENCE

- Worked with artists, jurors, and volunteers while coordinating all aspects of public relations, soliciting sponsors, and managing a national juried photographic art exhibition.
- Excelled in adapting to a variety of situations and getting along with people from many different backgrounds as a "temporary" clerk and receptionist.
- Served as the chairperson for a summer 2003 program of art exhibits: scheduled/managed volunteers, displayed artwork, designed the layout.
- Learned to do in-depth research of artist's biographical data for files, shows, and instructors in a summer job as a Research Assistant at Temple University's Farthing Gallery.

EDUCATION & TRAINING

B.S., Art Marketing, Temple University, Pennsylvania, PA, 2001.
- Held membership and offices in the art and interior design clubs and in Alpha Omicron Pi sorority.

Attended seminars on video production, desktop publishing, and proofreading.

PERSONAL

Am an enthusiastic individual with a high energy level. Offer excellent verbal and written communication skills.

WHILE ATTENDING THE GREENVILLE ARTS & DESIGN ACADEMY ART SCHOOL, I RECEIVED INSTRUCTION FROM A WIDE VARIETY OF ESTABLISHED ARTISTS.

JOSEPHINE COLLINS, illustrator
Liberty University, Lynchburg, VA
School of the Arts
Slade School, University of London

ILLUSTRATOR & PAINTER

Instead of the cover letter which accompanied her resume, here you see a description of the painters and artists with whom she studied. Typically such a page would be included in her portfolio.

SETH MCFADDEN, graphic designer/illustrator
James Madison University
M. F.A., College of Arts and Design, Harrisburg, VA

CARL WESLEY, curator/printmaker
Greenville Arts & Design Academy
Fine Arts School & Museum
Greenville, SC

CLINTON CARTELLE, painter
University of Southern California
Fine Arts Academy

LONNELL ROBERTS, art historian
M.A., Oxford University,
School of European Arts
United Kingdom

DEMOND GROVE, graphic designer
Northern Arizona University
Museum & School of the Arts

LAVARD NELSON, painter
Savannah College of Arts and Design, SCAD
Savannah, Georgia

MICHAEL BRISBANE, printmaker
State University of New York
K.D. Perrins Art Institute
Albany, NY

DARRYL REXX, painter
James Madison University
College of Arts and Design
Harrisburg, VA

ANDREW MARTIN, painter, printmaker
M.A., Oxford University,
School of European Arts
United Kingdom

KENNETH ELLISON, painter, printmaker
Northern Arizona University
Museum & School of the Arts
Flagstaff, AZ

VIRGINIA L. GARNETTE

1110½ Hay Street, Fayetteville, NC 28305   •   preppub@aol.com   •   (910) 483-6611

OBJECTIVE

To benefit an organization through my artistic talents in illustration, window/store display, interior design, painting, and designing, as well as my excellent customer relations skills and management experience.

EXPERIENCE

ILLUSTRATOR/PAINTER. Greenville, SC (2003-present). Involved in illustrating a series of children's books; painting; and preparing own works for various marketing projects.

COMMERCIAL ARTIST. Ethan Art Gallery, Greenville, SC (2002-03). Had the opportunity to design logos and art work for department stores, the newspapers, and specialty shops; created window and in-store displays.
* Created and managed this fine arts studio/gallery, the only commercial art firm in town.
* Developed skills as an instructor by teaching private art lessons.

INTERIOR DECORATOR. Kalston Home Furnishings, Greenville, SC (1999-02). Worked in customers' homes advising them on wallpaper, draperies, carpet and accessories, in addition to selling furniture.
* Organized display and sample rooms to better merchandise accessories.
* Commissioned own paintings to store customers/other decorators.

WINDOW DESIGN/DISPLAY SPECIALIST. Porterhouse Designs, Spartanburg, SC (1996-1999). Designed and organized store and window displays for two stores while gaining retail sales experience.
* Drew attention to one store with imaginative props and display, most notably a miniature western town. Organized and stocked display room.
* Learned techniques of creating illusion in display.
* Established advertising department which designed newspaper, radio, TV ads.

SALES MANAGER. Ivan Anheuser and Company, Inc., Greenville, SC (1994-1996). Managed a retail sales, matting/framing custom art work and controlled the inventory of art work, frames and supplies.
* Developed expertise in technical differences in types of framing.
* Gained valuable business/management experience.

PRODUCTION MANAGER/WATERCOLOR ARTIST. Natten Art Collections & Frames Inc., Greenville, SC (1991-93). Organized matt cutting, framing and shipping of original wildlife art; painted limited edition art work.
* Trained with Paula Lucey as commercial artist while learning how to market to specialty shops. Assisted with company catalog which was sent to East Coast Gift Shops.

HONORS

1997-1998: Voted as a juror in annual art show and auction.
             Honored with two first places, one second, one third.
1995-1996: Coastal Carolina State Fair, juried art show, third and fourth place.
1993-1994: Designed logo for the City of Greenville, SC.

EDUCATION

Studied Fine Art Painting/Illustration at the Greenville Arts and Design Academy, Greenville, SC, 1994.

PERSONAL

Confident and artistic. Get along well with people. Am quite involved in church activities. Strong planner with organizational skills.

Date

Exact Name of Person
Title or Position
Name of Company
Address (no., street)
Address (city, state, zip)

JOURNALIST
for a college
yearbook

Dear Exact Name of Person: (or Dear Sir or Madam if answering a blind ad.)

Can you use a talented young journalist who offers outstanding academic credentials along with extraordinary writing ability and creativity?

While earning my B.A. degree in journalism from the Loyola Marymount University, I have pursued the news-editorial sequence with broadcast option. In 2002, as a Television Intern with WSGI-TV in Monterey, I was involved in nearly all facets of television reporting and production, wrote some small features, and learned how to put a breaking story together.

I am considered by all who know my work to be a very skilled writer who has a good imagination as well as the ability to relay information in unique and exciting ways. Features I have written have been published in a newspaper and in a book. I am a hard worker who has learned from experience how to meet tight deadlines and how important a sales orientation is to the success of business activities.

I hope you will welcome my call soon to arrange a brief meeting at your convenience to discuss your current and future needs and how I might serve them. Thank you in advance for your time.

Sincerely yours,

Mitchell S. Thomas

Alternate last paragraph:
I hope you will call or write me soon to suggest a time convenient for us to meet and discuss your current and future needs and how I might serve them. Thank you in advance for your time.

MITCHELL S. THOMAS

1110½ Hay Street, Fayetteville, NC 28305   •   preppub@aol.com   •   (910) 483-6611

OBJECTIVE

I want to contribute to an organization that can use a talented young Journalist who has outstanding academic credentials along with extraordinary writing ability and creativity.

EDUCATION

B. A. degree in Journalism, Loyola Marymount University (LMU), Monterey, CA, 1999.
- Pursued the news-editorial sequence with broadcast option.
- Studied German and French.

PUBLICATIONS and RESEARCH

- Authored a detailed feature on the history and future of the Old Western Trade House, published in the Monterey Morning News in 1998.
- Wrote a lively feature depicting the LMU Spring Festival which will appear in the 1998 "New Beginnings" Yearbook.
- Am in the 11th year of a detailed research study of the royal family of England: after a decade of work, now possess many valuable collectibles.

EXPERIENCE

JOURNALIST and **ADVERTISING REPRESENTATIVE.** LMU New Beginnings Yearbook, Monterey, CA (2003-present). With a reputation as an exceptional writer who approaches language with creative flair and technical expertise, I produce feature articles for the yearbook that capture the spirit of life at LMU.
- Simultaneously conceive, organize, and implement campaigns to enhance yearbook sales and sell advertising space.
- Write and design layouts for newspaper ads, pamphlets, and mailings.
- Gain experience in preparing questionnaires to identify consumer interest and awareness.
- Excel in working under continuously tight deadlines.

TELEVISION INTERN. WSGI-TV, Monterey, CA (2002-2003). In the summer between my junior and senior years, was involved in nearly all facets of television reporting and production.
- Researched news stories; wrote small features.
- Assisted reporters, writers, producers, anchors, and camera professionals.
- Maintained communication between the station and organizations statewide.
- Gained insight into the inner workings of a newsroom.
- Observed how a show is put together, from start to finish.
- Learned how to take a breaking story, research it, and pull it together.

SALESMAN. Monterey Office Supply Co., Monterey, CA (1999-2002). While working in outside sales and in the office, gained skills in customer relations and came to understand that personal motivation is the key to success in sales.

PROFESSIONAL ACTIVITIES

Appointed the Advisor for Monterey Chapter, Association of Professional Journalist, 2002. Attended the Society of Professional Journalists' Convention: was involved in seminars in Washington, D.C., on the Freedom of Information Act, and on media versus privacy issues, 2001.

PERSONAL

Am computer literate; offer experience with Microsoft Word, Excel, and PageMaker. Am skilled with still cameras and darkroom processes. Have a good imagination and can relay information in interesting and unique ways. Take a positive and persistent approach to any job I tackle.

Date

Exact Name of Person
Title or Position
Name of Company
Address (number and street)
Address (city, state, and zip)

Dear Exact Name of Person: (or Sir or Madam if answering a blind ad)

With the enclosed resume, I would like to make you aware of my interest in becoming a part of your corporate communications team.

As you will see from my resume, I hold two Masters degrees —one in Communications and one in International Relations – in addition to my B.A. While traveling and living all over the country, I have worked as a freelance journalist and as a communications manager for corporations and nonprofit organizations.

Most recently as a freelance journalist and news stringer, I have earned respect for my investigative abilities while consulting for national news magazines, developing cover stories, and working as a news stringer. As a stringer for the *Chicago Tribune,* my work covering the World Trade Center disaster resulted in a front page story.

I am also experienced in managing organizational communications and public relations. As Corporate Public Relations Manager for a diversified medical corporation, I was responsible for all internal corporate communications including training videos, newsletters, and special projects. As Public Relations Coordinator for Carson Media Research, Inc., I supported the launch of new computer industry products through media liaison, industry trade shows, direct mail projects, and other activities.

A very community-oriented individual, I am skilled at rapidly assimilating myself into an organization and establishing excellent working relationships. My naturally enthusiastic personality and ability to infect others with my enthusiasm have proved to be valuable assets in corporate communications, and they have enabled me to develop a vast network of contacts within numerous industries and with journalists and communications professionals throughout the world.

I can provide excellent personal and professional references, and I hope you will contact me to suggest a time when we might meet in person to discuss your needs and how I might serve them. Thank you in advance for your time.

Yours sincerely,

Theresa Yolanda Rose

THERESA YOLANDA ROSE

1110½ Hay Street, Fayetteville, NC 28305 • preppub@aol.com • (910) 483-6611

OBJECTIVE To benefit an organization that can use an accomplished communicator and respected journalist who has created insightful written reports for national print and broadcast media and who has also managed corporate communications, public relations, and media relations.

AFFILIATION Member, Investigative Reporters and Editors

EDUCATION **Master of Arts (M.A.) in Communications**, Northwestern University, Evanston, IL, 1996.
Master of Arts (M.A.) in International Relations, UCLA, Berkeley, CA, 1992.
Bachelor of Arts (B.A.) in International Relations, Cornell University, Ithaca, NY, 1988.
- Was President of the Student Government and Editor of the Year Book.
- Received the Literary Award, International Studies Award, Leadership Award.

EXPERIENCE *Have excelled in a variety of jobs while traveling and living all over the country.*
JOURNALIST & NEWS STRINGER. Freelance (2001-present). Report a variety of features and news stories for nationally distributed magazines, television news magazine programs, and weekly newspapers.
- Was a consultant and reporter for the national news program *60 Minutes* on several occasions; one story resulted in an Emmy-nominated news-feature broadcast.
- Consulted on a *Prime Time Live* news feature.
- Developed cover stories for the nationally distributed magazine *Newsweek.*
- Was a News Stringer for the *Chicago Tribune* and *Louisville Guardian*; my work as a Stringer covering the World Trade Center disaster of 9/11/01 resulted in a *Chicago Tribune* front-page story. Earned respect for my investigative ability.

REPORTER. Peace Corps *Hand in Hand* monthly magazine and *Peace Corps Today* weekly newspaper, Springfield, VA (2000-01). Began as an Assistant to an Editor and, within three months, was assigned as a Feature Reporter for the national weekly newspaper; after six months, was promoted to Associate Editor.
- As the Business Reporter for the four-color monthly magazine, wrote approximately 10 news and feature-length articles per issue; developed cover stories.
- Refined editing skills while becoming skilled in newspaper and magazine layout/design.

CORPORATE PUBLIC RELATIONS MANAGER. United Healthcare Corporation, Fairfax, VA (1999). For a diversified corporation which included a hospital, nursing home, assisted living facility, medical imaging center, mobile blood testing clinic, and community outreach programs, was responsible for all internal corporate communications.
- Wrote and produced a corporate training video explaining a new benefits program.
- Planned and managed the corporate public relations budget.

PUBLIC RELATIONS COORDINATOR. Historical Williamsburg Society, Williamsburg, VA (1998-99). Coordinated special events such as the Christmas Candlelight Tour and Town Market Days while coordinating local and national media placement.

PUBLIC RELATIONS COORDINATOR. Carson Media Research, Inc., Chicago, IL (1996-98). Established an editorial calendar for international media placement while supporting product launches with media liaison, monitoring product reviews in trade magazines, assisting the public relations manager with industry trade shows, and supervising direct mail.

PERSONAL Enthusiastic professional with strong management skills with outstanding references.

Date

Exact Name of Person
Title or Position
Name of Company
Address (no., street)
Address (city, state, zip)

MARKET RESEARCHER

for this college radio
station

Dear Exact Name of Person: (or Dear Sir or Madam if answering a blind ad.)

I would appreciate an opportunity to talk with you soon about how I could contribute to your organization through my management potential, business education, and outstanding personal qualities.

Known as a hard worker who has a talent for rapidly learning new concepts as well as business equipment skills, I recently earned my B.A. degree in Business Management. While earning my degree I have excelled in handling responsibilities in the areas of market research, finance and banking, as well as office administration.

I have excelled in all my jobs so far because I have an exceptional ability to motivate and communicate with others. I sincerely enjoy serving each customer as well as helping co-workers develop to their maximum potential.

I hope you will welcome my call soon to arrange a brief meeting at your convenience to discuss your current and future needs and how I might serve them. Thank you in advance for your time.

Sincerely yours,

Eva C. Ernst

Alternate last paragraph:
I hope you will call or write me soon to suggest a time convenient for us to meet and discuss your current and future needs and how I might serve them. Thank you in advance for your time.

EVA C. ERNST

1110½ Hay Street, Fayetteville, NC 28305　　•　　preppub@aol.com　　•　　(910) 483-6611

OBJECTIVE　　To contribute to an organization that could benefit from the combination of my business education, customer service experience, ability to motivate others, and proven management potential.

EDUCATION　　**B.A. degree, Business Management,** University of Northern Colorado, Greely, CO, 1998.
- Concentrated in Personnel Management.
- Course work included:
  Labor/Personnel Management: estimating costs of hiring/firing
  Public Policy: dealing with government policies
  Marketing and Research: developing new products
- Earned Dean's List honors.

EXPERIENCE　　**MARKET RESEARCHER/WRITER.** University of Northern Colorado, Greely, CO (2003-present). For this college radio station, identify target market for a particular type of music through conducting field interviews, assembling data, and writing a final report presenting analyses and recommendations.
- Have been commended for my exceptional ability to motivate others in a team project situation.
- Exhibited my versatility as a "team player" through handling leadership responsibilities as well as field assignments.
- Refined my skills in collecting, analyzing, and presenting data for management decision making.

ACCOUNTS SERVICE REPRESENTATIVE. Colorado Federal Bank, Greely, CO (2001-2003). For a fast-growing federal bank, earned a reputation as a hard worker and learned to coordinate banking transactions and customer service functions related to:

check cashing	loan payments
deposits	account inquiries
operating an on-line	computer system

- Became knowledgeable of internal banking operations through exposure to policies and procedures of this branch bank.
- Consistently achieved a high monthly balance rate.

ADMINISTRATIVE ASSISTANT. Greely County School Board, Greely, CO (1998-2001). Gained insight into managing an office for maximum efficiency while handling a wide range of clerical functions.
- Performed wordprocessing, filing, and copying duties.
- Excelled in identifying priorities and meeting deadlines.

EQUIPMENT SKILLS　　Possess working knowledge of Microsoft Word, Excel, and Photoshop.
Have become known for my superior ability to rapidly learn to operate all types of business equipment.

PERSONAL
- Am enthusiastic, dependable, and maintain a positive attitude.
- Possess proven ability to work well with others as a "team player."
- Learn quickly and enjoy challenging opportunities.
- Am active in my church and enjoy working with children.

Date

Exact Name of Person
Title or Position
Name of Company
Address (no., street)
Address (city, state, zip)

MARKETING COORDINATOR & MEDIA LIAISON
for a recreational facility

Dear Exact Name of Person: (or Dear Sir or Madam if answering a blind ad.)

I would appreciate an opportunity to talk with you soon about how I could contribute to your organization through my marketing and public relations skills, combined with my expert ability to design and produce persuasive communication in forms ranging from flyers and brochures to radio spots and newspaper articles.

Superior writing, editing, and proofreading skills

After earning my B.S. degree in Journalism, I excelled in jobs that helped me sharpen my writing, editing, and proofreading skills. In one job at the corporate headquarters of Virginia National Bank, I was credited with significantly improving the quality of this prestigious bank's internal publications. In other jobs, I have developed newsletters "from scratch," trained and managed other journalists writing for a community newspaper, and prepared items ranging from newspaper articles to brochures and flyers. I am proficient in using Microsoft Word and PageMaker, and I am skilled in using a 35 mm camera and performing film processing.

Extensive expertise in marketing and public relations

In my most recent job, I have combined my written and oral communication skills with my public relations ability. I have become skilled in creating effective marketing plans for a wide variety of programs, services, and events, and I use every "tool of the trade" as a communicator to publicize those programs, services, and events. In earlier jobs I also managed publicity, public relations, and information services.

You would find me to be a cheerful and dynamic professional who enjoys combining my technical expertise with my creativity and interpersonal skills in ways that produce "bottom-line" results. In one job as a news manager, for example, I was credited with increasing circulation of a newspaper by 10%! I believe you would find numerous ways that my communication gifts could enrich your organization.

I hope you will welcome my call soon when I try to arrange a brief meeting to discuss your current and future needs and how I might serve them. Thank you in advance for your time.

Sincerely yours,

Summer Raftery

SUMMER RAFTERY

1110½ Hay Street, Fayetteville, NC 28305   •   preppub@aol.com   •   (910) 483-6611

OBJECTIVE

To benefit an organization that can use a creative self-starter and talented public relations professional who combines exceptionally strong written and oral communication skills with a proven ability to use those skills to produce teamwork and commitment to quality.

EDUCATION

Hold **Bachelor of Science (B.S.) degree in Journalism,** Virginia Commonwealth University, Richmond, VA, 1992.
Completed training under Source Publications in video scriptwriting, Richmond, VA, 2002.

TECHNICAL SKILLS

Computers: Proficient in using Microsoft Word and PageMaker.
Cameras: Operate 35 mm cameras; skilled in black-and-white film processing/printing.

EXPERIENCE

MARKETING COORDINATOR/MEDIA LIAISON & JOURNALIST/PHOTOGRAPHER. YMCA of Richmond, Richmond, VA (2003-present). Prepare and present marketing plans, and then create exciting printed and photographic materials, in order to publicize and promote the diversified services/programs/events offered through a vast network of recreational facilities.

- Write feature and news stories for local newspapers; write press releases for media.
- Author and proofread copy for brochures and flyers; develop scripts for briefings.
- Am an expert in using a 35 mm camera to take photographs and make slides. Produce a newsletter for 1200 members; the newsletter has been credited with increasing morale.
- Work with the press on a daily basis; schedule interviews for television and radio and provide media escort/information services. On a special project which involved producing a commercial, provided expertise to the Chamber of Commerce of Richmond.

NEWS MANAGER. *The Daily Voice,* Queens, NY (2001-2003). Increased circulation of this community newspaper by 10% while training new writers in reporting/writing skills; personally wrote half of all stories and took 2/3's of the photos.

PUBLICITY COORDINATOR. American International Group, New York, NY (1999-2001). Developed "from scratch" a newsletter which improved understanding and boosted teamwork among professional staff members at eight separate locations.

INTERNAL PUBLICATIONS ASSISTANT. Virginia National Bank, Richmond, VA (1997-1999). Was praised for improving the quality of the internal publications at this prestigious bank; played a key role in writing and proofreading publications reaching 3,000 people.

PUBLIC RELATIONS MANAGER. YWCA of Richmond, Richmond, VA (1992-1997). Became skilled in identifying target markets by age, income, and program preference while writing press releases and radio spots with potential for reaching more than 300,000 people.

Other experience:
PHOTO ARCHIVES TECHNICIAN. For the "Stars and Stripes" newspaper in West Italy, learned the importance of meticulously maintaining historical files while managing all photo files for the only newspaper serving the American armed forces in Europe.
FEATURE WRITER/PHOTOGRAPHER. Became a skilled interviewer and feature writer as the only civilian on the staff of a weekly newspaper serving a military community.

PERSONAL

Am an enthusiastic participant in competitive team sports, and in college led a traveling drill team to several winning performances over a two-year period. Will happily travel/relocate.

Date

Exact Name of Person
Title or Position
Name of Company
Address (no., street)
Address (city, state, zip)

Dear Exact Name of Person: (or Dear Sir or Madam if answering a blind ad.)

I would appreciate an opportunity to talk with you soon about how I could contribute to your organization through my strong written and oral communication skills as well as my experience in mass communications.

As you will see from my enclosed resume, I will soon graduate with a B.S. degree in Mass Communications and have excelled in coursework ranging from writing for broadcasters to corporate communications. In addition to my college courses, I aggressively sought out opportunities to involve myself in "hands-on" mass communications activities. For example, as a reporter with the student newspaper, I provided media coverage for special events, interviewed speakers for feature articles, and reported on festivals, pageants, and other social events. I used every "tool of the trade" as a communicator to publicize those programs, services, and events. I have recently been selected for a prestigious internship with one of Ft. Lauderdale's leading advertising agencies.

On numerous occasions, I have been selected for special jobs because of my strong written and oral communication skills. For example, I was selected by faculty advisors to edit the college yearbook during my sophomore year, and I provided leadership in producing one of the school's most attractive publications ever published.

You would find me to be a cheerful and dynamic professional who thrives on the challenge of meeting tight deadlines and solving problems under pressure. I have frequently been told that I am poised "beyond my years" and I credit my maturity to my extensive work background. For example, I have worked since I was 16 years old, and I held part-time jobs throughout college to finance my education. As a Sales Associate at Lord & Taylor for four years, I refined my public relations and customer service skills. Subsequently in part-time jobs during college, I excelled as an intern in a legal services environment and that gave me insight into the workings of our judicial system. In another part-time job while financing my college education, I strengthened my computer skills while providing administrative support to two bank vice presidents.

I hope you will welcome my call soon when I try to arrange a brief meeting to discuss your current and future needs and how I might serve them. Thank you in advance for your time.

Sincerely yours,

Bettina C. Hockensmith

BETTINA C. HOCKENSMITH

1110½ Hay Street, Fayetteville, NC 28305   •   preppub@aol.com   •   (910) 483-6611

OBJECTIVE   To contribute to an organization that can use an enthusiastic and creative professional who offers strong communication skills and the ability to develop ideas and provide assistance to others through natural leadership and multiple talents.

EDUCATION   **B.S. in Mass Communications,** Nova Southeastern University, Fort Lauderdale, 2003.
- Maintained a cumulative GPA of above 3.0 while excelling in course work in these areas:
  mass media   social work   psychology   marketing
  corporate communication research procedures   economics
  communications — writing, speaking, and acting; sound, filming, editing
- Was elected as secretary of the student government's Student Activities Committee.
- Through my affiliation with the student newspaper, I provided media coverage for functions, interviewed speakers for feature articles, reported on festivals, and pageants.

Attended National Institute for Broward Community College, FL, for my first two years of basic studies in the Liberal Arts.
- Selected by faculty advisors to edit the college yearbook during my sophomore year, applying my communication skills and creativity to produce an attractive publication.

EXPERIENCE   **MASS COMMUNICATIONS INTERN.** Marks & Morgan Advertising Group, Fort Lauderdale, FL (2003-present). Was specially selected for this prestigious internship with a leading advertising agency. Consistently meet aggressive sales goals through both my patience and persistence in public relations and customer service.
- Am known as a goal-driven, skilled professional who delivers customer satisfaction.

ADMINISTRATIVE ASSISTANT. Wachovia Bank, Boca Raton, FL (2002-03). Gained valuable experience in banking procedures and all phases of the loan process while providing clerical and administrative support to two regional vice presidents specializing in the area of consumer credit.
- Used my talent for organization and attention to detail while creating spreadsheets, typing, and maintaining files for two busy executives. Improved the filing system.
- Polished my knowledge of computer operations using the internet, Microsoft Word and Excel software while typing correspondence as well as handling financial record keeping.

LEGAL OFFICE INTERN. Wilson's Legal Services, Fort Lauderdale, FL (2000-01). Gained valuable exposure to the workings of the law while aiding attorneys in such activities as contacting witnesses to remind them of court appearances.
- Became familiar with the court system and legal procedures while learning to work with elected officials.

SALES ASSOCIATE. Lord & Taylor, Fort Lauderdale, FL (1996-00). In a part-time job while in high school and college, I became adept at completing sales while helping customers, ringing up their pur chases, and opening and closing my register.
- Consistently met or exceeded goals while developing an effective communication style.

TRAINING   Completed a seminar in modality training which aided me in learning to deal with people and to provide them with valuable training; also attended corporate-sponsored programs in Excel.

PERSONAL   Am an articulate speaker and skilled writer. Offer a creative and enthusiastic approach to project development and the organizational skills to see them to completion.

Date

Exact Name of Person
Title or Position
Name of Company
Address (no., street)
Address (city, state, zip)

Dear Exact Name of Person:

I would appreciate an opportunity to show you soon, in person, that I can benefit your organization through my excellent communication skills, public relations and media experience, combined with my recent degree from New York University in Journalism and Radio, TV, and Motion Pictures.

Most recently, I have excelled in using my teaching and "people" skills in a part-time job for the Inner City Youth Club while earning my degree. In a previous job as a news department summer intern for a television station, I developed expertise in writing, editing, and shooting for television as well as in preparing and delivering stories on-camera.

Prior to that, as a promotions aide for WDGI-FM radio station, I acquired valuable skills in effective telephone communication while refining my knack for putting people at ease.

I am sure I can make valuable contributions to your organization, too, and I am also sure you will find me to be a creative, energetic young professional who enjoys travel and meeting new people. I work well under the pressure of long hours and tight deadlines.

I hope you will welcome my call next week when I try to arrange a brief meeting at your convenience to discuss your current and future needs and how I might serve them. Thank you in advance for your time.

Yours sincerely,

Katherine L. James

Alternate last paragraph:
I hope you will call or write me soon to suggest a time convenient for us to meet and discuss your current and future needs and how I might serve them.

KATHERINE LYNN JAMES

1110½ Hay Street, Fayetteville, NC 28305   •   preppub@aol.com   •   (910) 483-6611

OBJECTIVE   I want to contribute to the success of an organization through my excellent written and oral communication skills combined with my experience in broadcast media, public relations, and promotion.

EDUCATION   Earned **B.A. degree, with a double major in Media and Broadcasting, as well as Radio, TV, and Motion Pictures,** New York University, New York, NY, 2003. Courses included:

Broadcast Scriptwriting	Newswriting
Production	Broadcast Journalism
Magazine and Feature Writing	Reporting
Video and Print Editing	Public Relations for Broadcasters

Earned an **A.A. degree, School of Visual Arts,** New York, NY 2000.

EXPERIENCE   **INSTRUCTOR AND SUPERVISOR.** Inner City Youth Club, New York, NY (2003-present). Am a popular instructor of water safety in a job that includes supervising pool safety and lifeguarding.
- Develop skills in coordinating effectively with the public, management, as well as other employees.
- Earn praise for my teaching and "people" skills.

NEWS DEPARTMENT SUMMER INTERN. WRER-TV, New York, NY (2002-03). Developed expertise in a wide range of areas, including these, related to television broadcasting and journalism:

Reporting. Originated and developed story ideas, authored scripts for video, and conducted interviews for on-camera and off.

Editing and shooting: Acquired skills in editing video footage as well as in using a variety of equipment, including the following, in the office and the field: videotape recorder (VTR) studio cameras editing machines "mini-cams."

On-Air Work. Prepared stories that aired on the 6 and 11 pm newscasts.
- Gained experience in both voiceover and stand-up reporting work.
- Learned techniques of effective media writing and production.
- Gained poise and increased my public relations skills in learning how to extract information from strangers in often hostile or strange situations.

PROMOTIONS AIDE. WDGI-FM Radio, Hawthorne Broadcasting Network, New York, NY (2000-2002). Developed expertise in many aspects of promotion in a job that involved wide-ranging duties for a radio station analyzing a possible programming change from "pop" to country music.
- Extensively interviewed and polled people, by phone and in person.
- Acquired valuable skills in effective telephone communication.
- Polished my knack for putting people at ease.

SPECIAL SKILLS   Familiar with Word and PowerPoint with some exposure to Pagemaker.

PERSONAL   Am a creative, energetic young professional who enjoys travel and meeting new people. Work well under the pressure of long hours and tight deadlines.

Date

Exact Name of Person
Title or Position
Name of Company
Address (no., street)
Address (city, state, zip)

Dear Exact Name of Person: (or Dear Sir or Madam if answering a blind ad.)

Can you use a creative young professional who offers excellent communication skills along with "newly-minted" degrees in Public Relations and Speech Communication?

A self-motivated and energetic person, I acquired experience in customer service and customer relations. As you will see from my resume, I am able to relate to and assist people in various situations through my helping and tactful personality.

My experience in planning, organizing, and advising members of an international organization have led me to recognition as a "natural" leader and have afforded me the opportunity to travel and become a valued speaker at district and national conferences.

I hope you will welcome my call soon to arrange a brief meeting at your convenience to discuss your current and future needs and how I might serve them. Thank you in advance for your time.

Sincerely yours,

Dana P. Powell

Alternate last paragraph:
I hope you will call or write me soon to suggest a time convenient for us to meet and discuss your current and future needs and how I might serve them. Thank you in advance for your time.

DANA P. POWELL

1110½ Hay Street, Fayetteville, NC 28305 • preppub@aol.com • (910) 483-6611

OBJECTIVE   To offer my outstanding communication skills to an organization in need of a dedicated and hard-working young professional who offers creativity and a background of supervisory experience.

EDUCATION   Received a **Bachelor of Arts (B.A.) degree, Public Relations,** University of West Florida, Pensacola, FL, 2002.
B.A. degree, Speech Communication, University of West Florida, 2001.
* Served as an Intern for Hope Harber (Ministry for the Homeless), planning fund-raising

COLLEGE COURSE WORK   Was a DEAN'S LIST student, excelling in specialized study including:

Organizational communication	Copy editing
Problems in public relations	Marketing methods
Writing for the electronic media	Business ethics

EXPERIENCE   *Have excelled in these and other jobs while attending college full-time:*
RESIDENTIAL LEASING AGENT. Moss Creek Apartments, Pensacola, FL (2002-present). For an apartment complex, process leases including typing forms, showing apartments to prospective tenants, and arranging for repairs.
* During a change in management, learn to handle irate tenants and difficult situations.

RETAIL CUSTOMER RELATIONS SPECIALIST. Altman's Department Store, Pensacola, FL (1999-2002). For a clothing store, helped customers find merchandise while also arranging merchandise displays, maintaining stock, and processing returns and exchanges.

CUSTOMER SERVICE REPRESENTATIVE. Bentall's Wholesale Company, Pensacola, FL (1997-1999). Developed my skills in communicating with customers while taking phone orders, processing credit checks, typing, and filing.

Earned a reputation as a "natural" leader with outstanding skills in organizing and planning with an international volunteer organization, Premier Outreach, Inc., Pensacola, FL:
DISTRICT ADVISOR. (2002-present). For a three-state district which also includes Pensacola, advise 80 local and area leaders while also preparing reports, planning meetings and conventions, and writing/editing articles for publication.
DISTRICT GOVERNOR. (2000-02). As leader of the district organization, guided the 150 members while earning a reputation as a valued speaker at meetings and conventions.
DISTRICT TREASURER. (1999-00). Learned budget planning and control handling $1,500 in funds for a 180-person district while advising two other chapters and leading them to increased membership and levels of activity.
CHAPTER PRESIDENT. (1997-98). Was involved in planning and managing a wide variety of fund-raising events including coordinating volunteer workers and providing publicity while also editing monthly bulletins.

AFFILIATIONS   Am currently a charter member of the Florida Association of Public Relations.
Selected as Vice President of the University of West Florida Communication Club in 2000.

PERSONAL   Offer knowledge of word processing. Speak, read, and write Greek. Can handle the pressure of working under deadlines and time constraints.

Date

Exact Name of Person
Exact Title or Position
Name of Company
Address (no., street)
Address (city, state, zip)

**MEDIA & PUBLIC
AFFAIRS MANAGER**

for a public relations firm

Dear Exact Name of Person:

I would appreciate an opportunity to talk with you soon about how my experience in public relations and management could benefit your company.

In my current position as Media & Public Affairs Director for Cook Public Relations, I work in a contractual relationship in charge of media and public relations for a major Fortune 500 company. I am involved in projects that require me to effectively manage people, time, and resources in order to meet the needs of my clients. While directing multiple simultaneous projects, I have gained considerable skills in personnel motivation and in human relations while dealing with business officials and national media. In addition to coordinating advertising campaigns with national and local media, I have developed numerous internal public relations tools which have been credited with improving employee morale.

Although I am held in high regard by my current employer, I have made the decision to selectively explore opportunities with leading public relations firms globally.

You would find me to be a versatile professional with superb public relations and management skills. I hope you will welcome my call soon to arrange a time at your convenience to discuss your current and future needs and how I might serve them. Thank you in advance for your time.

Yours sincerely,

Wesley Singleton

Alternate last paragraph:
I hope you will call or write me soon to suggest a time at your convenience for us to meet and discuss your current and future needs and how I might serve them. Thank you in advance for your time.

WESLEY SINGLETON

1110½ Hay Street, Fayetteville, NC 28305   •   preppub@aol.com   •   (910) 483-6611

OBJECTIVE

I want to offer my experience in effectively managing people, time, and resources, combined with my state-of-the-art electronic, computer, and data processing maintenance experience, to a company seeking a versatile manager.

EDUCATION

Earned a **Bachelor of Arts (B.A.) degree in Media Studies and Public Relations,** University of Colorado, Denver, CO, 2002.
Earned an **Associate of Science (A.S.) degree in Computer Science**, Community College of Denver, Denver, CO, 1999.

EXPERIENCE

MEDIA & PUBLIC AFFAIRS DIRECTOR. Cook Public Relations, Rafael, CA (2003-present). In a contractual relationship with a Fortune 500 company, excel in directing all aspects of media and public relations while supervising a staff of 25. Present briefings to top executives and business leaders within the California area.
- Plan and organize VIP trips throughout the U.S.
- Write, edit, and produce a weekly publication "Cook Announcements" which provides corporate information to employees.
- Improved community involvement within the corporation through special informational activities, one event attended by 250,000.
- Have refined my communication skills managing simultaneous projects.

PUBLIC RELATIONS INTERN. BPA and Associates, Denver, CO (2002-03). Selected for this internship because of my 3.7 GPA. Officially evaluated as one of the top six of 18 employees in the parent organization and as "a superb performer with unlimited drive and initiative," supervised two junior interns.
- Edited documentary scripts and videotapes produced by publishers and authors of news shows.
- Coordinated individual and group seminars for authors and publicists on how to be booked for TV news, talk, and documentary programs.
- Planned, scheduled, selected potential guest speakers for upcoming shows.

Other experience:
SALES REPRESENTATIVE. Lucent Technologies, Denver, CO (1999-02). Provided customer service for clients needing assistance with voice mail equipment.
- Acted as a computer technician for my department because of current knowledge of Windows 98 and Microsoft Word and Excel programs.
- Provided maintenance, troubleshooting, and repair of sophisticated electronic computer systems.
- Gained expertise in public speaking; provided guidance and personnel motivation.

COMPUTER SKILLS

Offer experience in using software including Illustrator, Microsoft Publisher, and PageMaker. Experienced in creating PDF files for printers.

PERSONAL

Have a thorough knowledge and "hands on" public relations and extensive computer experience. Have superior oral and written communication skills. Work well under pressure. Flexible; willing to relocate.

Date

Exact Name of Person
Exact Title or Position
Name of Company
Address (no., street)
Address (city, state, zip)

**MEDIA & PUBLIC
AFFAIRS MANAGER**

for a media corporation in
Washington

Dear Exact Name of Person:

I would appreciate an opportunity to talk with you soon about how I would like to contribute my public relation skills and experience to your organization. I am skilled at managing people, time, and resources, and I am seeking a company in need of a versatile public affairs manager.

My resume highlights my most notable accomplishments in the public relations field. I have an M. A. in Public Administration from Norfolk State University, and I have a B. A. in Media and Public Relations from Longwood College in Farmville, VA. I have completed courses in media studies, corporate communications law, and media writing. These courses have prepared me for a lasting career in Public Affairs.

Most recently, as a Public Affairs Director for the Media Training Corporation, I have excelled in directing all aspects of public relations within the organization. While overseeing several concurrent projects, I gained considerable skills in personnel motivation and in human relations dealing with local, national, and international media officials.

Previously, as an Events Coordinator and a Public Affairs Intern, I have consulted with business executives on the most effective ways of advertising their products. I have also organized local, national and international media conferences for clients as well as created press releases and promotional packages.

You would find me to be a versatile professional with superb communication and computer skills. I hope you will welcome my call soon to arrange a time at your convenience to discuss your current and future needs and how I might serve them. Thank you in advance for your time.

Yours sincerely,

Harold V. Lawrence

Alternate last paragraph:
I hope you will call or write me soon to suggest a time at your convenience for us to meet and discuss your current and future needs and how I might serve them. Thank you in advance for your time.

HAROLD V. LAWRENCE

1110½ Hay Street, Fayetteville, NC 28305 • preppub@aol.com • (910) 483-6611

OBJECTIVE   To offer my experience in effectively managing people, time, and resources, combined with my state-of-the-art computer skills, to a company seeking a versatile public affairs manager.

EDUCATION   **M.A. in Public Administration,** Norfolk State University, Norfolk, VA, 2003.
B.A. in Media and Public Relations, Longwood College, Farmville, VA, 2001.

EXPERIENCE   **MEDIA & PUBLIC AFFAIRS MANAGER.** Media Training Corporation, Washington, DC (2003-present). Excel in directing all aspects of public relations in the company's public affairs and supervising staff.
- Plan and organize trade shows throughout the U.S. using a budget of $1,140,038.
- Create, write, and edit a weekly newsletter with a circulation of 5,000 subscribers to keep clients in the industry informed of up and coming events.
- Receive Employee-of-the-Year award for successfully using my communication skills to manage several concurrent projects and interacting with many foreign and domestic officials and businessmen.

EVENTS COORDINATOR Gibson Media Consultants, Norfolk, VA (2001-03). Advised clients on the most efficient and effective advertising mediums.
- Consulted advertising executives, directed news telecast and a closed-circuit TV operations in order to fulfill client requests.
- Organized local, national, and international media conferences for all Gibson clients.
- Refined my time management skills coordinating two successful national fund-raising telethons.

PUBLIC AFFAIRS INTERN. Virginia Inc. Marketing Group, Farmville, VA (1999-01). Selected for this internship program because of my 3.8 GPA status.
- Prepared press releases, and promotion packages for clients.
- Supervised database technicians in all direct mail distribution projects.
- Participated in strategic planning involving multiple advertising campaigns.
- Created marketing surveys and data reports to monitor our success in the industry.
- Acquired computer skill using the most updated software programs in producing flyers, brochures, and correspondence.

Other experience:
TEACHING ASSISTANT. Garret Junior High School, Farmville County Public Schools, Farmville, VA (1998-1999).
- Assisted an English instructor while strengthening my communication skills by interacting on a personal level with all 30 students.
- Concentrated on teaching the students proper grammar, public speaking, and motivational skills.

COMPUTER   Knowledge of Microsoft Word, PowerPoint, and PageMaker.
SKILLS   Skilled in working with CorelDraw and Photoshop to create TIF and JPEGs.

PERSONAL   Have a thorough knowledge and "hands on" experience in public relations. Have superior oral and written communication skills. Work well under pressure. Am flexible; willing to relocate.

Date

Exact Name of Person
Exact Title or Position
Name of Company
Address (street, no.)
Address (city, state, zip)

MEDIA SALES
MANAGER

for an advertising sales
operation in St. Louis

Dear Exact Name of Person:

I would appreciate an opportunity to show you soon, in person, how my excellent management, marketing, and sales skills combined with my creativity could be of great value to you and your company.

As you will see from my resume, I have had experience in both retail and advertising sales. I enjoy every aspect of a sale, from the initial contact with a prospective client, through the follow-up consultations and revisions, to the delivery of an advertising package that clinches the account.

My personal sales approach has achieved powerful results in my present position. For example:

- Under my management, broadcast sales doubled, bringing the monthly quota to $400,000 in less than 2 months.
- My contributions added professional style and polish to a promotional campaign which successfully introduced a new FM station this year.

I am certain that my talent and expertise could produce similar results for your company, and I am sure that you would find me a warm, enthusiastic professional who prides herself on "getting things done through people."

I hope you will welcome my call next week when I try to arrange a brief meeting at your convenience to discuss your present and future needs and how I might serve them.

Yours sincerely,

Dorothy M. McWilliams

Alternate last paragraph:
I hope you call or write me soon to suggest a time convenient for us to meet and discuss your current and future needs and how I might serve them.

DOROTHY M. MCWILLIAMS

1110½ Hay Street, Fayetteville, NC 28305   •   preppub@aol.com   •   (910) 483-6611

OBJECTIVE

I want to benefit a company that needs an enthusiastic, creative professional who has demonstrated versatility, management "know-how," and superior marketing skills in both retail and advertising sales.

EXPERIENCE

SALES MANAGER. A. H. Belo Corp, St. Louis, MO (2003-present). Manage an advertising sales operation which handles local and national accounts totalling $400,000 monthly.
- Conduct daily sales meetings, demonstrate presentations and review individual sales portfolios.
- Handle all national accounts, consult personally with clients by telephone and design ad packages to fit their specifications.
- Doubled average monthly sales in less than 2 months.
- Play a key role in designing a promotional campaign which successfully launched a new FM station.
- Organized my department "from scratch," and personally handpicked and trained my 5-person sales staff.

SALES MANAGER. Acme Television Holdings, LLC, St. Louis, MO (2001-03). Managed a broadcast sales office, supervising personnel, payroll, and sales accounts.
- Hired, trained, and supervised a 4-person sales division.
- Oversaw the work of 6 office personnel, encouraging cooperation and efficiency within the department of Acme.
- Ensured the promptness and accuracy of a $17,000 monthly payroll.
- Maintained updated records on all accounts.
- Earned a reputation as the most innovative broadcast salesperson in town in less than 6 months.
- Successfully made the transition from retailing, where customers came to me, to broadcast advertising sales, where I sought out my clients.

DEPARTMENT MANAGER. Service Merchandise, St. Louis, MO (1998-2001). Managed the jewelry department in a large retail facility, supervising both showroom and warehouse operations.
- Supervised a floor sales staff of nine people.
- Oversaw inventory documentation and control.
- Enforced strict security measures, safeguarding a valuable stock of diamonds and other expensive jewelry.
- Was promoted to manager in 6 months in recognition of my superior sales, communication, and administrative skills.
- Maintained the company's lowest personnel turnover rate in my two years as manager.
- Excelled in a 6-month course which qualified me as a diamond consultant.

EDUCATION

Earned a **Bachelor of Science (B.S.) degree,** Business Administration, St. Louis University, St. Louis, MO, 2001.
Received an Associate of Science (A.S.) degree in Business Management, St. Louis Community College at Florissant Valley, St. Louis, MO, 1998.

PERSONAL

Am a creative, hard-working professional who believes that teamwork produces the best results. Thrive on tackling new challenges and enjoy the satisfaction of a job well done. Flexible; willing to relocate.

Date

Exact Name of Person
Title or Position
Name of Company
Address (no., street)
Address (city, state, zip)

MEDIA WEATHER PERSONALITY
for a national station

Dear Exact Name of Person:

I would appreciate and enjoy an opportunity to meet with you soon, in person, to demonstrate how my excellent live television experience, combined with specialist expertise in weather, news, and special features, could make a valuable contribution to your organization.

As you will see from my enclosed resume, I have had 8 years of on-air television experience. My early weekend weather positions permitted me to learn the basic techniques of live production and the specific technology used in forecast preparation. At the same time, I gained additional studio and on-location experience taping television commercials.

In my current job at WMC-TV in Memphis, I appear twice daily on live broadcasts, enjoying wide popularity both as a regular weather director, features' host, and commercials' personality. I have demonstrated my ability to handle a wide range of television activities, from interviewing celebrities for talk shows to producing and hosting the station's weekly adoptable child series.

I hope you will find it interesting that my last two television jobs, at which I have excelled, have come about because a program director and a news director sought me out because they both saw in me that indefinable quality that "sells" or "appeals" on-camera. My success as a local TV personality has led to numerous advertising appearances and speaking engagements. I enjoy promoting my station and its programs through my extensive community involvement and public contact.

I feel certain that my "television personality," on-camera experience, and production skills would be great assets to your organization, too, and I am also sure that you would find me a warm and articulate professional equally comfortable in scripted and ad-lib situations.

I hope you will welcome my call next week when I try to arrange a brief meeting at your convenience to discuss your current and future needs and how I might serve them. Thank you in advance for your time.

Yours sincerely,

Tabitha K. Mitchell

TABITHA K. MITCHELL

1110½ Hay Street, Fayetteville, NC 28305   •   preppub@aol.com   •   (910) 483-6611

OBJECTIVE   I would like to offer my excellent live television experience and on-camera know-how, combined with specialist expertise in weather and special features, to a broadcasting corporation in need of an articulate, popular television professional experienced in all aspects of live production.

EXPERIENCE   *Excelled in a "track record" of promotions from a special features producer position to a weather director with Raycom Media Inc.:*
WEATHER PERSONALITY. WMC-TV, Memphis, TN (2003-present). Was specially recruited for this versatile live television position.
* Write and deliver daily 2 live weathercasts on evening and nighttime news programs.
* Compile forecasts based on National Weather Service wire data.
* Prepare studio map and graphics for television viewing.
* Utilize the standard chyron graphics system.
* Have acquired expertise in news reporting as well as production.
* Have developed into a popular TV personality through communication skills that convey personal warmth in an articulate manner.

SPECIAL FEATURES PRODUCER. WMC-TV (2002-03). Produced a variety of regular and special feature programs. Organized and host "A Light Of Hope," WMC's weekly series about adoptable children. Became the personality in numerous regional commercials.
* Interviewed television stars and celebrities for local talk shows.
* Occasionally co-produced "6 o'clock news."
* Have learned video editing and other basic television production techniques.
* Have developed public relations expertise through hosting and speaking at numerous public events.

WEATHER ANNOUNCER. WKUP-TV of Lynnberg Broadcasting, Little Rock, AR (1999-02). Arranged and presented the weather segment of weekend news broadcasts.
* Learned to use chroma-key in forecast preparation.

HOME-SCHOOL COORDINATOR. Murray Bearden's Youth Center, Little Rock, AR (1998-99). Coordinated a program to involve parents in their children's school experiences.

WEEKEND WEATHER ANNOUNCER. WJVD-TV, Little Rock, AR (1996-98). Presented weekend weather forecasts and appeared on local commercials.
* Mastered live television techniques and meteorology fundamentals.

Other experience. Little Rock, AR (1995). Refined my planning, research, communication, and public speaking skills through teaching experience as a 6th grade teacher and education specialist for students with learning disabilities.

EDUCATION   Earned a **Master of Science (M.S.) degree,** University of Memphis, Memphis, TN, 2003. Received a **Bachelor of Arts (B.A.) degree,** University of Arkansas, Little Rock, AR, 1999.

PERSONAL   Possess superior communication skills; am a careful listener and handle ad-lib situations comfortably. Have a warm, poised, articulate style and am able to put others at ease. Will cheerfully relocate if needed.

Date

Exact Name of Person
Title or Position
Name of Company
Address (no., street)
Address (city, state, zip)

**MILITARY JOURNALIST &
MEDIA STUDENT**

is offering public affairs
experience in the military

Dear Exact Name of Person: (or Dear Sir or Madam if answering a blind ad.)

I would appreciate an opportunity to talk with you soon about how I could contribute to your organization through my experience and education related to media and broadcasting.

As you will see from my resume, after proudly serving my country for four years as an enlisted soldier, I attended college and will shortly be a magna cum laude graduate of New York University with a B.A. degree in Media and Broadcasting.

You will also see from my resume that I was handpicked for several jobs in the military which involved writing and communicating, and I am accustomed to dealing with major media sources such as Newsweek, USA Today, Philadelphia Inquirer, US News & World Report, as well as CNN and ABC. I feel certain that my experience working in media relations and public affairs could be a valuable asset to your organization.

You would find me in person to be an amiable individual who prides myself on my ability to interact well with people of all backgrounds. I can provide outstanding personal and professional references upon request.

I hope you will call or write me soon to suggest a time convenient for us to meet and discuss your current and future needs and how I might serve them. Thank you in advance for your time.

Sincerely yours,

Richard Howser

Alternate last paragraph:
I hope you will welcome my call soon to arrange a brief meeting at your convenience to discuss your current and future needs and how I might serve them. Thank you in advance for your time.

RICHARD HOWSER

1110½ Hay Street, Fayetteville, NC 28305   •   preppub@aol.com   •   (910) 483-6611

OBJECTIVE   To contribute to an organization that can use a hard-working young professional who offers versatile skills related to writing and public relations, law enforcement and security, sales and customer service, as well as personnel and project management.

EDUCATION   **Bachelor of Arts** (B.A.) degree, double major in Media and Broadcasting, New York University (NYU), New York, NY, degree anticipated 2004.
- Inducted into Pi Gamma Mu Honor Society for Broadcasting; elected Vice President of NYU Media Club; was handpicked by faculty as a Delegate at regional United Nations conference.
- Previously studied Broadcasting, Fordham University, New York, NY.

PUBLICATIONS   Have published more than 20 newspaper articles and four editorials in *The Aviator*, a
& MEDIA SKILLS   newspaper distributed throughout Ft. Benning's military base.
- Video news stories I created and photographs I took were picked up by major media including *The Chronicle, Newsweek, USA Today, Philadelphia Inquirer, US News & World Report*, as well as CNN and ABC.
- Knowledgeable of Associated Press Style Guide for media publications and outlets.

EXPERIENCE   **COLLEGE STUDENT.** New York University, Albany, NY (2002-present).

CUSTOMER SERVICE REPRESENTATIVE. Inter-American Foundation, Rochester, NY (2001-02). After my honorable discharge from the military and prior to enrolling in college full time, worked in a busy eight-person office and served hundreds of people weekly while providing information on membership, driving, maps, and hotel reservations.

COMMUNICATIONS SPECIALIST/SUPERVISOR. U.S. Army, Ft. Benning, GA (1999-01). As an E-4, was selected for a position normally held by an E-6; trained and managed six people while maintaining and installing communications equipment valued at $4 million including radios, antennas, telephones (office and mobile), and cameras (video and still).
- Received the prestigious Army Achievement Medal for my managerial performance.

JOURNALIST/PUBLIC AFFAIRS ADVISOR/MEDIA SPECIALIST. U.S. Army, Ft. Benning, GA (1998). Earned the respected Army Achievement Medal for my work while acting as an advisor to an executive on media matters and media relations while also authoring articles and creating videos to capture key organizational events.
- Worked closely with AP, UPI, and newspapers/magazines all over the U.S. while also authoring articles for the base newspaper.

PUBLIC AFFAIRS ASSISTANT. U.S. Army, Ft. Benning, GA (1997). After being handpicked for this job, taught myself video camera operations and then collected hours of valuable historical footage of engineer operations; acted as a liaison reporter to national media including CNN, *USA Today*, and *US News and World Report* during the war in the Middle East.

COMMUNICATIONS SPECIALIST. U.S. Army, Ft. Benning, GA (1996-97). Oversaw radio operations for airborne projects; installed/maintained field wire lines and telephones.

PERSONAL   Have an amiable disposition and the ability to get along with anyone. Possess a knack for being able to juggle numerous simultaneous projects and to rapidly master new tasks.

Date

Exact Name of Person
Title or Position
Name of Company
Address (no., street)
Address (city, state, zip)

**MORNING TALK
SHOW HOST**

for a Chicago radio station

Dear Exact Name of Person: (or Dear Sir or Madam if answering a blind ad.)

I would appreciate an opportunity to talk with you soon about how I could contribute to your organization through my extensive radio broadcasting and public relations experience.

After earning my B.A. degree in Broadcast Communications, I excelled in jobs that helped me sharpen my public relation skills by gaining local celebrity status through dedicated community involvement. At one radio station, WCKZ-FM, I was successful in increasing market share ratings and I developed professional relationships with celebrity and public figures. I was nominated twice for Medium Market Radio Personality of the Year and also won the Afternoon Personality of the Year contest.

You would find me to be an aggressive and dynamic professional who enjoys combining my creativity and interpersonal skills in ways that produce "bottom-line" results. I am capable of capturing audiences by presenting national, pop cultural, and political issues to the general public.

Although I am held in high regard in my current position, I have decided to selectively explore opportunities in other major markets. I would appreciate your holding in confidence my expression of interest in your station.

I hope you will welcome my call soon when I try to arrange a brief meeting to discuss your current and future needs and how I might serve them. Thank you in advance for your time.

Sincerely yours,

Lance Ketchum

Alternate last paragraph:
I hope you will call or write me soon to suggest a time convenient for us to meet and discuss your current and future needs and how I might serve them. Thank you in advance for your time.

LANCE KETCHUM

1110½ Hay Street, Fayetteville, NC 28305 • preppub@aol.com • (910) 483-6611

OBJECTIVE

I want to contribute to an organization that can use a popular and dynamic radio personality who has played a significant role in increasing market share in every position I have held while also gaining local celebrity status through my aggressive and dedicated community involvement.

EXPERIENCE

Worked for two different entities owned by Tribune Broadcasting Inc., Chicago, IL, which was acquired in December 1999 by Cumulus Media:
MORNING TALK SHOW HOST. WXTC AM/FM, Chicago, IL.
Feb 2003-present
Raised the AQH share of younger listeners 6a-10a with my opinionated style of entertainment.
- Became known for my popular style of localizing national issues and for my ability to focus on lifestyle, pop cultural, and political issues.
- Won awards in 2002 for "Largest New Team" and "Most Money Raised by a Media Team" in the March of Dimes Walkathon.

MORNING DRIVE PERSONALITY. TALK 88 WZCP-AM, Chicago, IL.
July 2001-Feb 2003
Brought Mornings from #3 to #2 in key demos by developing and refining techniques used later at WXTC AM/FM.

FINANCIAL PLANNER. Menton Financial Resources, Chicago, IL.
May 2000-July 2001
Sold 402 (K) plans to small businesses; led seminars and developed financial plans for city and state employees.
- Resigned my position when I was recruited by Tribune Broadcasting.

MORNING DRIVE PERSONALITY. JAMZ-109 WCKZ-FM, Chicago, IL.
July 1999-May 2001
- Increased market share ratings through entertaining style of community involvement.
- Developed professional relationships with many local celebrities and public figures.
- Was twice nominated **Medium Market Radio Personality of the Year.**
- This company was bought by new owners, who then released all the airstaff; I then embarked on a career change in the financial services field.

MORNING DRIVE PERSONALITY. K-97 WAPI-AM, Peoria, IL.
Sept 1997-May 1999
- Significantly increased market share ratings to #1 in key demos.

AFTERNOON DRIVE PERSONALITY. SKY-1390 WSDK-AM, Macomb, IL.
April 1996-September 1997
Was the winner of the **Afternoon Personality of the Year** based on reader votes in the local newspaper.
- Increased the station's market share ratings.

AFTERNOON DRIVE PERSONALITY. WKRC-AM, Macomb, IL.
April 1995-April 1996
- Achieved #1 rankings in multiple key demos.

EDUCATION

B.A. Broadcast Communications, Western Illinois University, Macomb, IL 1995.

Date

Exact Name of Person
Exact Title
Exact Name of Company
Address
City, State, Zip

**NEWSPAPER CLASSIFIED
MANAGER**

for a publishing company

Dear Exact Name of Person: (or Dear Sir or Madam if answering a blind ad)

With the enclosed resume, I would like to express my interest in exploring employment opportunities with your organization. I am an experienced newspaper industry professional with an extensive management background.

I was recruited for my current position by Washington's oldest continuously owned newspaper. As Classified Manager, I took over a department which had lacked a manager for more than a year, and I have made numerous contributions to profitability and efficiency while managing 17 people. While training and motivating the staff, I provided leadership in selecting and then installing a new front-end system which replaced a nonWindows, nonmouse system and interfaced it with the billing system. I managed our simultaneous transition to a 50-inch web and new press installation..

In a previous position with *Spokane News*, I was promoted from Classified Director to Publisher by one of the nation's largest weekly alternative newspaper publishers, which owned eight publications in major U.S. cities. As the Publisher of *Summit Classifieds*, I managed 50 people while producing a weekly shopper in the Spokane area. Through my leadership, we revamped rates, increased revenues, and cut costs. As a result of the upgrades, 60% of the subsidiary was sold for the largest amount ever paid at that time for a product of its type in the U.S. Prior to my promotion to Publisher, I performed with distinction as Classified Director and, in that capacity, I managed 12 inside and outside sales professionals while upgrading the front-end and generating an additional $415,000 yearly by establishing a voice personals audiotext system.

Although I am held in the highest regard by my current employer and can provide outstanding references at the appropriate time, I have decided to selectively explore opportunities. In every community in which I have worked, in my spare time I have assumed leadership roles in local, state, and national organizations and have been a highly visible representative of the newspaper. In Seattle, I have been active in the United Way and other organizations. In Tacoma, I was chairman of numerous fund drives, membership drives, and professional organizations. In Spokane, I received numerous awards for my leadership in the Kidney Foundation.

If you can use a results-oriented and technologically knowledgeable newspaper person with a proven ability to translate new concepts into operating realities that positively impact the bottom line, I hope you will contact me to suggest a time when we might discuss your needs.

Sincerely,

Geraldine T. Epstein

GERALDINE T. EPSTEIN

1110½ Hay Street, Fayetteville, NC 28305   •   preppub@aol.com   •   (910) 483-6611

OBJECTIVE   To contribute to an organization that can use an experienced publisher, advertising sales manager, and newspaper staff manager who has excelled in organizing and implementing new ventures, projects, and programs that have improved profitability and productivity.

EDUCATION   Earned **Bachelor of Science in Journalism**, minor in Advertising, University of Puget Sound, Tacoma, WA.

EXPERIENCE   **CLASSIFIED MANAGER & SPECIAL PROJECTS MANAGER.** The Seattle Publishing Company, Seattle, WA (2003-present). Was recruited by the oldest continuously owned newspaper in WA (*The Seattle Times*) to take over its classified advertising department; manage a classified department which had not had a manager for over a year and, through my extensive newspaper background, made numerous contributions which modernized internal operations while managing up to 17 people.
- Provided leadership in selecting and then installed a new front-end system which replaced a nonWindows, nonmouse system and interfaced it with the billing system; trained the staff to use the new system.
- Provided leadership in switching to a 50-inch web and new presses at the same time.
- Established a new telemarketing staff of two which exceeded their sales goal by 40%.
- Created new sales positions for outside real estate and inside/outside recruitment specialists. Took charge of and motivated the inside sales staff that sold for three subsidiary publications.
- Redesigned the classified section to create a new look with attractive fonts; changed categories and rates. Was instrumental in the startup and subsequent sale of a new weekly real estate quarterfold magazine.

PUBLISHER. Spokane News, Spokane, WA (1992-02). Was promoted from **Classified Director** to **Publisher,** *Summit Classifieds,* by one of the nation's largest weekly alternative newspaper publishers, which owned eight publications in Phoenix, Denver, Miami, Dallas, Houston, San Francisco, and Los Angeles.
- **1998-01:** As **Publisher,** *Summit Classifieds,* managed a staff of 50 employees, including five supervisors, while producing a free weekly classified newspaper with a 60,000 circulation. Increased revenues and cut costs by combining three zoned editions. Revamped all rates, marketing, format, and size within five months. Modernized all production, front-end, and accounting systems. *(**As a result of upgrades, 60% of the subsidiary was sold for the largest amount ever paid for a product of this type in the U.S. I decided not to continue with the new owners.**)*
- **1992-98:** As **Classified Director,** trained and managed 12 inside and outside sales personnel. Restructured accounting/credit procedures which increased prepaids and decreased monthly uncollectibles. Increased revenues 85% over a five-year period. Upgraded classified front-end and saved $200,000 compared to the costs of installing a new system. Generated an additional $415,000 yearly by establishing voice personals audiotext system for *Seattle Times.*

NATIONAL ADVERTISING MANAGER. *Tacoma Tribune,* Tacoma, WA (1990-1992). Began as an Advertising Executive and was promoted to Classified Advertising Sales Manager; then to National Advertising Manager.
- As **National Advertising Manager**, managed a department generating $4 million annually. As **Classified Advertising Sales Manager,** managed 12 inside, outside, and telemarketing personnel. Increased recruitment revenues by 25%.

Date

Exact Name of Person
Title or Position
Name of Company
Address (no., street)
Address (city, state, zip)

NEWSPAPER DISTRICT MANAGER

for a local Texas newspaper

Dear Exact Name of Person: (or Dear Sir or Madam if answering a blind ad.)

I would appreciate an opportunity to talk with you soon about how I could contribute to your organization through my experience in my most recent position as a newspaper district manager as well as through my proven ability to coordinate all factors of production including recruiting, training, supervising, and service/support.

As you will see from my resume, I have had extensive experience in managing newspapers. As an executive aide for *The Toledo Gazette*, I was well known for my expertise in coordinating a team of test directors to develop, evaluate, and analyze the cost of a new newspaper manufacturing system. I have lived up to my reputation as a "fast learner" and talented strategic thinker in this job.

As a graduate of the Central Texas University at Houston, I also have earned my M.A. degree in Media Management and have excelled in specialized training for executives related to maintenance, supply, and logistics. While serving my country as an Air Force pilot instructor, I became personally dedicated to training successful individuals. I also took the initiative to cut training program costs by 15%.

You would find me to be a bright and inquisitive professional who excels in training and motivating employees, both in groups and one-on-one as well as a natural leader who is comfortable and effective when working with people of various educational, religious, and racial backgrounds. I hope you will welcome my call soon to arrange a brief meeting at your convenience to discuss your current and future needs and how I might serve them. Thank you in advance for your time.

Sincerely yours,

Timothy D. Thompson

Alternate last paragraph:
I hope you will call or write me soon to suggest a time convenient for us to meet and discuss your current and future needs and how I might serve them. Thank you in advance for your time.

TIMOTHY DENNIS THOMPSON ("TIM")

1110½ Hay Street, Fayetteville, NC 28305   •   preppub@aol.com   •   (910) 483-6611

OBJECTIVE   I want to contribute to the success of an organization that can use an experienced communicator with proven skills in teaching and motivating others, a dynamic manager with superior planning and organizational ability, and a hard-working professional who subscribes to high personal standards of loyalty, honesty, and reliability.

EDUCATION   **M.A. degree, Media Management**, Central Texas University, Houston, TX, 2003. Earned this degree at night while excelling in my full-time job.
B.S. degree, Industrial Management, University of South Carolina, Columbia, SC, 1985. Completed three years of elite management graduate schools for Air Force executives.

EXPERIENCE   **DISTRICT MANAGER**. *The Houston Chronicle*, Houston, TX, (2003-present). Recruit, train, and supervise newspaper representatives; responsible for sales, service, collection, and route audits of the district while exceeding set goals in all categories.
- Conduct an extensive district realignment with a 20 percent increase in circulation.

OPERATIONS CHIEF. Anderson Publishing Co., Houston, TX, (2000-03). Routinely coordinated with vendors while supervising 159 people. Organized/managed a security force protecting people and assets.
- Installed a new web operation which improved manufacturing capability. Employees working on three shifts and the three shift supervisors reported to me.

EXECUTIVE AIDE. *The Toledo Gazette*, Toledo, OH (1998-02). Was handpicked for this special assignment because of my reputation as a talented strategic thinker and analyst; provided expertise in designing the test and then led a team of test directors in the development, evaluation, and cost analysis of a new newspaper manufacturing system.
- Coordinated extensively with industry and with top-level Air Force policy makers.
- Produced all project plans and final reports well ahead of schedule.

DIVISION CHIEF. The National Association of Newspapers and Magazines, Washington, DC (1996-98). Directed 11 project directors in masterminding the concepts, procedures, and criteria to be used in evaluating products and operational techniques for proposed use by newspapers and magazines in the U.S.

INSTRUCTOR and **ADMINISTRATOR**. University of North Carolina at Chapel Hill, Chapel Hill, NC (1992-96). Instructed and evaluated students in the manufacturing and management program.

Highlights of prior military experience:
INSTRUCTOR. U.S. Air Force, Pope AFB, NC (1990-92). Became a polished platform and one-on-one instructor as one of only 56 pilots in the Air Force qualified to instruct others in the most sophisticated airdrop systems. Cut training program costs 15% by creative consolidations. Became personally dedicated to the philosophy that training is the most critical ingredient in the success of any organization.

GENERAL MANAGER/TRAINING PROGRAM COORDINATOR. U.S. Air Force, Rickenbacker AFB, OH (1985-90). Supervised assets maintenance, personnel training, and program planning related to the training of 19 copilots.

PERSONAL   Am known for my "poise under pressure." Am confident in my ability to motivate people.

Date

Exact Name of Person
Title or position
Name of Company
Address (no., street)
Address (city, state, zip)

NEWSPAPER JOURNALIST

for an 84,000-circulation newspaper

Dear Exact Name of Person: (or Dear Sir or Madam if answering a blind ad.)

I would appreciate an opportunity to talk to you soon about how my people skills, public relations expertise, and extensive background in preparing and presenting public information could ideally fit your need for a public relations and information specialist.

As you will see from my resume, I am currently coordinating and writing a column for the *Columbia Evening Post*. I have earned recognition for good judgement in writing and editing features for the paper as well as earning a reputation for quickly and easily establishing a rapport with the large number of people from diverse backgrounds with whom I come into contact. Previously, I gained experience in most areas of information administration through jobs as media coordinator, public relations intern, publicity chairwoman, and news assistant.

While working for the *Columbia Evening Post*, I had the unique opportunity to serve as a Winston Cup pit crew member on Walter Stevenson's team. This was a childhood dream come true, as all my life I have eagerly followed all types of racing, including NASCAR, Winston Cup, and dirt-track.

You would find me to be a versatile, creative, and innovative professional who thrives on the responsibility of new challenges. I am certain my media and public relations background could significantly contribute to your communication and public information efforts.

I hope you will welcome my call soon to arrange a brief meeting at your convenience to discuss your current and future needs and how I might serve them. Thank you in advance for your time.

Sincerely,

Sheila M. Ireland

Alternate last paragraph:
I hope you will call or write me soon to suggest a time convenient for us to meet and discuss your current and future needs and how I might serve them. Thank you in advance for your time.

SHEILA MAE IRELAND

1110½ Hay Street, Fayetteville, NC 28305 • preppub@aol.com • (910) 483-6611

OBJECTIVE   To offer my superior communication and writing skills to an organization in need of a creative and versatile professional experienced in public relations, print and broadcast journalism, and project management.

EDUCATION   **Bachelor of Arts degree in Communication Arts, with a concentration in radio/television/film**, Maryville University, St. Louis, MO, 1995.

EXPERIENCE   **NEWSPAPER JOURNALIST.** *Columbia Evening Post,* Columbia, SC (2003-present). Was recognized for subject expertise and promoted from reporter to columnist in charge of coordinating and writing a weekly community section for this 84,000-circulation newspaper.
- Organize all material for calendar events, including charity functions, reunions, personnel close-ups, and sports events. Write the "My Town" column, detailing the concerns and experiences of local families and a wide range of other special story features.
- Have received excellent feedback from readers through letters to the editor.
- Built a reputation for sound judgement and thorough reporting.

REPORTER. *Community Forum Newsletter*, Columbia, SC (2001-03). Acted as a stringer coordinating and writing a monthly column discussing social events in a humorous style.

PUBLICITY COORDINATOR. Officers' Wives Club, Ft. Jackson, SC (1998-01). Performed writing and public relations functions for an active community volunteer organization as well as serving as a liaison between the Officers' Wives Club and local media.
- Promoted special fundraising events and created press releases, slogans, and graphic designs. Wrote and released press releases and PSA's to several area newspapers, including *Columbia Evening Post, The Viper*, and other local media.
- Utilized public relations skills and print media to raise $25,000 for scholarship funds.

PROGRAM COORDINATOR. Burnes Elementary School, Columbia, SC (1996-1998). Worked in a volunteer capacity organizing a wide range of fundraisers and recreation activities for over 160 elementary disabled students. Served as mediator between families and faculty.

PUBLIC RELATIONS INTERN. Department of Public Affairs, Buffalo International Airport, Buffalo, NY (1995-1996). Wrote press releases on current events and issues concerning the airport for submission to area media.
- Acquired expert communication skills handling a wide range of functions, including preparing press releases, a new long-range marketing plan, and business announcements.
- Assisted director with a wide range of special events and activities such as attending monthly Commission meetings, organizing the airport's anniversary celebration, and coordinating the Delta Airlines welcoming service.

NEWS ASSISTANT. NBC Affiliate/WSOG-TV, St. Louis, MO (1994-1995). Developed expertise in writing and public relations skills while working as an intern at a respected television news station. Prepared daily news broadcast scripts.
- Produced, wrote, and directed an educational videotape, *The Rules of the Newsroom*.
- Gathered information for news reports by working with area law enforcement agencies.

COMPUTERS   Proficient with Microsoft Word, Access, Corel Draw, Harvard Graphics, and Pagemaker.

PORTFOLIO   Available upon request.

Date

Anne McKinney
Publisher
PREP Publishing
Box 66
Fayetteville, NC 28302

Dear Mrs. McKinney:

I am writing to express my strong interest in the position of News Photographer, which was posted on the employee web page. With the enclosed resume, I would like to make you aware of my background as an articulate young professional whose has proven skills in editing news features, conducting interviews, and gathering pertinent information for future stories. My strong leadership ability have been tested in versatile and challenging positions in sales, management, and broadcast journalism.

Most recently, I have been excelling in a number of broadcast journalism positions with ABC, NBC, and Fox affiliates on the east coast. Currently with WFLX-TV in West Palm Beach, FL, I shoot and edit a wide variety of feature stories and photoessays while serving as editor and photographer for general assignment and sports.

In a similar job with WRVI-TV in Daytona Beach, FL, my exceptional efforts in these areas earned me an Emmy nomination in the News/Public Affairs/Community Issues category from the National Academy of Television Arts and Sciences. In these and other positions with various network affiliates, I have demonstrated my outstanding communication skills while assisting in the preparation of scripts for news anchors, as well as providing exceptional editing and photography. I am also an expert at setting up, troubleshooting, and operating the ENG live broadcast truck.

Although I am highly regarded by my present employer, and can provide outstanding personal and professional references at the appropriate time, I am interested in exploring other career opportunities. I feel that my extroverted personality, strong communication skills, and natural salesmanship would be a valuable addition to your sales or management team.

If you can use an outgoing, articulate young professional with an aptitude for sales and strong leadership skills, then I look forward to hearing from you soon. I can assure you in advance that I have an excellent reputation, and would rapidly become an asset to your organization.

Sincerely,

Jerome P. Decker

JEROME P. DECKER

1110½ Hay Street, Fayetteville, NC 28305   •   preppub@aol.com   •   (910) 483-6611

OBJECTIVE
To benefit an organization that can use an articulate, versatile young professional with outstanding communication skills who offers an outgoing personality, natural sales ability, and a background in broadcast journalism, route sales, and transportation management.

AFFILIATIONS
Current member, National Press Photographers Association (NPPA).

EXPERIENCE
NEWS PHOTOGRAPHER, EDITOR, and **ENG TRUCK OPERATOR.** WFLX-TV, Fox Broadcasting Company, West Palm Beach, FL, (2003-present). Shoot and edit a wide variety of news, feature, sports, and general assignment stories as a cameraman and live truck operator.
- Conduct interviews with subjects related to the assignment; gather facts pertinent to the story and assist in assembling news features.
- Assist in the preparation of scripts for news anchors. Provide expert editing of news features to achieve the greatest impact from all feature and photoessay footage.
- Serve as editor and photographer for all general assignment and sports features.
- Set up and operate a wide range of audio and video recording and broadcast equipment while preparing features for broadcast from the live truck.

NEWS PHOTOGRAPHER, EDITOR, and **ENG TRUCK OPERATOR.** WRVI-TV, Daytona Beach, FL (2002-2003). Excelled in a number of challenging roles while supporting the broadcast journalism efforts of this large ABC affiliate.
- Filmed and edited news features and photoessays; interviewed subjects and gathered facts on featured stories; served as editor and photographer for general assignment and sports.
- Set up and operated a wide range of audio and video recording and broadcast equipment while preparing features for broadcast from the live truck.
- Nominated for an Emmy award for News/Public Affairs Segments/Community issues by the National Academy of Television Arts and Sciences, South Florida Chapter, 2002.

NEWS PHOTOGRAPHER, CHIEF EDITOR, and **ENG TRUCK OPERATOR.** WEKW-TV, Atlanta, GA (2000-02). Served as Chief Editor of the 10:00 PM weekend broadcast; shot and edited spots, features, and photoessays; served as editor for general assignment and sports; and set up and operated the live truck.

CHIEF EDITOR, NEWS PHOTOGRAPHER, and **ENG TRUCK OPERATOR.** WEXD-TV, Atlanta, GA (1998-00). Performed a variety of tasks while providing photography, editing, and operating the live truck for this busy NBC affiliate. Served as Chief Editor for the 5:00 and 6:00 PM newscasts while shooting and editing general assignments, news, and features.

Other experience:
SALES MANAGER. Kitzmiller Sales & Marketing, Atlanta, GA (1996-98). Coordinated business meetings for marketing executives. Prepared marketing packets for potential clients.

ROUTE SALESMAN. Simmons Distributing Company, Macon, GA (1993-1996). Serviced existing accounts and developed new business while excelling as a route driver and salesperson.

EDUCATION
Completed two years of college course work towards Associate's degree, Macon State College.

PERSONAL
Excellent personal and professional references are available upon request.

Date

Exact Name of Person
Title or Position
Name of Company
Address (no., street)
Address (city, state, zip)

Dear Exact Name of Person: (or Dear Sir or Madam if answering a blind ad.)

I would appreciate an opportunity to talk with you soon about how I could benefit your organization through my office management abilities, as well as through my education and experience related to reporting and broadcasting.

In my current position as a News Reporter for a Pittsburgh television station, I deliver live broadcasts for the evening news show. Although I am excelling in this position and can provide excellent references at the appropriate time, I am selectively exploring opportunities in the major markets. I am an award-winning newspaper journalist who offers a proven ability to bring stories "to life" and communicate effectively on television.

In a previous position outside the newspaper industry, I refined my administrative skills working as an Office Manager and Human Resources Specialist. In that job I earned recognition for my creativity in developing marketing strategies as well as for my ability to oversee the smooth preparation of accounts payable transactions in excess of $500,000 monthly. Recognized for my high degree of initiative, I made important contributions to my employer. I developed "from scratch" the idea for a regular corporate newsletter and now write and edit a monthly publication for the 1,200 area employees.

I hope you will welcome my call soon to arrange a brief meeting at your convenience to discuss your current and future needs and how I might serve them. Thank you in advance for your time.

Sincerely yours,

Amber D. Hanson

Alternate last paragraph:
I hope you will call or write me soon to suggest a time convenient for us to meet and discuss your current and future needs and how I might serve them. Thank you in advance for your time.

AMBER D. HANSON

1110½ Hay Street, Fayetteville, NC 28305   •   preppub@aol.com   •   (910) 483-6611

OBJECTIVE

I want to contribute to an organization that can use my office management and administrative abilities, along with my professional knowledge related to public relations, marketing, and broadcasting.

EDUCATION

Earned a **Bachelor of Arts (B.A.) degree in Broadcast Journalism,** minored in Business and English, Edinboro University, Edinboro PA, 1999.

AWARDS

Produced stories on abused children and neglected animals which were nominated for national awards in recognition of their creativity and investigative thoroughness.

EXPERIENCE

BROADCAST ANNOUNCER and **NEWS REPORTER.** WELE Television, Pittsburgh, PA (2003-present). As a General Assignment Reporter, gather information, write news stories, and produce material for evening news broadcasts; deliver live newscasts.

FILM EDITOR and **NEWS REPORTER.** WEJI-TV and Radio, Pittsburgh, PA (2001-03). Produced radio and television news reports, including gathering news, filming live reports, editing film for broadcast, and appearing on camera reporting news stories.
* Learned to use a 16mm camera and editing equipment to collect information and process for broadcast use.

OFFICE MANAGER and **HUMAN RESOURCES SPECIALIST.** Sodexho Food Services, Inc., Edinboro, PA (1998-00). For the corporate headquarters of this food service franchise management organization, compile, write, and edit a monthly newsletter, which is distributed to the corporation's 1,200 employees in five area locations.
* Handled monthly accounts payable transactions in excess of $500,000.
* Worked closely with proposal writers to research and wrote responses used by the company in bidding for future accounts.
* Processed supply orders totaling $50,000 for four divisions.
* Prepared exhibits for company marketing and public relations use.
* Created the company's first-ever employee newsletter and now write and edit information for monthly publication.
* Developed company marketing activities which have included the initiation of the use of exhibits to increase company visibility.
* Set up an in-house library, using my knowledge of the Dewey decimal system for proper organization of printed material.
* Am recognized as a creative individual with outstanding planning and organizing abilities who excels in human resources/personnel management.

TRAINING

Completed corporate training related to making effective presentations and office management principles, as well as a 40-hour training program on marketing strategies at the Carnegie Mellon University, Pittsburgh, PA.

EQUIPMENT

Am skilled in operating a variety of equipment including cameras, lighting, and studio equipment. Proficient with software including PageMaker and QuarkExpress as well as PowerPoint.

PERSONAL

Read and write Spanish. Have completed continuing education courses related to marketing. Enjoy the challenge of mastering new ideas and procedures.

Date

Anne McKinney
Publisher
PREP Publishing
Box 66
Fayetteville, NC 28302

PHOTOGRAPHER
for a traveling studio

Dear Mrs. McKinney:

With the enclosed resume, I would like to express my interest in employment opportunities within your organization and acquaint you with my professional skills as a photographer and videographer. I am interested in relocating, and I am single and available to travel as your needs require.

As you will see from my resume, I have recently excelled as a Photographer for Allan A. Philiba, Inc., a traveling studio. While handling numerous administrative responsibilities including collecting money, preparing paperwork, and assuring the correct assembly and adjustment of all equipment, I have become respected for my technical expertise as well as my ability to relate to people and put them at ease. I have specialized in portrait photography of children and have a knack for working with children and their parents.

As a Photographer and Videographer with Tom Stacks & Associates, I create graphics and video reports used in historical documentation and visual information processing. In a prior job as a Photo Lab Technician, I gained practical experience in the technical aspects of commercial photography. I have also volunteered as a gallery assistant for a visual studies workshop in which I have gained experience in grant writing, curating exhibitions, and preparing press releases.

In 1994, I received my Bachelor of Fine Arts (B.F.A.) degree in Photography from the Florida Institute of Technology (FIT) in Melbourne, FL. While earning my degree I worked as a Photographic Equipment Clerk with the FIT School of Printing, I completed internships with an arts program and an art gallery. Both of those internships helped me refine my writing and media relations skills.

I hope you will contact me to arrange a brief meeting at your convenience to discuss your current and future needs and how I might serve them. I can provide excellent references at the appropriate time, and I thank you in advance for your time.

Sincerely yours,

Jane A. Vigor

JANE ANNE VIGOR

1110½ Hay Street, Fayetteville, NC 28305   •   preppub@aol.com   •   (910) 483-6611

OBJECTIVE

To offer my reputation as a dynamic and creative professional to an organization that can use a talented writer, videographer, photographer, and production specialist.

EDUCATION

Bachelor of Fine Arts (B.F.A.) degree in Photography, Florida Institute of Technology (FIT), Melbourne, FL, 2000.
- Excelled in course work including Photography, Applied Photography, Photomedia, Photo as Fine Art, Photo Media Survey, Introduction to Portable Video I & II, and Newswriting.

SPECIAL SKILLS

Offer experience with equipment such as:
Cameras: still 35 mm and 4X5; and video
Other equipment: B&W and color enlargers, linear and nonlinear editing systems
Lighting: Various studio and location lighting
Software: MacWrite, Microsoft Word, PageMaker, Photoshop, CorelDraw

EXPERIENCE

PHOTOGRAPHER. Allan A. Philiba Inc., Orlando, FL (2003-present). As a Portrait Photographer with a traveling studio, have become a respected photographer of children.
- Am respected for my technical expertise as well as my gracious customer service skills; offer an ability to put people at ease so that I can capture their personality on camera.
- Have been complimented on creativity of visual effects. Maintain all studio equipment; assembled and adjusted photography equipment.
- Handle administrative duties including collecting money and completing paperwork.

PHOTOGRAPHER & VIDEOGRAPHER. Tom Stack & Associates, Key Largo, FL (2002-03). Excelled in extensive professional training in the videography field; provide visual imagery acquisition and exploitation support. Created visual information products, including graphics and video reports used in historical documentation and visual information processing.

PHOTO LAB TECHNICIAN. XenoLab Photo Center, Tampa, FL (2001-02). Built on my strong educational background in photography and gained practical experience in the technical aspects of commercial photography as well as the day-to-day business side.
- Recognized as a mature and dependable individual, was selected to relieve the manager of certain daily responsibilities such as opening and closing the store.
- Assisted in processing film, printing enlargements, running the cash register, and sales.

PHOTOGRAPHER & ARTS PROGRAM INTERN. Visual Pursuit, Tampa, FL (2000-01). Cited by the director for "quickly grasping the complexities" of an arts in education program, contributed ideas which helped expand the program and make it a success; used my photography skills to document Visual Pursuit events.
- Was exposed to all aspects of this program which links more than 130 performing, visual, and literary artists with schools which presented more than 3,300 workshops, performances, and artists in residence programs in 250 schools for 1994.
- Provided new artists with information on the program's history, goals, and procedures and then maintained files on each artist after they began participating.

EDUCATIONAL ASSISTANT and **INTERN.** Panorama Art Gallery, Melbourne, FL (1998-2000). During a three-month internship, made important contributions by creating a self-guided tour for families and a mailing list, which helped make community programs successful.

PERSONAL

Am able to communicate with people of all ages, walks of life, and backgrounds. Single.

Date

Exact Name of Person
Title or Position
Name of Company
Address (no., street)
Address (city, state, zip)

**PHOTOGRAPHER &
VIDEO TECHNOLOGY
SPECIALIST**

for a digital imaging and
videography company

Dear Exact Name of Person: (or Dear Sir or Madam if answering a blind ad.)

I would appreciate an opportunity to meet with you in person to discuss my versatile skills and expertise related to broadcasting, public relations, computer operations, photography, and videography.

As you will see from my resume, I have recently received a BA degree in Mass Communications from Morgan State University of Baltimore, Maryland. I have also received a FCC Broadcaster License which has allowed me to gain experience through previous internships as a radio announcer, writer/producer, editor, and public relations officer. I am also familiar with Pagemaker, QuarkXpress, CorelDraw, and other software programs as well.

In my current position as a video technology specialist, I am required to use every aspect of my skills in photography and videography. I have used a variety of equipment such as digital cameras and electronic imagers while working on extensive editing projects for Sam Blates Associates.

So I hope this demonstrates to you my dedication to excel in this field. You would find me in person to be a congenial, multi-talented individual who could enhance your team through my versatile abilities as well as through my personality, character, and strong work ethic. I can provide outstanding personal and professional references.

If you can use a hard-working individual with a desire to enhance the quality and reputation of your organization, I hope you will call or write me to suggest a time when we could meet to discuss your needs and how I might serve them. Thank you in advance for your time.

Yours sincerely,

Sean McGrane

SEAN MCGRANE

1110½ Hay Street, Fayetteville, NC 28305 • preppub@aol.com • (910) 483-6611

OBJECTIVE To offer training, experience, and strong interest in photography/videography as well as all aspects of public relations and mass communication to an organization in need of a creative professional with excellent written/verbal communications and technical electronics skills.

EDUCATION & TRAINING Earned B.A. degree in **Mass Communications** with a concentration in **Public Relations and Photography** Morgan State University, Baltimore, MD, 2003.

EXPERIENCE **VIDEO TECHNOLOGY SPECIALIST.** Sam Blate's Imaging, Montgomery Village, MD, (2003-present). Study electronic imaging, digital cameras and imaging techniques, videography, editing, and TV studio techniques as well as basic photography; am the company leader for this intense video documentation training program.

INTERNSHIPS AS A FULL-TIME STUDENT: Morgan State University, Baltimore, MD (1999-2003). Earned a bachelor's degree; learned to manage my time effectively while pursuing an education and participating in internships:
2002-03: PUBLIC RELATIONS INTERN. For the university's Office of Public Information, wrote and edited articles for publication in *The Morgan Prospect* and *The Morgan Times* while also preparing public service announcements and news releases.
• Conducted research on scholarship donors and university benefactors.

2001-02: COMMUNICATIONS INTERN. For the Maryland Forestry Association, applied my written and verbal communication skills while conducting research, preparing news releases, and coordinating public relations activities.
• Applied my technical computer abilities while working with the association's data base to update their records. Worked closely with various state and corporate officials and association members while planning news releases and press conferences.

Other experience:
RADIO ANNOUNCER, WRITER, AND PRODUCER. (2000-01). Represented the university at a local radio station (WCCE in Briar Creek, Baltimore) by coordinating, researching, writing, and producing public service announcements and advertisements.
• Operated audio production and broadcast equipment doing two daily segments.

COMPUTER LAB ASSISTANT. (1999-00). Provided technical support to students in computer lab. Established working knowledge of the following programs:

Apple Color One Microtek 600ZS Scanners	Microsoft Word
QuarkXpress	Macintosh/Apple Power Book
Apple Talk/Local Talk/Apple Works	Stuff It Deluxe Expander
Adobe /Aldus PageMaker	Adobe Photoshop
Adobe Illustrator	Microsoft Power Point
Adobe Premier	Corel Draw
Corel Graphics	Macinotsh McPaint

COMMUNICATIONS SYSTEMS OPERATOR AND MECHANIC. WPOC-FM Nationwide Communications, Inc., Baltimore, MD (1996-99). Consistently maintained extremely high levels of serviceability for a wide range of equipment including AM and FM radio systems. Was selected as the Operator and Manager of a Maryland Radio Station; wrote and produced material for public broadcast while also maintaining equipment.
• Coordinated public affair programs and interviewed potential guests.

CAREER CHANGE

Date

Exact Name of Person
Exact Title
Exact Name of Company
Address
City, State, Zip

**PROGRAM
COORDINATOR**

for a department of social
services

Dear Exact Name of Person: (or Dear Sir or Madam if answering a blind ad)

With the enclosed resume, I would like to make you aware of my desire to become involved in your organization in some capacity in which you could utilize my extensive background in program management, public relations, and human services administration.

As you will see from my resume, I earned a B.A degree in Sociology and Political Science and then completed my M.S. in Guidance and Counseling/Psychological Counseling. I was specially selected to manage a wide range of human services and executive support programs in Charleston, SC. I excelled in earlier positions as a Management Consultant, Social Services Coordinator and Field Supervisor. In one job as a Guidance Counselor, I was commended on my success in inspiring many employees to set and achieve high goals.

While managing programs providing assistance to neighborhoods and business executives, I maintain an active public speaking schedule, briefing up to **2,000** people monthly. I also plan and manage large-scale events, and my efforts resulted in our annual Community Expo increasing from 684 issues received in one year to 1933 the next. I author and publish numerous how-to and self-help publications while recruiting, training, managing, and motivating the dozens of volunteers who make our support programs successful. I also supervised an eight-person paid staff.

A naturally gregarious individual, I am accustomed to excelling in positions which require excellent negotiating and motivational skills. In my current position as a Public Relations Coordinator, I am continuously "selling" the concept of needed programs to business executives who determine funding priorities, and I have trained hundreds of individuals, supervisors, and human services professionals in effective communication techniques.

Although I am highly regarded in my current position and can provide outstanding references at the appropriate time, I am approaching your organization because I feel there might be a "fit" between your needs and my versatile management and public speaking experience. I would appreciate the opportunity to meet with you personally to discuss your needs and how I might serve them. I was widowed at a young age and have no children, so I am willing to relocate and travel as your needs require. I appreciate in advance your consideration of my skills and talents.

Sincerely,

Amy K. Strohme

AMY K. STROHME

1110½ Hay Street, Fayetteville, NC 28305   •   preppub@aol.com   •   (910) 483-6611

OBJECTIVE

I want to contribute to an organization that can use an articulate professional who is skilled at coordinating and implementing large-scale events, authoring and publishing materials ranging from handbooks to policy manuals, as well as managing teams of dedicated specialists.

EDUCATION

Master of Science in **Guidance and Counseling/Psychological Counseling**, Charleston Southern University, Charleston, SC, 1996.

Bachelor of Arts, majors in **Sociology and Political Science** and minor in **Media Studies**, College of Charleston, Charleston, SC, 1994.

Completed executive development programs related to human services administration, service program development, crisis intervention program management, and program coordination.

EXPERIENCE

PROGRAM COORDINATOR. Department of Social Services, Charleston, SC (2003-present). Supervise eighty individuals while directing a wide range of human services and neighborhood support programs.

- Am considered the country's leading technical expert in establishing community events; wrote the *Neighborhood Support Handbook* for the City of Charleston and have trained hundreds of managers and supervisors.
- Plan and implement the annual Community Expo and train all facilitators, recorders, and delegates; increased the number of issues for the *Neighborhood Support Handbook* received from 684 in 2002 to 1933 in 2003.
- Have excelled in recruiting, training, and managing dozens of volunteers, many of whom give up to 40 hours per week to the Community Expo which I plan and coordinate.
- Handle public speaking responsibilities; conduct briefings for 2,000 people monthly.
- Offer highly developed written communication skills; wrote the *Guide to Living Handbook*, and wrote weekly articles on family issues for *The Lowcountry Daily* and *The Evening Post* newspaper.
- Manage a wide range of programs designed to assistant low-income families.
- Train hundreds of managers and professional supervisors in counseling techniques.

MANAGEMENT CONSULTANT. BMR Associates, Charleston, SC (2001-03). Taught numerous classes including Leadership Effectiveness, Employment Workshops, and courses in Communication Skills.

- Created a new executive information directory for this community after developing the fact sheets and other data collection tools used in obtaining and compiling information.
- Interviewed and counseled individuals and referred them to appropriate agencies.

SOCIAL SERVICES COORDINATOR. Department of Health and Human Services, Mt. Pleasant, SC (1998-00). Provided protective services, crisis intervention, counseling, investigation, and short-term therapeutic intervention to individuals living in Mt. Pleasant.

TRANSITIONAL HOME DIRECTOR. Charleston County Health Center, Charleston, SC (1996-1998). Achieved an **85% success rate** in placing clients from mental hospitals in jobs and foster homes while in charge of instruction of clients in a mental health facility; taught interpersonal and social skills while also providing group and individual therapy and coordinating services for follow-up and screening.

PERSONAL

Offer highly refined public speaking skills, and am known as an outstanding communicator.

Date

Exact Name of Person
Exact Title
Exact Name of Company
Address
City, State, Zip

Dear Exact Name of Person: (or Dear Sir or Madam if answering a blind ad)

With the enclosed resume, I would like to make you aware of my interest in exploring employment opportunities with your organization.

I am a graduate with a B. A. degree in Marketing, from Portland State University, Portland, Oregon who is currently working in a position as Public Affairs Director for J. J. Spector & Associates. I have coordinated advertising campaigns with international, national, and local media for our extensive list of clients. Because of my strong written communication skills, I have had an opportunity to be involved in The Fashion Fair Expo in Los Angeles, California. During this event, I handled numerous behind-the-scenes responsibilities in an effort to help produce this major fashion extravaganza which draws several thousand buyers, retailers, and members of the local and national press to Los Angeles to see American designers present their collections.

Although I have excelled in this job normally held by older business executives, I also had an opportunity in 2002 to work for First Impressions Agency for public relations. I was able to coordinate advertising expeditions in major cities such as Los Angeles, New Orleans, Miami, and New York City in order to improve our status within the industry.

I am well known for my ability to step into a new situation and quickly master the key ingredients for success. I have demonstrated strong organizational and leadership skills as a I managed the advertising and marketing departments. One formal performance evaluation, while employed by First Impressions Agency, described me as "an absolutely outstanding leader with the ability to remain calm while thinking quickly in demanding situations."

I am confident my highly creative nature and experience in public affairs would be assets to any organization which values self-motivated individuals who aspire to excellence in all things. I can provide excellent references at the appropriate time, and I hope you will contact me to suggest a time when we could meet to discuss your needs.

Yours sincerely,

Octavia M. Tookes

OCTAVIA M. TOOKES

1110½ Hay Street, Fayetteville, NC 28305   •   preppub@aol.com   •   (910) 483-6611

OBJECTIVE   To contribute to an organization that can use a creative professional with a proven ability to communicate effectively with worldwide media through my strong written and oral communication skills along with experience in producing effective news segments and special events including entertainment for the general public.

EDUCATION   Graduated with a **B.S. degree in Marketing,** Portland State University, Portland, OR, 2001.

EXPERIENCE   **PUBLIC AFFAIRS DIRECTOR.** J. J. Spector & Associates, Portland, OR (2003-present). Was specially selected for this position in which I serve as the "voice and face" of 20 different organizations with 500 employees who work in both Oregon and California.
- Plan the strategic public affairs "personality" of the organizations I represent.
- Perform as a liaison with national, and local media; brief media on organization's mission.
- Process and distribute digital images and information. Redesign a new Web page that is more interactive, informative, and user-friendly.
- Write speeches for a department executives.

Experience in producing advertising segments for the following companies:
- Produced nearly 20 advertisement videos for the following clients:

Petite Sophisticate	The Limited	Fifth Avenue
Casual Corner	Express	Old Navy

Involvement in "The Fashion Fair Expo" in Los Angeles, CA:
- Coordinated an event called "The Fashion Fair Expo" in Los Angeles. Assisted in creating the seating charts, acting as hostess, assisting dressers backstage, coordinating media opportunities, and helping with security. This is a major show which draws the attention of several thousands of buyers, retailers, and members of the national and international press to runway shows at which American designers present their collections.

Major accomplishments:
- Significantly increased my organization's presence on the local and national market.
- Created a new internal newsletter called the *Market Informer* which has been credited with improving communication, morale, and decision making.
- Streamlined the public affairs budget in order to optimize the utilization of every dollar.
- Produced dozens of luncheons for VIPs and special groups.

PUBLICIST. First Impressions Agency, Portland, OR (2002-03). Motivated and supervised 15 individuals while assuming personal responsibility for providing new and creative advertising ventures. Demonstrated strong organizational and leadership skills as I managed the advertising and marketing departments. Organized advertising expeditions in major cities such as Los Angeles, New Orleans, Miami, and New York City in order to network with others to improve our status in the industry.

PUBLIC AFFAIRS INTERN. Weis Public Relations, Portland, OR (2001-02). Gained experience in a one-year internship while attending Portland State on a full-time basis:
- Provided press releases for local television, radio stations, and print publications concerning new clients. Developed advertising and publicity campaigns for clients.

CUSTOMER SERVICE REPRESENTATIVE. *The Portland Daily News*, Portland OR (1999-01). Worked part-time while attending college. Gained experience in dealing with the public. Refined my verbal communication skills in training new employees.

PERSONAL   Participate in volunteer work for the Homeless Hotline and the Red Cross in Portland.

Date

Exact Name of Person
Title or Position
Name of Company
Address (no., street)
Address (city, state, zip)

Dear Exact Name of Person: (or Dear Sir or Madam if answering a blind ad.)

Can you use an aggressive, articulate, and innovative professional with a reputation as a persuasive individual with well-developed sales and communication skills?

As a Director of Public Affairs at the American Association of Advertising Agencies, I have become adept at developing marketing plans, molding teams, and ensuring the success of organizational goals. I have managed companies with as many as 25 employees, coordinated advertisement strategies for multimillion-dollar companies.

I have been consistently praised for my dynamic and productive job performance while working as a General Manager and Territory Manager for Phoenix based marketing firms. I have received extensive training and experience in the field of marketing, advertising, and public relations. I have directed a variety of activities ranging from training programs and formal classroom instruction, to long-range advertisement planning and development. Currently, I am completing requirements for a M.A. in Public Administration, and I have been placed in the honors society for the past three semesters.

I am well-accustomed to dealing with people of all cultures. In a previous position, I was a marketing instructor at the University of Phoenix. On that job, I have been commended for my natural skills in dealing a with people and for my ability to "sell" ideas. From a young age, I learned how to set and achieve difficult goals; for example, I earned my Eagle Scout rank in Boy Scouts at age 12!

I hope you will welcome my call soon to arrange a brief meeting at your convenience to discuss your current and future needs and how I might serve them. Thank you in advance for your time.

Sincerely yours,

Robert James Polk

Alternate last paragraph:
I hope you will call or write me soon to suggest a time convenient for us to meet and discuss your current and future needs and how I might serve them. Thank you in advance for your time.

ROBERT JAMES POLK

1110½ Hay Street, Fayetteville, NC 28305   •   preppub@aol.com   •   (910) 483-6611

OBJECTIVE

To add value to a company that can use a persuasive communicator, creative organizer, and talented manager who has excelled as a public affairs director while earning respect for the ability to develop and implement ambitious plans, perform under pressure, and "sell" ideas.

EXPERIENCE

DIRECTOR OF PUBLIC AFFAIRS. American Association of Advertising Agencies, New York, NY (2003-present). Apply my outstanding human relations and communication skills while managing an organization which provides public affairs support to companies whose employees are on nationwide assignments.
- Oversaw a two-month project to combine interaction with west coast offices.
- Edited a bi-weekly newspaper for 550 advertisers involved in the set up.
- Represented U.S. corporate and issued press releases in cooperation interests while coordinating visits by more than 20 international executives.
- Taught seminars training business executives in public speaking, editing, and media.

ASSISTANT PROFESSOR and **PROGRAM ADVISOR**. University of Phoenix, Phoenix, AZ (2001-03). Credited with doubling the enrollment in the University of Phoenix's Marketing Department, developed a very demanding training program for public relation students.
- Polished my skill at long-range planning while working with representatives of actual marketing agencies to develop a successful and highly effective 18-month training program while teaching at the university.
- Served as advisor and took on a critical role in selling talented and highly motivated young adults on the advantages of a marketing career. Praised for creative projects and teaching techniques that developed student interest the marketing field.

GENERAL MANAGER. HSP Enterprises, Phoenix AZ (1999-01). Promoted based on my success in running a highly marketing support center, transformed a group of poorly motivated, low-performing employees into a team recognized for its high morale and outstanding selling performance.
- Controlled sales and public relation operations which increased sales by more than $10 million. Managed a 25-person organization assigned to identifying successful target markets in the surrounding Phoenix areas.

TERRITORY MANAGER. Direct Marketing Solutions, Phoenix, AZ (1997-99). Honed my ability to work under the pressure of ensuring the smooth operation of a 24-hour-a-day customer service support center while overseeing activities including inputting and relaying constantly changing data.
- Reached department sales goals weekly using my extensive communication and negotiation skills; sold over $25,000 in marketing contracts.
- Managed executive accounts in the southwestern region with over 46 clients.

ADVERTISING ASSISTANT INTERN. Fuller Associates, Tempe, AZ (1996-97). Developed innovative marketing strategies which led to outstanding company recognition.
- Coordinated advertising campaigns with potential clients .

EDUCATION & TRAINING

Completing **M.A. in Public Administration,** University of Phoenix, AZ, degree expected in 2004. **B.S., Media and Public Relations,** Arizona State University, 1996.

PERSONAL

Became an Eagle Scout at age 13. Am known for remaining calm and unflappable in difficult situations. Have a highly developed ability to express myself verbally and in writing.

Date

Exact Name of Person
Exact Title
Exact Name of Company
Address
City, State, Zip

Dear Exact Name of Person: (or Dear Sir or Madam if answering a blind ad):

With the enclosed resume, I would like to make you aware of my desire to become involved in your organization in some capacity in which you could utilize my extensive background in public speaking, public relations, and management.

As you will see from my resume, I earned a B.A in Communication and Public Relations at McNeese State University. Then I was specially selected to work as a Public Relations intern at the Television Communicators-Media Training Center in Lake Charles, LA. I gained experience in coordinating individual and group seminars for public instructors for the publishers at the firm as well as editing scripts and videotapes for future documentaries.

In 1999, I was selected to attend an intensive training program in marketing and public relations, and I have had an opportunity to refine my abilities related to public relations and marketing as the Public Affairs Officer for WDSU-TV of Pulitzer Broadcasting. I routinely perform liaison with media including TNN, NBC, PBS, FOX, the Travel channel, and the Learning channel as well as numerous magazines and newspapers. I have coordinated five film projects and three book projects, and I have developed highly successful community relations programs that sparked civic involvement and community-wide problem-solving.

With outstanding written and public speaking skills, I am proficient with numerous software applications including PowerPoint and other presentation software. I was strongly encouraged by my peers to excel in the public relations field because of my natural talent in relation to people. I was also commended on my success in inspiring many employees to set and achieve higher performance goals.

If you can use an astute communicator and experienced manager who could contribute strong problem-solving and strategic thinking skills to your staff, I hope you will contact me to suggest a time when we might meet to discuss your needs. I can provide excellent personal and professional references at the appropriate time.

Yours sincerely,

Jeremy O. Seick

JEREMY O. SEICK

1110½ Hay Street, Fayetteville, NC 28305   •   preppub@aol.com   •   (910) 483-6611

OBJECTIVE   To offer strong planning, organizational, and communication skills along with exceptional abilities in developing and implementing projects, mediating disputes, and solving problems through an innovative style of management, marketing, and public relations.

EDUCATION   **B.A. in Communication and Public Relations**, McNeese State University, Lake Charles,
&   LA, 2001.
TRAINING   Completed intensive executive education program in marketing and public relations, The Media Studies Program for Public Relations, Bossier City, LA, 1999.

EXPERIENCE   **PUBLIC AFFAIRS MANAGER.** WDSU-TV Division of Pulitzer Broadcasting, New Orleans, LA (2003-present). Was recruited for this position which involves coordinating with newspapers, magazines, and media including TNN, NBC, PBS, FOX, the Travel channel, Learning channel, and numerous other broadcasting media while acting as the "voice" of the WDSU-TV.
- Coordinate five film projects and three book projects.
- Trained more than 200 people in media relations and public relations.
- Developed community relations programs that helped resolve community problems and ignited civic pride and citizen involvement; work with film crews to create community awareness.
- Coordinate internal and external information releases; conduct media content analyses.
- Develop and publish public affairs guideline seminars; conduct seminars regarding guidelines. Write articles for network magazine *Pulitzer Post*.

PUBLICATIONS MANAGER. Codra Enterprises Inc., New Orleans, LA (2002-03). Handpicked from among 19 well-qualified managers, excelled in planning and scheduling long-range training for an organization with 1,000 employees in four departments; developed a two-year comprehensive training plan for corporate communications department while managing projects nationwide.
- Integrated communication operations and administrative support.
- Managed an operations control center and integrated its functions into joint and international activities directed at the highest levels of national security management.

PUBLIC RELATIONS INTERN. Television Communicators-Media Training, Lake Charles, LA (2000-02). Officially evaluated as one of the top six of 18 employees in the parent organization and as "a superb performer with unlimited drive and initiative," supervised two junior interns.
- Edited documentary scripts and videotapes produced by publishers and authors of news shows. Coordinated individual and group seminars for authors and publicists on how to be booked for TV news, talk, and documentary programs.
- Planned, scheduled, selected potential guest speakers for upcoming shows.

CUSTOMER SERVICE REPRESENTATIVE. Southwestern Communications, Inc., Bossier City, LA (1998-00). Earned respect for my sound judgment and effectiveness as a leading representative in customer service. Transformed a group of 28 customer representatives into a cohesive team of enthusiastic professionals.
- Provided outstanding customer service to local clientele.
- Interacted well with coworkers to achieve a dedicated work ethic.

PERSONAL   Excellent references. Computer skills include PowerPoint, Word, Excel, PageMaker, Corel Draw.

Date

Exact Name of Person
Exact Title
Exact Name of Company
Address
City, State, Zip

Dear Exact Name of Person: (or Dear Sir or Madam if answering a blind ad)

With this letter and the enclosed resume, I would like to express my interest in receiving consideration for the Public Affairs Manager position available in your organization.

As you will see from my resume, I am presently employed with the U.S. Department of Internal Affairs in Atlanta, Georgia. In this position which frequently calls for me to serve as Acting Chief, Public Affairs, I am known as an effective strategic planner with "rare insight" and exceptional written and verbal communication skills. I am excelling in a career field which calls for high degrees of diplomacy and the ability to communicate ideas and concepts to a wide range of audiences worldwide while representing the department involving print and broadcast media.

With a B.A. in Communications and a M.A. in Political Science and minor in Public Relations, I have completed courses in media writing, corporate communications law, media studies, marketing, and management. I have also completed a Public Affairs Officers Course while serving in the U. S. Army. During my career, I have been awarded numerous medals and honors in recognition of my accomplishments and professionalism. I am confident that with my background and accomplishments I would be a valuable asset to a public relations company and am especially interested in being considered for a position in either Atlanta, GA or Washington, DC.

I am confident that I am the candidate who can well represent your organization and be a valuable liaison to the civilian industry through my articulate and persuasive style. If I offer the type of background the program is currently seeking for positions in public affairs, I hope you will call or write me soon to suggest a time when we might have a brief discussion of how I could contribute to your organization. I can provide excellent professional and personal references at the appropriate time.

Sincerely,

Christina L. Cantrell

CHRISTINA LOUISE CANTRELL

1110½ Hay Street, Fayetteville, NC 28305   •   preppub@aol.com   •   (910) 483-6611

OBJECTIVE
To offer my background of accomplishments as a military officer to the Training in Industry program in an assignment in the public affairs department of a public relations company where my strong base of knowledge and results-orientation will allow me to contribute.

EDUCATION
M.A., Political Science and minor Public Relations, University of Georgia, Columbus, GA, 1998.
B.A., in Communications, Georgia Southern University, Statesboro, GA, 1995.

EXPERIENCE
PUBLIC AFFAIRS PLANS AND OPERATIONS MANAGER. U. S. Department of Internal Affairs, Atlanta, GA (2003-present). Officially cited for my skills as a strategic planner of "rare insight" whose attention to detail made me a key factor in public affairs effectiveness, currently responsible for the development, implementation, and management of public affairs activities.
- Advise the Chief of Public Affairs for civilian communities worldwide and keep him informed and up-to-date on public affairs activities and operations worldwide.
- As a specialist in public relations, develop communications plans and crisis communications. Conduct media relations, representing a civilian community to the American public through the regional, national, and international media.
- Act as liaison and PA representative in an Emergency Operations Center which oversees corps activities in response to short-notice worldwide missions.
- Coordinate with reserve and national guard public affairs units.
- Frequently serve as Acting Chief, Public Affairs, XVIII.
- Was singled out for my attention to detail and "unrelenting dedication" while planning corporate-level operations. Cited as "absolutely comfortable working with the press," was described as having a "unique ability as a communicator suited to represent the Department of Internal Affairs."

PUBLIC AFFAIRS COORDINATOR. U.S. Department of Defense, Atlanta, GA (2001-2003). Trained, mentored, and guided the performance of a team of six print and broadcast journalists working along with the Department of Public Affairs.
- Provided oversight for photojournalism as well as print and electronic news gathering while also managing media training for all departments.
- On a formal citation for the Government Service Achievement Medal, was commended for "outstanding professionalism and exceptional leadership" as the primary coordinator of all local, regional, and international media coverage. Was praised for producing "positive international media coverage of soldiers, sailors, airmen, Marines, and Forces from all Coalition nations" while coordinating media coverage for more than 1,000 international media.
- Was a significant factor in department personnel receiving public affairs awards from private industry as well as from the Departments of Defense in Washington, DC.

PUBLIC AFFAIRS OFFICER (PAO). Defense Nuclear Facilities Safety Board, Washington, DC (1998). Supervised members of the media and oversaw four broadcasters and journalists in a joint nations peacekeeping. Controlled a $350,000 media budget as a financial officer.
- Assigned to act as PAO for what was recognized as effective leader in a multinational division, developed a cohesive and responsive team and handled international, national, and local media on a daily basis.

PERSONAL
Enjoy world travel. Gourmet cook.

Date

Exact Name of Person
Title or Position
Name of Company
Address (no., street)
Address (city, state, zip)

Dear Exact Name of Person: (or Dear Sir or Madam if answering a blind ad.)

I would appreciate an opportunity to talk to you soon about how my people skills, public relations expertise, and extensive background in presenting public information could ideally fit your need for a public affairs manager.

In a recent position as a Public Affairs Manager for the Department of Defense, I gained experience working with government officials and feel that my capacity for developing productive relations with other agencies is one of my strong points. I have developed security and law enforcement policies, evaluated and inspected customer programs, established and conducted public speaking seminars, and been highly successful in motivating employees to produce quality services.

In a previous position as a Public Relations Administrator for the Federal Labor Relations Authority, I was also called on display my well-developed motivational abilities, leadership style, and team-building expertise. Also, while serving in the U.S. Army, I was regularly selected for positions requiring managerial, communication, and analytical skills.

I hope you will welcome my call soon to arrange a brief meeting at your convenience to discuss your current and future needs and how I might serve them. Thank you in advance for your time.

Sincerely yours,

Kelsey Marie Granger

Alternate last paragraph:
I hope you will call or write soon to suggest a time convenient for us to meet and discuss your current and future needs and how I might serve them. Thank you in advance for your time.

KELSEY MARIE GRANGER

1110½ Hay Street, Fayetteville, NC 28305 • preppub@aol.com • (910) 483-6611

OBJECTIVE To apply expertise in a public relations environment to an organization that can use a proven motivator and communicator with a "track record" of distinguished public affairs experience.

EXPERIENCE **PUBLIC AFFAIRS MANAGER/INSTRUCTOR**. U.S. Department of Defense, Houston, TX, (2003-present). Coordinate a wide variety of activities in order make arrangements for visits by Pulitzer Prize-winning journalists and broadcasters, providing advice to a senior executive, and conducting classes for mid-level executives.
- Establish the policies for handling visits by foreign dignitaries.
- Work closely with international executive officials from Argentina, Brazil, and Spain to set up VIP visits.
- Learn to control media operations and compiled the company's Public Affairs Directory.

PUBLIC INFORMATION OFFICER. Federal Communications Commission (FCC), Houston, TX (2001-03). Was awarded a Meritorious Federal Service Medal for my performance and expertise displayed while disseminating official government information.
- Established standard policies for major forms of media such as television and radio.
- Reviewed corporate laws for media types to ensure that they were being properly used in the state of Texas.
- Conducted seminars to inform FCC executives of public information procedures.

PUBLIC RELATIONS ADMINISTRATOR. Federal Labor Relations Authority, Dallas, TX (1999-01). Revitalized a regional labor law program while involved in establishing policies and procedures for employment for FCC offices in the Dallas area.
- Managed the 14 supervisors over the Public Affairs Department.
- Coordinated seminars for instruction on effectively provide jobs for citizens in the Texas area; highly recommended throughout the state as an effective speaker.
- Organized major conferences, seminars, and initiated staff-level evaluations and recommendations for organizational improvement.

PUBLIC AFFAIRS MEDIATOR. U.S. Department of Defense, Houston, TX (1996-1999). Acted as liaison between the police chiefs of 10 communities and the headquarters of the Texas law enforcement organizations.

Advanced rapidly with the U.S. Army Military Police:
DIVISIONAL GENERAL MANAGER. U.S. Army, Fort Hood, TX (1995-96). Directed a specialized 200-person company which provided prisoner-of-war and battlefield security; additionally trained peacetime law enforcement personnel.
- Earned a reputation as a "superb" manager of large-scale operations.

DIVISIONAL OPERATIONS ADMINISTRATOR. U.S Army, Fort Polk, LA (1994-95). Worked closely with military police agencies while managing all police-related operations.

EDUCATION & TRAINING **M.A., Media Management,** University of St. Thomas, Houston, TX, 2002.
B.A., Media and Public Relations with minor in Law Enforcement, Sam Houston State University, Huntsville, TX, 2000.

PERSONAL Hold a Top Secret/SBI security clearance. Am familiar with Microsoft Word and PageMaker.

Date

Exact Name of Person
Title or Position
Name of Company
Address (no., street)
Address (city, state, zip)

Dear Exact Name of Person: (or Dear Sir or Madam if answering a blind ad.)

I would appreciate an opportunity to talk with you soon about how I could contribute to your organization through my versatile skills related to marketing, promotions, public relations, advertising, customer service, and office administration.

As you will see from my resume, I have an extensive educational background and experience in the field of public relations. I have a B.S. in Business Administration with a minor in Public Relations. I have also received a Diploma for a course I took in Visual Information/Audio Documentation Systems and Audio-Television Production.

In my most recent job as a Public Affairs Supervisor for ARIQ Footage Inc., I gained experience working with a production team in which I am in charge of media relations. My main purpose in this position is to direct the production and editing of footage for our public relations instructional films. I am also skilled in drafting eye-catching press releases and fact sheets.

In addition to my exceptionally strong writing and public speaking skills, I offer extensive advertising, marketing, and promotional knowledge. I have developed and supervised all promotional events for a chain of ten graphic studios, while creating memorable multimedia advertising campaigns that included direct mail, print, television, and radio ads. I was a key player in the creation of a public service campaign called "Clean and Drug-Free Cincinnati"; I also planned and directed a one-day fundraiser which raised $20,000 for the Leukemia Society!

You would find me to be an adaptable person who takes pride in doing even the smallest job to the best of my ability. I am proficient with several popular software programs including Microsoft Word, Excel, Corel Draw, PageMaker, and dBase, and I would enjoy using that knowledge to benefit your organization.

I hope you will welcome my call soon to arrange a brief meeting at your convenience to discuss your current and future needs and how I might serve them. Thank you in advance for your time.

Sincerely yours,

Cynthia N. Cole

CYNTHIA NADIA COLE

1110½ Hay Street, Fayetteville, NC 28305 • preppub@aol.com • (910) 483-6611

OBJECTIVE
I want to contribute to an organization that can use a talented organizer and communicator who offers proven skills related to public relations, office administration, and operations management along with a broad knowledge of commonly used software programs.

EDUCATION
Bachelor of Arts (B.A.), *Summa Cum Laude*, in **Communications**, Xavier University, Cincinnati, OH, 1999.

EXPERIENCE
PUBLIC AFFAIRS SPECIALIST, ADMINISTRATIVE ASSISTANT, OFFICE MANAGER. Department of Commerce, Columbus, OH (1999-present). Began with the EPA as office manager in 1999, was rapidly promoted to administrative assistant in 2000, and was handpicked in 2002 as public affairs specialist to represent the EPA to the general public and to federal, state, and local officials.

- As **Public Affairs Specialist,** draft press releases and fact sheets; serve as a liaison with the media, citizens' groups, and government officials; excel in using my written communication skills to "translate" complex technical concepts related to hazardous waste and other emotional environmental issues into information tailored to the needs of concerned citizens.
- After promotion to the newly created position of **Administrative Assistant** (2000-2002), developed it into a vital coordination role within the EPA; as the "right arm" to the Director of the Office of External Programs, organized administrative and secretarial workflow for 15 employees while working with the national EPA Headquarters, the Regional Administrator, as well as the media, the general public, and federal, state, and local agencies.
- As **Office Manager** (1999-2000), mastered numerous popular software packages while managing a busy office which required my management/organizational abilities as well as my editing/proofreading skills; was selected as a member of a team which created a management skills development program that was implemented region-wide!

PROMOTIONS/MARKETING/ADVERTISING COORDINATOR. Direct Graphics Inc., Cincinnati, OH (1997-1999). Developed and supervised all promotional events for a chain of ten graphic studio services while scheduling, setting agendas for, and chairing weekly marketing/promotional meetings.

- Coordinated a one-day fundraiser which raised $20,000 for the Leukemia Society; the event was so successful that it made the front page of the Cincinnati newspaper.
- Created media campaigns that included direct mail, print, television, and radio ads.

INTERN IN PROMOTIONS & MUSIC DEPARTMENTS. WXDE 107.5 FM Radio, Cincinnati, OH (1995-1997). Implemented various station contests and promotions and represented the station at promotional events while also maintaining an extensive music library. Played a key role in developing the "Clean and Drug-Free Cincinnati" public service campaign and held fundraisers to promote antidrug messages.

CUSTOMER SERVICE REPRESENTATIVE. Champion Printing Inc., Cincinnati, OH (1993-1995). In this job which helped me finance my college education, learned to plan/manage large public events while providing customer service for trade shows/expositions.

TRAINING
Completed training related to software including Corel Draw, PageMaker, and dBase.

PERSONAL
Speak, read, and write Spanish. Am an adaptable self-starter with unlimited initiative.

Date

Exact Name of Person
Title or Position
Name of Company
Address (no., street)
Address (city, state, zip)

Dear Exact Name of Person: (or Dear Sir or Madam if answering a blind ad.)

I would appreciate an opportunity to talk with you soon about how I could contribute to your organization through my versatile skills related to marketing, promotions, public relations, and advertising.

In my most recent job as a Public Affairs supervisor, I have developed professional relationships with individuals and companies in the media industry. I have conducted seminars on requirements and guidelines for public relation executives. I have also gained experience in writing effective press releases.

In addition to my exceptionally strong skills, I offer an educational background in marketing and public relations. I have a B. S. in Business Administration with a minor Public Relations and I have taken courses in public affairs, corporate law, media studies, and management.

You would find me to be a versatile, creative, and innovative professional who thrives on the responsibility of new challenges. I am certain my experience could significantly contribute to your company's needs. I hope you will welcome my call soon to arrange a brief meeting at your convenience to discuss your current and future needs and how I might serve them. Thank you in advance for your time.

Sincerely yours,

John T. Rogers

Alternate last paragraph:
I hope you will call or write me soon to suggest a time convenient for us to meet and discuss your current and future needs and how I might serve them. Thank you in advance for your time.

JOHN T. ROGERS

1110½ Hay Street, Fayetteville, NC 28305   ·   preppub@aol.com   ·   (910) 483-6611

OBJECTIVE
To benefit an organization that can use a creative and highly skilled video production specialist with extensive marketing and advertising knowledge who offers a proven ability to meet tight deadlines and achieve the highest quality standards while operating within budgetary realities.

EDUCATION & TRAINING
B.S. in Business Administration with a minor in Public Relations, Harding Univ., Searcy, AR; 2003. Completed this degree at night while working full-time.
Diploma, Visual Information/Audio Documentation Systems Advanced Course, 2000.
Certificate of Training, Audio-Television Production Specialist Course, 2000.
- Experienced in script writing and in digital editing with Turbo cube editing system.
- Experienced with Macintosh and PC programs including Windows, spreadsheets, databases, Adobe Photoshop, Illustrator, Pagemaker, and Photoshop.

EXPERIENCE
PUBLIC AFFAIRS SUPERVISOR. ARIQ Footage Inc., Searcy, AR (2003-present). Because of my achievements in producing video products and technical expertise, was selected as Chief Videographer for the famed production of *One Bright Morning.* Am in charge of media relations while directing the production and editing of public relations films.
- Develop professional relationships with over 100 national TV stations; through my media liaison and communication skills, have obtained more than two hundred thousand dollars worth of publicity and free press coverage.
- Operate and maintain more than half a million dollars in editing equipment. Produce and edit footage for news, public service announcements, and historical documentation.
- Conduct tours for VIPs and dignitaries which involved creating media shows.
- Produced and directed a new TG 86 Public Service Announcement (PSA); on my own initiative, organized a film library utilizing 37 years of historical video footage.
- Was commended for superior editing judgement in producing PSAs for 500,000 people.

PUBLICITY COORDINATOR. Elaine Jesmer Public Relations, Little Rock, AR (2001-03). Supervised three people and managed a $500,000 budget while acting as the Director of local community events. Conducted seminars on media relations and public relations.
- Developed community relations programs that helped resolve community problems and ignited civic pride and citizen involvement. Coordinated internal and external information releases; conducted company-wide media content analysis. Prepared press releases.

PUBLIC RELATIONS INTERN. Leoleen-Durck Creations, Jackson, TN (2000-01). Selected for position because of GPA score of 3.5.
- Wrote press releases for media exposure within the advertising industry.
- Proofread copy for advertising brochures and flyers. Produced a newsletter for 1200 members; the newsletter has been widely credited with increasing advertising clientele.

PRODUCTION ASSISTANT. Powell Productions, Memphis, TN (1998-00). With a six-member crew and over $2 million in equipment which included.
- Produced and edited audio and video content for future news stories
- Coordinated local and network access to produce daily programming for the station.

PRODUCTION ASSISTANT. WROE-TV, Little Rock, AR (1997-98). Managed a mobile video unit recording live footage and edited scripts for evening news stories.
- Managed the inventory of syndicated materials. Selected the content for talk shows such as current events, community affairs, and minority issues. Integrated computer graphics to produce films for training; produced spots for local tv shows and news broadcasting.

Date

Exact Name of Person
Title or Position
Name of Company
Address (number and street)
Address (city, state, and zip)

PUBLIC INFORMATION
ASSISTANT

for a college in
Massachusetts

Dear Exact Name of Person: (or Sir or Madam if answering a blind ad.)

I would appreciate an opportunity to talk with you soon about how I could contribute to your organization through the application of my versatile experience and knowledge in the areas of sales and marketing as well as finance operations and business management.

As you will see from my resume I earned my B.S. in Business Management with a minor in Public Relations from The Springfield College. My leadership abilities and communication skills led to my election by the student body to hold a seat as a Student Government Senator, and I was then selected by the organization's president to serve on the Campus Hearing Board where my sound judgment and ability to listen to both sides and make fair decisions was valuable.

I am a highly self-motivated individual who can handle pressure and deadlines and mange time for maximum productivity and efficiency. While earning my degree and maintaining a 3.0 GPA, I worked at Springfield College as a Public Information Assistant. Active in my community and local politics, I am a community-minded person who enjoys working with others to achieve team objectives.

I am certain that I can provide a company or organization with sound abilities in multiple areas which range from financial management, to human resources and personnel administration, to creative marketing and sales abilities. Known as an energetic and enthusiastic professional, I excel in motivating others and organizing complex activities.

I hope you will welcome my call soon to arrange a brief meeting to discuss your current and future needs and how I might serve them. Thank you in advance for your time.

Sincerely,

Alice C. Paglia

Alternate last paragraph:
I hope you will call or write me soon to suggest a time convenient for us to meet and discuss your current and future needs and how I might serve them. Thank you in advance for your time.

ALICE C. PAGLIA

1110½ Hay Street, Fayetteville, NC 28305　　•　　preppub@aol.com　　•　　(910) 483-6611

OBJECTIVE　　To offer versatile experience in areas requiring communication, sales, training, and marketing skills to an organization that can use a detail-oriented professional with an eye for detail and ability to handle pressure, deadlines, and challenges.

EDUCATION　　**B.S., Business Management and minor in Media Studies,** Springfield College, Springfield, MA, 2003.
* Elected by the student body as a Student Government Senator, was appointed by the organization's president to serve on the Campus Hearing Board.

EXPERIENCE　　**PUBLIC INFORMATION ASSISTANT.** Springfield College, Springfield, MA (2002-present). Provide support services for faculty, staff, students, and campus visitors as well as controlling inventory for the student supply store to include ordering merchandise; supervise and schedule student employees.
* Present the university to potential new students.

STATE PUBLICITY COORDINATOR. Department of Housing and Urban Development, Springfield, MA (1998-02). Gained exposure to using computers and provided supervision for at least 12 employees while handling additional functional areas such as scheduling, collections, and inventory control.
* Developed a working knowledge of PageMaker, Microsoft Word, Access, and Excel.

TEACHING ASSISTANT. Halton County Public Schools, Worcester, MA (1998). Filled short-term vacancies in pre-kindergarten through senior high school classrooms; prepared lesson plans and dealt with as many as 35 students per class while earning a reputation as a highly effective teacher who provided a caring and supportive atmosphere for children.

CUSTOMER SERVICE REPRESENTATIVE. Berkshire Hathaway, Boston, MA (1994-98). Provided administrative support by ordering materials, preparing bids, preparing receipts for customers, and making determinations on the profitability of potential jobs.
* Utilized my verbal communication and human relations skills recruiting new customers through outside sales and by phone.

Highlights of prior sales and management experience:
SALES ASSOCIATE. Dillards, Boston, MA (1990-94). Developed and polished sales skills while assisting Dillards customers in selecting home accessories; also acted as a Home Interiors representative making in-home sales presentations of home accessories.

COMMUNITY INVOLVEMENT　　Have been active in community affairs including being personally invited by Halton County Commissioner Salsing to serve on his campaign committee.
* Played an important part in efforts which resulted in the commissioner being elected despite several polls predicting he would lose.
* Spearheaded a successful campaign to stop trains from carrying nuclear waste throughout Halton County: approached local and state-level elected figures as well as sports figures, distributed petitions, attended environmental seminars, and held rallies to make people aware of the potential for disaster; my leadership led to a grant for $300,000.

PERSONAL　　Attended several workshops and seminars sponsored by local colleges and which emphasized listening, leadership, teaching, and problem-solving skills. Am a creative thinker with a talent for dealing with people fairly and honestly.

Date

Exact Name of Person
Title or Position
Name of Company
Address (no., street)
Address (city, state, zip)

PUBLICIST
for a local library

Dear Exact Name of Person: (or Dear Sir or Madam if answering a blind ad)

I would appreciate an opportunity to talk with you soon about how I could contribute to your organization through my creativity and wide ranging skills in the field of corporate communications and graphics/visual arts.

As you will see from my resume, I hold an M.S. degree in Communications Education and a B.A. degree in Communications/Mass Media. In addition to my formal education, I am by nature a "hands-on" creative individual who has demonstrated an ability to master a wide variety of technical tools and media ranging from computer software and television equipment to woodworking utensils and automotive tools. In most of the jobs I have held, I have been selected to supervise my co-workers during the absence of the manager, so I offer a proven ability to train, motivate, and supervise others.

Experienced in all phases of educational/training program design and development, I am skilled in corporate/instructional video design and production. Knowledgeable of all aspects of television writing and production, I have won awards in both national and international photography contests.

You would find me in person to be a congenial individual who rapidly masters new technical skills. I can provide outstanding personal and professional references upon request.

I hope you will welcome my call soon to arrange a brief meeting at your convenience to discuss your current and future needs and how I might serve them. Thank you in advance for your time.

Sincerely yours,

Emily Moriarty

Alternate last paragraph:
I hope you will call or write me soon to suggest a time convenient for us to meet and discuss your current and future needs and how I might serve them. Thank you in advance for your time.

EMILY L. MORIARTY

1110½ Hay Street, Fayetteville, NC 28305　　•　　preppub@aol.com　　•　　(910) 483-6611

OBJECTIVE

To contribute to an organization that can use a creative "hands-on" professional with versatile skills related to writing, television production, and photography along with expertise in using automotive, wood working, and many other kinds of tools and equipment.

EDUCATION

Master of Science (M.S.) degree in Communications Education, Pratt Institute, Brooklyn, NY, 2000; excelled academically with a **3.8 GPA.**
Bachelor of Arts (B.A.) degree in Communications/Mass Media, Virginia Commonwealth University, Richmond, VA, 1992.
Associate of Arts (A.A.) degree in Liberal Arts, Western Wyoming Community College, Rock Springs, WY, 1989.

EXPERIENCE

PUBLICIST. City Library System, Brooklyn, NY (2002-present). Write and design publicity materials marketing books, upcoming events, and programs while applying my expertise in creating original art and graphics, utilizing clip-art, and performing cut-out and paste-up.
- Handle publicity and public relations for a wide range of events. Supervise three employees.
- Organize author signings; personally worked with Mary Higgins Clark in a special signing for her best-selling anthology. Communicate with national magazine and newspaper editors in the process of publicizing library functions.
- Contribute a monthly column to *The Village Voice.*
- Work freelance as a book reviewer for *Publisher's Weekly* and *Book Review Monthly.*

PRINTER/ENGRAVER. Brooklyn Community Recreation Center, Brooklyn, NY (1998-01). Worked for over three years at this community recreation center that offered automotive shop courses as well as a variety of arts and crafts activities.
- Assisted in teaching custom printing and engraving of and on a variety of surfaces.
- Coordinated the first annual "Arts and Crafts Christmas Fair" at the center; made crafts to sell, arranged for prizes, selected craft participants, and handled publicity.

PRODUCER/WRITER & EDUCATIONAL TRAINING SPECIALIST. Department of Wildlife, Yellowstone National Park, WY (1996-98). Worked on a special project which involved creating an educational training program called Project Wild which teachers used to teach children basic concepts of wildlife ecology.
- Wrote, produced, and created an audio-visual slide program.

TELEVISION OPERATIONS ENGINEER. KMNT Television, Jackson, WY (1994-96). Acted as both Master Control Operator, Video Tape Operator, and Remote Broadcast Operations Engineer in this job which required me to have an FCC Radio Operators License.
- Produced mini-documentaries concerning wildlife for the Wyoming State Game Department and Grand Teton National Park; developed pre-production ideas and transformed them into outlines, scripts, continuity, storyboards, and graphics.

Other experience: Worked as a television News Photographer, television Production Assistant, and was Hostess, Producer, Writer, and Camera Operator for a public television series.

HONORS, PROFICIENCIES
- Have won awards in worldwide photography contests.
- Am skilled in corporate/instructional video design and production.
- Knowledgeable of all aspects of television writing and production.
- Experienced in all phases of educational/training program design and development.

Date

Anne McKinney
Publisher
PREP Publisher
P.O. Box 66
Fayetteville, NC 28302

Dear Mrs. McKinney:

I would appreciate an opportunity to talk with you soon about how I could contribute to your organization through my public relations experience gained through employment with some of the most successful public relations firms in the country.

As you will see from my resume, I have a M.A. in Public Administration and a B.A. in Media and Public Relations. I am a Honors Graduate from the class of 2002 and have received numerous public speaking awards because of my presidential position with the National Public Speakers Association. I have been honored with several awards for my humanitarian efforts as well.

I offer a reputation as a professional who can "think on his feet" in difficult assignments and be counted on for wise decision making under conditions of pressure and hardship. I am currently employed with Media Distribution Services in which my main objective each day is to ensure that all personnel adhere to proper communication laws and guidelines when disseminating information to the public. I have first hand knowledge of creating press releases and coordinating media conferences in Washington DC.

You would find me to be a professional business executive who is known for my ability to creatively apply my public relations training and experience in order to find the best solution for difficult problems. I am willing to relocate anywhere. I hope you will welcome my call soon to discuss your current and future needs and how I might serve them. Thank you in advance for your time.

Sincerely yours,

Daniel Clay Simmons

DANIEL CLAY SIMMONS

1110½ Hay Street, Fayetteville, NC 28305 • preppub@aol.com • (910) 483-6611

OBJECTIVE   To apply my excellent public relations and managerial skills, to an organization that can use my broad knowledge and experience in all aspects of public relations.

EDUCATION   **M.A., Public Administration,** University of the District of Columbia, Washington, DC, 2002. **B.A., in Media and Public Relations,** Georgetown University, Washington, DC, 1999. Graduated *with honors.*

EXPERIENCE   **PUBLICITY DIRECTOR.** Media Distribution Services, Washington, DC (2003-present). Direct the public relations division ensuring that all personnel adhered to the proper communication laws.
  - Create an online database system for media distribution clients. Create press releases, fax review copies, and media announcements to critics other journalist in all forms of media.
  - Develop instructional materials and conduct training seminars on communication law.

MEDIA ASSISTANT. PR Newswire, Washington, DC (2002-03). Managed 26 employees in the corporate communication department. Transmitted full text of press releases to more than 200 news organizations within the country.
  - Coordinated media coverage for local, national, and international organizations.
  - Assistant in the provision of news lines for sports, entertainment, and financial services nationwide. Created new research strategies to enhance our specialized database systems.

MARKETING COORDINATOR. Shandwick USA, Washington, DC (1999-2002). Worked in marketing department for a full service public relations firm with additional expertise in broadcast communications and promotions.
  - Prepare and present marketing plans, and then create exciting printed and photographic materials, in order to publicize and promote the diversified services/programs/events offered through a vast network of recreational facilities.
  - Wrote feature and news stories for local newspapers; write press releases for media.
  - Authored and proofread copy for brochures and flyers; develop scripts for briefings.
  - Produced a newsletter for 300 subscribers; the newsletter has been widely credited with increasing morale and building membership.
  - Worked with the press on a daily basis; schedule interviews for television and radio and provide media escort/information services.

COMPUTER SKILLS   Developed working knowledge of the following software programs:

Microsoft Word	Access	Excel
PowerPoint	Front Page	PageMaker
MacIntosh OS 9.1	Corel Draw	Dbase

VOLUNTEER   Volunteered with the D. C. Humane Society, contributed 32 hours per month. Received honorary awards from the National Public Speakers Association in Washington, D. C.

PERSONAL   Known for my strong, proven work ethic. Can provide personal and professional references. Willing to relocate.

Date

Exact Name of Person
Title or Position
Name of Company
Address (no., street)
Address (city, state, zip)

Dear Exact Name of Person: (or Dear Sir or Madam if answering a blind ad.)

Can you use a hard-working young public relations professional who has some experience in writing for newspapers, editing, a corporate newsletter, and improving internal employee relations?

Although I only recently received my B.A. degree in Communications and English, I have already gained valuable experience in my field through a summer internship at PR Newswire in Atlanta, GA. As one of only two interns selected by the company after conducting extensive interviews with candidates throughout GA, FL, AL, and TN, I had the opportunity to acquire a "wealth of experience" in one summer (2002):

- As Editor/Writer of the company's employee newsletter, I became skilled in most aspects of publishing.
- As a **Project Manager**, I planned special events such as dances and speeches while managing the summer softball league.
- As **Employee Relations Supervisor**, I worked with department managers and participated in seminar on "Problem Solving."

You would find me to be a cheerful and adaptable young person with a sincere desire to contribute to my employer's success.

I hope you will welcome my call soon to arrange a brief meeting at your convenience to discuss your current and future needs and how I might serve them. Thank you in advance for your time.

Sincerely yours,

Tasha N. Barnes

(Alternate last paragraph:
I hope you will call or write me soon to suggest a time convenient for us to meet and discuss your current and future needs and how I might serve them. Thank you in advance for your time.)

TASHA N. BARNES

1110½ Hay Street, Fayetteville, NC 28305 • preppub@aol.com • (910) 483-6611

OBJECTIVE

To contribute to an organization that can use a hard-working young public relations professional who has had experience in writing for newspapers, editing a corporate newsletter, and improving internal employee relations.

EDUCATION

Earned a **Bachelor of Arts (B.A.) degree, Communications and English,** Emory University, Atlanta, GA, 1999.
- Concentrated my course work in the following areas:

Advanced reporting	Radio and TV speaking	Public speaking
Copy editing	Speech communication	Basic reporting

EXPERIENCE

PUBLIC RELATIONS INTERN, PROJECT MANAGER, and **EMPLOYEE RELATIONS SPECIALIST.** PR Newswire, Atlanta, GA (2002-present). After being selected by this company as one of only two summer interns on the basis of intensive interviews with prospective candidates from all over GA, FL, AL and TN, excelled in wearing the following "hats:"

EDITOR/WRITER. Edit and write articles for the weekly corporate newsletter, "Newswire Presents."
- Am proficient at these and other aspects of publishing:

Planning content	Preparing layout	Managing production
Coordinating w/printers	Directing distribution	Writing articles

- Am respected for my creative approach, outstanding writing skills, and excellent editorial judgement.

PROJECT MANAGER. Enjoyed the challenge of planning, organizing, and managing several unique projects and events.
- Chose speakers for special engagements and handled logistical arrangements.
- Planned and organized dances for employees.
- Supervised a softball league for the company's 2,400 summer employees.
- Earned a reputation as a flexible and adaptable young professional who enjoys working with people.

EMPLOYEE RELATIONS SPECIALIST and **WORKSHOP SUPERVISOR.** Gained deep insights into effective methods of promoting employee satisfaction while serving as an apprentice in the employee relations area.
- Interviewed department managers in order to get an understanding of their operations.
- Participated in a workshop for supervisors on "Skills for Problem Solving."

Other experience:
SALES CLERK. Presto Windows, Atlanta, GA (1999-2001). As the business's only employee, was meticulously reliable in opening/closing this retail store and in preparing exciting window displays.
- Prepared advertisements for the newspaper.
- Learned how to interact with customers and help them make satisfying decisions.

SOCIAL CHAIRMAN. Delta Sigma Sorority, Atlanta, GA (1999-2000). Applied my creativity in organizing social events for hundreds of people.

PERSONAL

Have a very positive attitude towards life as well as a knack for motivating others.

Date

Exact Name of Person
Title or Position
Name of Company
Address (no., street)
Address (city, state, zip)

Dear Exact Name of Person: (or Dear Sir or Madam if answering a blind ad.)

Can you use a talented and creative marketing professional who offers strong personal qualities along with outstanding communication and organizational skills?

As you will see from my resume, I recently completed my B.S. degree magna cum laude from a campus of the Central Texas College in Killeen, TX.

- Through my experience in public relations, sales, and teaching I have worked on the "front line" learning about what influences consumer behavior and purchasing decisions.
- I credit my extensive worldwide travel with also giving me an "education" related to marketing and consumer decision making.

You would find me to be a loyal and hard-working professional who is respected for my ability to rapidly "size up" people and situations. I am sincere in my desire to contribute to your strategic goals and "bottom line".

I hope you will welcome my call soon to arrange a brief meeting at your convenience to discuss your current and future needs and how I might serve them. Thank you in advance for your time.

Sincerely yours,

Karen L. Patterson

Alternate last paragraph:
I hope you will call or write me soon to suggest a time convenient for us to meet and discuss your current and future needs and how I might serve them. Thank you in advance for your time.

KAREN L. PATTERSON

1110½ Hay Street, Fayetteville, NC 28305   •   preppub@aol.com   •   (910) 483-6611

OBJECTIVE

I want to contribute to an organization that can use a talented marketing professional who combines a dedicated and persistent attitude with a proven flair for identifying and communicating the appeal of a product or service.

EDUCATION

Earned **B. S. and A. A. degrees, Business Administration and Marketing,** Central Texas College, Killeen, TX, 2003.
- Graduated magna cum laude and was inducted into Beta Phi Business Administration Honor Society. Named "Student of the Year" 2003.

TRAVEL EXPERIENCE

Am relocating permanently to the Iowa City area after living throughout the United States and Asia and traveling all over the world with my husband while he was serving his country in the U.S. Marines.
- Gained insights into the factors that influence consumer buying decisions.
- Acquired the ability to "size up" and adapt easily to new situations.

EXPERIENCE

PUBLIC RELATIONS LIAISON. Covington Place Community, Killeen, TX, (2003-present). Refined my communication skills while managing the communication process between a military community and its hospital, dental, and veterinary services.
- Prepare, distribute, and analyze the results of a questionnaire designed to sample consumer opinions related to public transportation.
- Am skilled at "selling" ideas, both orally and in writing.

MARKETING/BUSINESS ADMINISTRATION STUDENT. Central Texas College, Killeen, TX (1999-03). With honors, finished my B.S. degree; also completed courses at a local community college which strengthened my computer knowledge and typing skills.
- Excelled in course work related to these and other areas:
    Developing marketing strategies and programs
    Creating marketing and advertising for diverse audiences
    Conducting marketing research, surveys, and analysis
    Preparing effective direct mail materials
    Developing and implementing promotions and public relations

TEACHING ASSISTANT. Newport News Elementary School, Newport News, VA (1996-99). Assisted the full-time teacher in all aspects of teaching and managing a class: prepared lessons, graded papers, counseled students and parents.

PROOFREADER. Wuest Business Forms, Newport News, VA (1995-96). Became known for my persistent attention to detail and my ability to rapidly edit large volumes of work while proofreading business forms.

SALES REPRESENTATIVE and **INVENTORY CONTROLLER.** Wells & Manning Retail Distribution Center, Newport News, VA (1993-95). Worked with vendors as well as customers in a wide range of income brackets; learned how to quickly assess a buyer's preferences, and became skilled in selecting merchandise from vendors that would sell quickly.

Other experience: Held leadership roles in the Officer's Wives Club.

PERSONAL

Am regarded by all who know me as an energetic and intelligent self-starter who exhibits a loyal and persistent attitude in everything I do.

Date

Exact Name of Person
Title or Position
Name of Company
Address (number and street)
Address (city, state, and zip)

PUBLIC RELATIONS MANAGER

for a pet grooming facility

Dear Exact Name of Person: (or Sir or Madam if answering a blind ad.)

I would appreciate an opportunity to talk with you soon about how I could contribute to your organization through the application of my versatile experience and knowledge in the areas of public relations and business management.

As you will see from my resume I earned my B.A. in Media and Public Relations Fairfield University in Connecticut. My leadership abilities and communication skills led to internships that refined my skills and allowed me to gain knowledge in media relations and business operations.

In my most current position as a Public Events Coordinator at the Fairfield Pets Inn, I have used my enthusiastic personality to develop good working relationships with my fellow co-workers and clients. I have a developed a highly successful publication called *The Pet Gazette* that will keep our existing clients and potential customers informed of our multi-service organization. I have also gained experience working as a Publicity Intern for the Mayor of West Haven, CT. My duties included writing press releases and radio advertisements to develop a strong campaign for his office.

I am a highly self-motivated individual who can handle pressure and deadlines and mange time for maximum productivity and efficiency. I am certain that I can provide a company or organization with sound abilities in multiple areas of marketing and sales. I hope you will welcome my call soon to arrange a brief meeting to discuss your current and future needs and how I might serve them. Thank you in advance for your time.

Sincerely,

Karen Suzanne Ellis

Alternate last paragraph:
I hope you will call or write me soon to suggest a time convenient for us to meet and discuss your current and future needs and how I might serve them. Thank you in advance for your time.

KAREN SUZANNE ELLIS

1110½ Hay Street, Fayetteville, NC 28305   •   preppub@aol.com   •   (910) 483-6611

OBJECTIVE   To offer my strong organizational and project development skills along with my ability to conceptualize and find ways to meet goals to an organization that can use an enthusiastic, detail-oriented young professional with dynamic public relation, motivational, and computer skills.

EDUCATION   **B.A. in Media and Public Relations,** Fairfield University, Fairfield, CT, 2002.

EXPERIENCE   *Was promoted on the basis of my earlier performance part time while in college at the Fairfield Pets Inn in Fairfield, CT:*
2002-present: PUBLIC RELATIONS & PUBLIC EVENTS MANAGER. Applied my education in business administration and special interest in public relations to create programs which increased the company's customer base and led to higher sales for the retail store portion of the business.
* Develop good working relations with related operations including pet groomers, the county SPCA (Society for the Prevention of Cruelty to Animals), and area veterinary hospitals.
* Established a highly successful publication, *The Pet Gazette*, which supported the county's rescue and pet placement efforts in addition to contributing to the already successful monthly newsletter, *My Pet's News.*

2000-02: SALES REPRESENTATIVE. Became acquainted with small business operations while checking boarders in and out. Contributed to planning and organizing special events including photo sessions and a "free flea dip" promotion.

Refined my public relations skills while attending college, working in a variety of part-time and summer jobs, and engaging in student leadership roles:
PUBLICITY INTERN. Department of Public Relations, Fairfield, CT (2000). Prepared press releases for local and national publications.
* Used graphic software programs to prepare layouts for in-house publications and print advertisements. Wrote radio advertisements and public service announcements.
* Worked with members of the administration as well as trustees and alumni.

COMPUTER LAB ASSISTANT. Fairfield University, Fairfield, CT (2000-02). Gained increased knowledge of computer software while helping students operate equipment.

Highlights of other public relations experience:
CAMPAIGN COORDINATOR. Mayor Ryan Vincent's Office, West Haven, CT (1999). Coordinated campaign functions during the 1999 Mayoral election in Connecticut.
* Answered phones and tallied poll votes at different locations for local mayor's office.
* Wrote press releases directed toward the News Election Service in West Haven.

ADVERTISING ASSISTANT. Weller/Grossman Productions, Greenwich, CT (1999-2000). Gained knowledge of production operations and the practice of media law while taking care advertisement accounts. Coordinated meetings with potential clients; sold advertising spots.
* Designed flyers, newsletter, and brochures for trade expeditions.
* Developed an interest in the public relations field while refining my skills in handling multiple tasks simultaneously in a hectic and fast-paced environment.

PERSONAL   Speak, read, and write French. Prepared several press releases which were published in various Connecticut newspapers. Played varsity softball for three years in college.

Date

Exact Name of Person
Title or Position
Name of Company
Address (no., street)
Address (city, state, zip)

**RADIO ACCOUNT
EXECUTIVE**

for a multimedia television
station

Dear Exact Name of Person: (or Dear Sir or Madam if answering a blind ad.)

Can you use a dynamic communicator and hard-working account executive who offers a proven ability to sell television advertising, produce revenue, generate new business, and assist in video/commercial production? I am very familiar with Missouri and am positive I could enhance your media sales and professional image in that region.

As you will see from my resume, I have excelled as an account executive and media consultant for KSDK-TV. A proven performer in this field, I am told by clients that they appreciate and trust my knowledgeable approach to television sales.

I feel sure you would find me to be a friendly and conscientious professional who could make your station even more competitive in your viewing area.

I hope you will welcome my call soon to arrange a brief meeting at your convenience to discuss your current and future needs and how I might serve them. Thank you in advance for your time.

Sincerely yours,

Lana F. Aaron

LANA F. AARON

1110½ Hay Street, Fayetteville, NC 28305   •   preppub@aol.com   •   (910) 483-6611

OBJECTIVE

I want to benefit an organization that can use a creative, self-motivating, and hard-working sales professional who has excelled as a media consultant and account executive with a major television network affiliate.

EDUCATION & TRAINING

B. A. in Media Studies, St. Louis University, St. Louis, MO, 1997.
Informal training provided by Multimedia Inc.; learned to overcome objections.

EXPERIENCE

RADIO ACCOUNT EXECUTIVE and **MEDIA CONSULTANT.** KSDK-TV, Division of Multimedia, Inc., St. Louis, MO (2003-present). Because of my excellent communication skills and "natural sales personality," was promoted to generate new business and serve existing local and regional clients in all aspects of television advertising.

> Cost-effectively purchase commercial air time.
> Write script copy for aired commercials.
> Assist in producing videos.
> Collect outstanding debts.
> Conduct "cold calling" to produce new business.
> Prepare correspondence and maintained files.

- Am a consistent revenue producer for this station.
- Am highly skilled in introducing new clients to electronic media benefits.
- Am considered highly skilled in developing promotions that delight the customer.
- Have been told by numerous clients that they appreciate and trust my knowledgeable approach to advertising sales.

SALES SECRETARY. KCTV, St. Louis, MO (2001-2003). Learned to write and edit script copy while excelling in supporting the administrative needs of a general sales manager and four account executives.

OFFICE MANAGER. E. S. Hudson Tennis and Golf Resort, St. Louis, MO (1999-2000). In my hometown, supervised 15 full-time and part-time employees while handling these and other areas:

accounts receivable	payroll	purchasing
accounts payable	bookkeeping	apartment rentals

- Wrote a monthly newsletter for the E. S. Hudson Resort.
- Learned to manage my time wisely.

EXECUTIVE SECRETARY. Fields, Price & Associates, St. Louis, MO (1998-1999). For two attorneys, transcribed dictation, prepared contracts and deeds, maintained files, and served customers.

Other experience:
CREDIT ASSISTANT. Assisted a busy manager in collections.
SALES SECRETARY. For five account executives, organized and maintained client files, prepared minutes of sales meetings, handled customers, and performed extensive telephone canvassing.
SALES CLERK. For the retail giant Burdines, sold merchandise and worked with the department manager to control inventory and create displays.

PERSONAL

- Work comfortably under pressure and tight deadlines.
- Am regarded by all who know me as friendly, conscientious, —and competitive!

Date

Exact Name of Person
Title or Position
Name of Company
Address (no., street)
Address (city, state, zip)

RADIO ANNOUNCER
for an FM radio station

Dear Exact Name of Person: (or Dear Sir or Madam if answering a blind ad.)

Would you be interested in considering a new talented professional with extensive experience in radio announcing to join your broadcasting team?

As you will see from my resume, I am an experienced radio broadcasting professional with talents that equip me for this opened position. I am proud of the fact that, at every station with which I have been associated, I have boosted ratings because of my effervescent personality and enthusiastic, likable style of relating to people. I have brought to broadcasting an understanding of people which I have acquired through versatile work experience which includes sales, retail management, fashion merchandising, and modeling.

At Greater Media Broadcasting, I was praised for my creative in writing. I offer not only my ability to originate new ideas but also the practical skills to implement new concepts on the air. A true broadcasting professional with excellent interviewing skills as well as the ability to provide sensitive leadership to others when they are discussing sensitive or controversial subjects, I can provide outstanding personal and professional references.

After earning my B.A. degree in Media and Public Relations, I excelled in jobs that helped me sharpen my public relation skills by gaining local celebrity status through dedicated community involvement. At one radio station, WHYY-FM, I was successful in increasing market share ratings and I developed professional relationships with celebrity and public figures.

If you would like to talk in person about your needs, I would be delighted to make myself available at your convenience by phone or in person. I am certain you would find me to be someone who could become a valuable new personality for your organization.

Yours sincerely,

Lisa Marie Dennison

LISA MARIE DENNISON

1110½ Hay Street, Fayetteville, NC 28305　　·　　preppub@aol.com　　·　　(910) 483-6611

OBJECTIVE

I want to transfer to television broadcasting my proven skills as a radio broadcaster and talk-show host along with my demonstrated ability to boost station ratings through my ability to relate to the audience and to motivate them to specific actions through my charm, wit, empathy, and personality.

EDUCATION

B.A. in Media and Public Relations, La Salle University, Philadelphia, PA, 2001.
Studied Broadcasting and Journalism, Pierce College, Philadelphia, PA, 1999.
Have completed numerous professional development courses in public relations, public speaking, management, broadcasting, and other areas.

EXPERIENCE

RADIO ANNOUNCER. JAZZ-108.5 FM, Philadelphia, PA (2003-present). Am a popular radio announcer for a station which appeals primarily to "oldies" connoisseurs aged 35-50 in an area with a population of more than 250,000.

RADIO ANNOUNCER. Greater Media Broadcasting, Philadelphia, PA (2002-03). Developed many creative programming ideas which boosted station ratings; for example, provided leadership in developing a "love" program which resulted in a popular dating game show. Utilized my expert knowledge of rhythm and blues and soul music.
- Handled daytime drives and acted as announcer for on-air contests. Performed remotes and promotional work.

RADIO ANNOUNCER. WUSL-FM of Chancellor Media Broadcasting, Philadelphia, PA (2002). Was credited with being the major factor behind the increase in station ratings; was recruited away from this "oldies" station by Greater Media Broadcasting.
- Handled commercial voice overs and new broadcasts.

RADIO BROADCAST ASSISTANT. Mercury Radio Communications, Philadelphia, PA (1999-02). Highly creative with proven ability to develop and implement new ideas.
- Extensive experience in working on broadcasting teams and equipment.
- As a host, have a likable personality with the ability to get people to open up and talk about sensitive subjects. Handled commercial voice overs and new broadcasts.
- Can provide a fresh new image along with a professional understanding of broadcasting.
- Interviewed personalities Jill Scott and Maxwell as well as the 'Philadelphia Trio' after their return from Olympic Trials where they won gold, silver, and bronze medals.

PRODUCTION ASSISTANT. WHYY-FM, Philadelphia, PA (1997-1999). Began as a part-time announcer with some sales responsibilities and was promoted to full-time announcer.
- Performed commercial reading and writing, live broadcasting promotions, remotes, and participation in all station projects.
- Was the driving force behind several community projects which raised money and collected food baskets for needy families; enhanced the station's public image through my charismatic motivational skills.

Other experience: SALES ASSOCIATE. Sak's Fifth Avenue, Philadelphia, PA (1996-1997). Hired, trained, motivated, and managed employees at two different retail operations while directing all aspects of merchandising, including visual displays, while handling accounting and bookkeeping.

LICENSE

Hold an FCC license in Radio and TV Communications

Date

Exact Name of Person
Title or Position
Name of Company
Address (no., street)
Address (city, state, zip)

Dear Exact Name of Person: (or Dear Sir or Madam if answering a blind ad.)

I am sending a resume in response to your recent ad for television production professionals.

With a B.A. degree from Williamette University in Salem, OR, I am skilled in operating a video camera, hanging lights, and providing the "behind-the-scenes" support critical to flawless television broadcasting.

As a television production specialist at WWEO-TV in Portland, I gained experience as a floor manager in operating the studio camera and in taking care of all the details that make a station look good on the air.

You would find me to be a hard-working young professional who is committed to a career in television production.

I hope you will welcome my call soon to arrange a brief meeting at your convenience to discuss your current and future needs and how I might serve them. Thank you in advance for your time.

Sincerely yours,

Jack P. Kronquest

JACK P. KRONQUEST

1110½ Hay Street, Fayetteville, NC 28305   •   preppub@aol.com   •   (910) 483-6611

OBJECTIVE   I want to contribute to an organization that can use a hard-working young professional who offers excellent skills related to all aspects of television production.

EDUCATION   **Bachelor of Arts (B.A.) degree in Radio, Television, and Motion Pictures,** Williamette University, Salem, OR, 1998.
- Concentrated in broadcast journalism while studying newswriting, media speech, and television production.
- Was elected a dorm senator and sergeant-at-arms of my fraternity.
- As an orientation counselor, became a mentor to new students.

PRODUCTION SKILLS   Skilled in operating a video camera, hanging lights, and providing all the "behind-the-scenes" support critical to flawless broadcasting.

EXPERIENCE   **RADIO NEWS ANCHOR**. WVIO-Radio, Portland State University, Portland, OR (2003-present). Am learning how to write under the pressure of tight deadlines while writing and reporting nightly news, sports, and weather.

TELEVISION PRODUCTION SPECIALIST. WWEO-TV, Portland, OR (2001-2003). In a "no-room-for-error" job, became known for my strict attention to detail while performing all the behind-the-scenes production activities that make the on-the-camera professionals look good.
- Gained experience with all aspects of television studio production including lighting, camera operation, and audio.
- Ran videotapes for newscasts; rewrote news items; edited stories.
- Skillfully took care of all the little details that no one sees: set up desks for the anchors; took care of lights, phones, water glasses, teleprompters, etc.
- Work with a large staff of teaching professionals while managing audiovisual services and production.
- Refined my skills in television production.

TELEVISION PRODUCTION SPECIALIST. WKID-TV, Portland, OR (1999-2001). Acted as Floor Manager, operated the studio camera, and rewrote the news when needed. Became respected for my careful attention to detail.

Other experience: Learned good work habits in these jobs (1998-1999):
PRESS BOOTH USHER. At Williamette University, worked with newspaper writers from all over the United States.

MAINTENANCE WORKER. At a restaurant and at an airport, performed behind-the scenes maintenance upkeep.

CASHIER. Managed a convenience store at night.

PERSONAL   Truly enjoy handling all the background details that make broadcasting effective. Am an effective communicator who enjoys working with people.

Date

Exact Name of Person
Title or Position
Name of Company
Address (no., street)
Address (city, state, zip)

RADIO PERSONALITY
for a radio broadcast
company

Dear Exact Name of Person: (or Dear Sir or Madam if answering a blind ad.)

I would appreciate an opportunity to talk with you soon about how I could contribute to your organization through my marketing experience, broadcasting knowledge, and public relations skills. Enclosed you will find a resume that I am sending in response to your advertisement for a radio personality.

After reading your ad, I believe I can assure you that my background is "tailor-made" to your specifications. With considerable expertise in the broadcasting field, I have created and implemented promotional strategies, handled media buying, and developed direct mail campaigns.

Companies that I have worked for have looked to me for leadership in a variety of areas. In one corporate "start-up" I helped the company reach its break-even point in only three weeks. For another company I designed and implemented its largest advertising campaign for the year. At another company I used my computer operation skills to computerize many manual functions.

You would find me to be a proven self-starter who offers a "track record" of achievements along with extensive business management and marketing skills and unlimited personal initiative.

I hope you will call or write me soon to suggest a time convenient for us to meet and discuss your current and future needs and how I might serve them. Thank you in advance for your time.

Yours sincerely,

Celeste Rhimer

CELESTE RHIMER

1110½ Hay Street, Fayetteville, NC 28305   •   preppub@aol.com   •   (910) 483-6611

OBJECTIVE

To benefit an organization that can use a resourceful self-starter who offers proven business marketing knowhow, expert knowledge of broadcasting, and a skilled public relations style.

EDUCATION

Bachelor of Arts (B.A.) degree program, Franklin Pierce College, Rindge, NH, **major in Communications, minor in Music;** degree expected in 2003.

SPECIAL SKILLS

Am skilled in analyzing/tracking media resources and consumer trends.
Am proficient with various software for broadcasters.
Hold FCC Restricted Radio Operator's Permit and am knowledgeable of FCC regulations.

EXPERIENCE

RADIO PERSONALITY. Foster-Bryant Broadcasting, Manchester, NH (2003-present). In my second ratings period, claimed the #1 market position for 18-34 year olds and stayed in first place throughout my employment; wore multiple "hats" as:

air personality	PSA director	remote broadcaster
copy writer	news team member	artist interviewer

- Produce innovative special programming related to artists including Bradford Marsalis, Brian Sullivan, and Maxwell.
- Create a week-long program on blues music and its influence on rock.

MARKETING COORDINATOR. WPDI Radio, Division of Buckley Broadcasting Corp., Manchester, NH (2001-2003). Developed, implemented, and evaluated promotional strategies and tactics designed to attract and retain advertisers.

- Landed the company's largest broadcast sale for 2002 — $16,500 for a 5-week campaign.
- Became skilled in tracking/identifying consumer profiles and designing advertising campaigns.
- Worked with demographic analysis and rate negotiations.

TRAFFIC & CONTINUITY DIRECTOR. SKYE, Inc., Rindge, NH (1999-01). Provided the leadership in computerizing company operations while maintaining billing data/accounts receivable, daily logs, and commercial production.

- Handled advertising agencies; used my cooperative specifications knowledge.

SALES/ADVERTISING MANAGER. Coldwell Advertising Inc., Rindge, NH (1998-99). In this corporate "start-up," helped the company reach its break-even point in only three weeks.

- Managed more than 25 employees.
- By the end of its first year, had opened five new markets and added three new popular client services for the company.
- Conducted sales seminars; developed sales packages which increased client loyalty; created employee incentive programs.
- Created all advertising and handled all advertising buying: print, broadcast, billboard, direct mail, and billing inserts.

Other experience:

writer/producer for public radio	researcher
voice talent for advertising agencies	TV audio technician

PERSONAL

Believe creativity and persistence are the keys to success in marketing.

Date

Exact Name of Person
Title or Position
Name of Company
Address (number and street)
Address (city, state, and ZIP)

Dear Exact Name of Person: (or Dear Sir or Madam if answering a blind ad.)

I would appreciate an opportunity to talk with you soon about how I could apply my creativity and maturity as well as my track record of excellent performance in rapidly changing and fast-paced entertainment environment.

As a Television Program Director, I earned a reputation as a dynamic leader and responsible manger of production and media resources while developing a broad base of skills in diverse settings. With a degree in Media and Public Relations, I have become an expert in the field of producing and directing informative and responsible broadcast products. Through a position as a director of audio-visual services and internships throughout the state of California, I have become known as a subject matter expert.

While advancing in this field, I have directed day to day activities of 51 employees including video film, and still crews who provided video products in response to the needs of our audience. I have also worked on local telethons and charity events in the area. These projects earned the praise of senior officials for my creativity in finding ways to keep costs down while improving quality.

I am a results-oriented professional who offers a detail orientation, proven intellectual and creative abilities, and an effective leadership style which consistently results in superior products. Through my many years as a producer and director, I have excelled in capturing important events which have directly impacted local communities in the western region of the U.S.

I hope you will welcome my call soon to arrange a brief meeting at your convenience to discuss your current and future needs and how I might serve them. Thank you in advance for your time.

Sincerely yours,

Matthew A. McGrew

Alternate last paragraph:
I hope you will call or write me soon to suggest a time convenient for us to meet and discuss your current and future needs and how I might serve them. Thank you in advance for your time.

MATTHEW ALAN MCGREW

1110½ Hay Street, Fayetteville, NC 28305 • preppub@aol.com • (910) 483-6611

OBJECTIVE

To contribute to an organization that can use a producer and director of informative and responsible broadcast products who offers expertise in managing projects, communicating with people at all levels, developing successful programs, and negotiating contracts.

EDUCATION & TRAINING

M.A. Public Administration, University of California, Berkeley, CA 2001.
B.S. Media and Public Relations, California State University, Fresno, 1999.

EXPERIENCE

TELEVISION PROGRAM DIRECTOR. Horizon Broadcasting Network, Los Angeles, CA (2003-present). Monitor existing daily programs; negotiate contracts for new productions.
- Increased advertising sales by 35% within last 3 months. Totally revitalized this broadcasting organization. Located new satellite equipment which improved reception.

DIRECTOR OF AUDIO-VISUAL PRODUCTIONS. KCAH-TV, Santa Clara, CA (2001-03). As the senior official in charge of audio-visual products with KCAH-TV, supervised 18 staff members production of international documentaries.
- Managed a total annual operating budget of $230,000 and $400,000 worth of state-of-the-art equipment. Received a commendation medal for my accomplishments while documenting current events and community involvement projects.
- Provided the audio-visual products using a still video satellite system.
- Officially evaluated as **"the best video producer/director for the station."**

PRODUCTION MANAGER. KOVR of Sinclair Broadcasting, West Sacramento, CA (1999-01). Directed the day-to-day activities of 51 employees including video, film, and still crews who provided products in response to the needs our audience.
- Managed a $1 million annual operating budget and $300,000 worth of equipment.
- Established a satellite unit which gave improved reception to the Sacrament area.

PRODUCTION ASSISTANT. A & E, San Francisco, CA (1996-1999). During this internship at A & E, I acted as production specialist, cameraman, floor director, and director of an early morning news program.
- Produced a video clip used by the university for recruiting purposes.
- Assistant Senior Producer with contract negotiations; prepared needed documentation.
- Produced and directed the still video product shoots for local advertisement ventures.
- Personally oversaw the processing, printing, and editing videos used for daily shows.

TELEVISION BROADCAST ASSISTANT. WHUD-TV, Oakland, CA (1994-1996). Wrote, produced, and directed television productions which focused on community activities from a facility with three production professionals and $1.5 million worth of equipment.
- Produced a program rated as the best of its type during a project in Oakland.
- Gained experience as a cameraman, gaffer, key grip, and technical director on local Oakland TV productions such as local telethons and charity events in the area.

COMMUNITY SERVICES ANNOUNCER. WJHR AM Talk Radio, Oakland, CA (1993-1994). Gained radio announcing experience working full-time for a local station.
- Wrote news stories from AP wire service reaching a 7,000-person community.
- Conducted telephone interviews. Recorded national public radio evening newscasts.

SKILLS

Familiar with video and still cameras, post-production equipment including CMX editor and Grass Valley switcher. Experienced with Microsoft Word, PageMaker, Photoshop, Corel Draw.

Exact Name of Person
Title or Position
Name of Company
Address (number and street)
Address (city, state, and ZIP)

RADIO NEWS DIRECTOR
for a college
communication
department

Dear Exact Name of Person: (or Dear Sir or Madam if answering a blind ad.)

I would appreciate an opportunity to talk with you soon about how I could apply my creativity and maturity as well as my track record of excellent performance in rapidly changing and fast-paced entertainment environment.

As an Radio News Director, I earned a reputation as a dynamic leader and responsible manger of production and media resources while developing a broad base of skills in diverse settings. With a degree in Media and Public Relations, I have become an expert in the field of producing and directing informative and responsible broadcast products. Through various positions as a Radio News Reporter throughout Detroit, I have become known as a subject matter expert.

While advancing in this field, I have become quite knowledgeable of writing press releases, public service announcements, and feature news and sports stories for publication and broadcasting. I am well aware of current environmental issues and am familiar with the Associated Press (AP) News Desk and AP database. I am very knowledgeable of the all radio and audio equipment.

I am a results-oriented professional who can offer a detail orientation, proven intellectual and creative abilities, and an effective leadership style to your organization. I hope you will welcome my call soon to arrange a brief meeting at your convenience to discuss your current and future needs and how I might serve them. Thank you in advance for your time.

Sincerely yours,

Erin Christine Magnuson

Alternate last paragraph:
I hope you will call or write me soon to suggest a time convenient for us to meet and discuss your current and future needs and how I might serve them. Thank you in advance for your time.

ERIN CHRISTINE MAGNUSON

1110½ Hay Street, Fayetteville, NC 28305   •   preppub@aol.com   •   (910) 483-6611

OBJECTIVE   I want to contribute to the public relations image and activities of an organization that can use an experienced young news reporter who offers an excellent understanding of the media and how companies can maximize media relations.

EDUCATION   **Master of Arts in Public Administration,** University of Detroit, Detroit, MI, 2003.
Bachelor of Arts in Media and Public Relations, Marygrove College, Detroit, MI, 2002.
- Staff writer for The Specialist at the University of Detroit, Detroit, MI.
Studied English, Marygrove College, Detroit, MI.
- Copywriter for *The Rockwell Report*, Atlantic Christian College Annual.

SKILLS   Offer the ability to prepare publicity materials and press kits. Knowledgeable of how to write press releases, public service announcements, as well as feature, news, and sports articles for publication and broadcast. Knowledgeable of environmental issues and trends. Familiar with the Associated Press (AP) News Desk and the AP data base. Have earned a reputation as a creative professional with a knack for making complex issues understandable to the public. Skilled in video, writing, and production.

EXPERIENCE   **RADIO NEWS DIRECTOR.** Michigan State University Communication Arts Department, Detroit, MI (2003-present). Was promoted to this job after excelling as a part-time reporter while in school on a full-time basis. I am in charge of making assignments for a three-person staff in the news room of this radio station; handle numerous administrative responsibilities related to maintaining the news room's productivity and efficiency.
- As a Reporter, cover local government and other issues.
- Am respected for my skills in identifying, researching, and developing interesting stories.
- Learned to manage a news operation. Covered a wide variety of environmental issues.

RADIO NEWS REPORTER. Infinity Broadcasting, Detroit, MI (2001-2003). Sharpened my creative writing skills and interpersonal/interviewing abilities in building news beats.
- Covered county/community issues, and developed stories about education and environmental issues for use in regular newscasts; generated much public awareness/ discussion based on stories I produced on saving natural resources and a proposal for a new incinerator.
- Anchored and occasionally produced special reports on issues of local interest.

REPORTER/NEWS DIRECTOR. WCSX-FM Division of Greater Media Inc., East Lansing, MI (1999-2001). Was solely responsible for local news production and anchoring.
- Through my hard work and initiative, greatly strengthened this station's coverage of local government issues, educational matters, and spot news events.
- Was commended for my soothing voice and professional manner of delivering the news.

NEWS ASSISTANT and **PUBLIC AFFAIRS PRODUCER.** WOMC, Detroit, MI (1998-1999). Developed and produced stories of local interest to morning news casts.
- Originated the concept for and produced a weekly public affairs show focusing on issues in the station's city of license.

VOLUNTEER   Have extensively volunteered my time to perform on-the-air radio reading for the blind.

PERSONAL   Excellent interpersonal skills have helped me build solid working relationships with government officials, politicians, business people, and citizens. Easygoing style of interviewing.

CAREER CHANGE

Date

Exact Name of Person
Title or Position
Name of Company
Address (no., street)
Address (city, state, zip)

RADIO NEWS INTERN

for an AM and FM radio

station

Dear Exact Name of Person: (or Dear Sir or Madam if answering a blind ad.)

Can you use a hard-working young professional who offers an education in Mass Communications along with a reputation as an articulate and gifted writer and communicator?

As you will see from my resume, I have excelled in jobs requiring skills in customer and public relations, sales, and marketing. I am known as a fast learner who can be depended on to find ways to increase efficiency and ensure quality performance from others based on my own high standards.

As a Radio News Intern, I was called on to coordinate special events for our daily talk shows. I researched future topics with potential to increase market share ratings for the station. In another internship as a Media Assistant, I was given the liberty of editing scripts for evening news anchors. I also earned praise for my exceptional public relations skills in setting up media contacts.

I feel that the combination of my education, experience, and ability to learn quickly while applying what I have learned would make me a productive asset to your organization.

I hope you will welcome my call soon to arrange a brief meeting at your convenience to discuss your current and future needs and how I might serve them. Thank you in advance for your time.

Sincerely yours,

Shannen L. Stokes

Alternate last paragraph:
I hope you will call or write soon to suggest a time convenient for us to meet and discuss your current and future needs and how I might serve them. Thank you in advance for your time.

SHANNEN LYNN STOKES

1110½ Hay Street, Fayetteville, NC 28305　　•　preppub@aol.com　•　(910) 483-6611

OBJECTIVE

To contribute to an organization that can use my outstanding written and oral communication skills, my education in mass communications, and my public relations, sales, personnel management, and office administration experience.

EDUCATION & TRAINING

Bachelor of Arts (B.A.), Mass Communications with a concentration in **and Electronic Media**, San Francisco State University, San Francisco, 2003.
Completed this degree at night while excelling in my full-time job.
- Completed an internship as a radio news director and a professional media internship in a television station.

EXPERIENCE

RADIO NEWS INTERN. WMIK-AM/FM, San Francisco, CA (2003-present). Research potential topics for future shows and coordinate special events.
- Manage incoming calls for talk shows.
- Interview potential guests; arrange dates and times for their appearances.
- Prepare statistical reports regarding local listening audiences.

MEDIA ASSISTANT INTERN. WJRJ-TV, San Francisco, CA (2002). Evaluated as an outstanding communicator with exceptional skills as a writer regarding statistical reports and press releases.
- Edited scripts for news anchors.
- Earned praise for exceptional organizational abilities in setting up media contacts.

Highlights of previous experience:
NEWSLETTER EDITOR. IGA Publications, San Diego, CA (2000-02). Served as **Newsletter Editor**; produced biweekly newsletter which contained human interest stories and information on upcoming events.
- Also served as **Benefits Coordinator** for full and part-time employees; notified employees of benefits and eligibility requirements.
- Used PageMaker desktop publishing software.

CUSTOMER SERVICE REPRESENTATIVE/CASHIER. Verizon Communications, San Diego, CA (1999-00). Processed new and existing accounts and programmed equipment for mobile services.
- Received payments for purchases from customers in a retail sales store.
- Excelled in providing courteous professional customer service.

RECREATION CENTER EQUIPMENT MANAGER. High-Valley Recreation Center, San Diego, CA (1998-99). Controlled an inventory of recreation equipment: checked equipment in and out, completed daily inventories, and sent damaged equipment for repairs.
- Maintained daily records of facility use by making periodic counts of how many customers were using each type of equipment.
- Applied my attention to detail in keeping/completing accurate records of baseball, volleyball, and softball statistics.

SPECIAL SKILLS

Working knowledge of Microsoft Word, PageMaker, and QuarkXPress.

PERSONAL

Possess secret security clearance. Am FCC-licensed as a radio operator. Speak/read Spanish.

Date

Exact Name of Person
Title or Position
Name of Company
Address (no., street)
Address (city, state, zip)

RADIO SALES DIRECTOR
for an Ohio radio group

Dear Exact Name of Person: (or Dear Sir or Madam if answering a blind ad)

Now working as a Director of Sales and Market Manager with Carver Radio Group, I feel it is time for a change. Before coming aboard with the Carver Group, I was Vice President of Sales for Better Broadcasting Inc., responsible for the oversight of fourteen stations in Minnesota.

Through the years working in radio, I have learned that there is no secret to the success each market has had: it is **hard work, everyday**.

Remember, the only difference between a failure and a success is that success decides to get up one more time.

Needless to say, I have gotten up more than once or twice in my career.

I hope you will welcome my call soon to arrange a brief meeting at your convenience to discuss your current and future needs and how I might serve them. Thank you in advance for your time.

Sincerely,

Gene H. Overstreet

GENE H. OVERSTREET

1110½ Hay Street, Fayetteville, NC 28305   •   preppub@aol.com   •   (910) 483-6611

OBJECTIVE

I want to contribute to an organization that can use a dynamic broadcasting executive with a proven ability to boost ratings and improve market share.

EDUCATION

Associate's degree from American Broadcasting School, Minneapolis, MN, 1995.
Bachelor of Arts (B.A.) degree in Communications, University of Minnesota Twin Cities Campus, Minneapolis, MN, 1989.
Associate's degree in Business, Concordia College, Moorhead, MN, 1986.

EXPERIENCE

RADIO SALES & MARKET DIRECTOR. Carver Radio Group, Akron and Medina, OH (2003-present). Responsible for the oversight of seven radio stations with $5.6 million in sales.

- Was promoted to Market Manager in Akron where I am responsible for the oversight of four stations.
- Q-1 was $191,000 over budget and $102,000 over BCF. Due to my intervention, the stations that were $191,000 over budget and $102,000 over BCF are now on target to generate $6 million in revenue this year.

VICE PRESIDENT OF MINNESOTA OPERATIONS. Better Broadcasting, Inc., Bloomington, MN (2001-03). Responsible for the oversight of 14 radio stations throughout the state of MN with billings totaling $4.5 million.

GROUP GENERAL MANAGER. Thomas Broadcasting, Saint Paul, MN (1999-01). Responsible for the oversight of 13 stations including promotions, sales training, and recruiting of managers.

- Worked with all station General Managers on their station activities and concerts.
- Was in charge of Thomas Network sales throughout the state of MN.
- As Group Manager, took billing of 13 stations to $4.7 million with collections of 98%.
- After being challenged to increase sales by 20% in 2001, ended the year with a 31% increase.

GENERAL MANAGER AND SALES MANAGE. KERM-KTWC Radio Stations, Minneapolis and Saint Paul, MN (1997-99). Increased sales by 41% annually while ensuring budget compliance and meeting quotas.

GENERAL SALES MANAGER. KTWC Radio, Cooper Entertainment, Minneapolis, MN (1995-97). Was in charge of all national and local sales. Increased sales 47%.

GENERAL SALES MANAGER. Mainstage Productions, Columbia, MO (1992-95). Handled annual revenues over $3 million in national sales and production. Directed television advertisements.

REGIONAL SALES MANAGER. Rogers Industries, Saint Louis, MO (1990-92). Responsible for the entire midwest region for a company selling maintenance equipment.

PERSONAL

Excellent references available upon request.

Date

Exact Name of Person
Title or Position
Name of Company
Address (no., street)
Address (city, state, zip)

Dear Exact Name of Person: (or Dear Sir or Madam if answering a blind ad.)

I would appreciate an opportunity to talk with you soon about how I could benefit your organization through my office management abilities, as well as through my education and experience related to news reporting.

As you will see from my resume, I am presently working as a Reporter for Parade Publications in New York. In this job, I have earned recognition for being a hard worker with a high energy level, and I have "broke" major stories through my persistence and investigative skills.

Recognized for my high degree of initiative, in the three years I have worked for Long Island University, I have made important contributions to my employer. I excelled in a variety of functional areas related to operating a tri-weekly student newspaper while completing a B. S. in Business Administration and a B. A. in Journalism.

I hope you will welcome my call soon to arrange a brief meeting at your convenience to discuss your current and future needs and how I might serve them. Thank you in advance for your time.

Sincerely yours,

Andy McKinsey

ANDY MCKINSEY

1110½ Hay Street, Fayetteville, NC 28305   •   preppub@aol.com   •   (910) 483-6611

OBJECTIVE

To offer the versatility of my formal education in both business management and chemistry to an organization in need of a hard-working young professional with outstanding communication, public relations, and sales skills.

EDUCATION

Earned two Bachelors' degrees, Long Island University, Brooklyn, NY, 2000: **Bachelor of Science in Business Management; Bachelor of Arts in Journalism.**

- Earned 60% of my educational funds while maintaining a 3.27 GPA in my major area of concentration.
- Excelled in specialized course work including:

Economics of the firm	Business statistics
Personnel management	Biochemistry
Investment and portfolio management	Organic chemistry
Systematic inorganic chemistry	Quantitative analysis

- Am familiar with chemistry lab procedures and equipment including:

IR spectra generation and analysis	NMR spectra analysis
Liquid column & gas chromatography	TLC analysis
Reference materials including Dowell Index and Organic Synthesis	

- Gained experience in word processing using Microsoft Word, Excel, and PageMaker software.

EXPERIENCE

REPORTER. Parade Publications, Inc., New York, NY (2003-present). Write news stories concerning county court activities in a system handling 20,000 cases annually; report on federal and U.S. Supreme Court cases which impact in some way on New York area residents.

- Was selected to handle specialized assignments in a field outside the focus of my formal education.
- Am known as a hard worker with a high energy level, "broke" major stories through persistence and investigative skills.

GENERAL MANAGER, STUDENT NEWSPAPER. Long Island University, Brooklyn, NY (2001-03). Excelled in a variety of functional areas related to the operation of a tri-weekly student newspaper at the state's largest university while increasing circulation, improving efficiency, and reducing costs.

- As the **Editor**: Saved $9,000 by reducing production costs 5% and increasing circulation 27%; controlled a $340,000 operating budget.
- As the **Managing Editor**: Increased productivity by reorganizing staff assignments while managing daily newsroom operation.
- As **Production Manager**: Trained and directed a production staff of as many as 10 people while controlling supplies.
- As a **Layout Artist** and **General Assignment Reporter**: Simultaneously assisted in designing and pasting up the front page, writing headlines, and covering news stories.

TRAINING

Attended seminars and training programs related to financial management, public relations, time management, and conflict resolution.

PERSONAL

Am an effective speaker with exceptional "people" skills. Feel that my versatility and adaptability are among my strongest attributes.

Date

Anne McKinney
Publisher
PREP Publishing
P.O. Box 66
Fayetteville, NC 28302

Dear Mrs. McKinney:

With the enclosed resume, I would like to make you aware of my experience in sales and management and my desire to put my talents to work for you. I began my broadcast career at KSOP, as a Yellow Page, back-room, thought-you-read-the-rating-book-down-one-side-and-start-over-on-the-next-page trainee. I left KSOP to assume a major list and promotion opportunity at KSDN-TV in Louisville. (No one advised me that moving from the 25th market to the 75th market was a normal career path!)

You will see from my resume that I am currently a Local Sales Manager at WJFT, TV 53 in Kentucky, where I am managing a sales force covering a market (Louisville and Lexington) which is the 32nd largest market. While managing a sales force of six account executives, I have exceeded all expectations in terms of revenue generation as well as personnel training and development. Although I am highly regarded by this employer and can provide excellent references at the appropriate time, I am interested in relocating to Lexington, KY, and am very interested in the possibility of returning to KSOP.

In a prior position with KSDN-TV in Louisville, Kentucky, I excelled in a track record of promotion and was credited with being the driving force behind the station's being recognized as a "Top Performing" station in Goldstein's TV's national survey. I began with the station as an Account Executive and achieved the status of Top Salesman each year while also winning all the sales incentive contests. Then I was promoted to National Sales Manager, and I took the national revenue share from less than rating share to greater than audience delivery. After my promotion to General Sales Manager, I made numerous contributions to the bottom line while expanding the local staff from four to eight account executives.

I have had significant success with many forms of value-added selling: vendor, doorknob delivery, and musical themes (jingles). When our vendor specialist pitched KPJO-TV, the Sales Manager called me to verify our unbelievable sales figures. Our achievements with the Top-of-the-Scale promotion were equally spectacular. My broadcast experience includes experience with major networks – ABC at KSDN, MSNBC at KSOP, and UPN, as well as my current position at an independent.

I hope you will contact me to suggest a time when we might meet to discuss your needs and how I might serve them. I can provide excellent professional references. Thank you in advance for your time.

Yours sincerely,

Dion Estes

DION ESTES

1110½ Hay Street, Fayetteville, NC 28305   •   preppub@aol.com   •   (910) 483-6611

OBJECTIVE   I want to offer my broadcast experience with major networks – ABC, MSNBC, and UPN as well as my retail management and sales background which makes me ideally suited to your need for a General Sales Manager at KSOP-TV.

EXPERIENCE   **SALES MANAGER.** WJTF-TV 53, Louisville, KY (2003-present). While managing a sales force of six account executives, have exceeded all expectations in terms of revenue generation as well as personnel training and development.
- Have achieved a 45% increase in sales compared to last year.
- Cover a market (Louisville and Lexington areas) which is the 29th largest market.

BROADCAST SALES MANAGER . WESC-TV 12, Louisville, KY (2002-03). Supervised 10 employees in the sales division. Created new avenues of improvement concerning customer service needs.
- Increased sales by 25% in one year and reduced labor by 8%. Increased regional market share costs by 4% while restructuring and retraining the staff for a more aggressive customer service orientation.

GENERAL SALES MANAGER. KHJK-TV 42, Louisville, KY (2000-02). Increased sellout by 22% and raised unit costs by 12% while excelling in this sales management role.
- Increased local market share by 3% in one year. Increased revenue each year by 11% and 19% respectively. Increased regional market share by 6% in one year.

Excelled in the following track record of promotion with KSDN-TV, **Louisville, KY:**
1999-00: BROADCAST SALES MANAGER. Through my aggressive bottom-line orientation and strong personal initiative, led the sales department to be recognized as a "Top Performing" station in Goldstein TV's national survey.
- Realized a 19% revenue share difference over audience delivery.
- Initiated a revenue-generating vendor program that generated over one million dollars.
- Achieved almost 2 months of local budget in 1st quarter with the Top-of-the-Scale Promotion. Achieved and maintained market leadership in sponsorship selling and new account development. Expanded local staff from four to eight account executives.

1997-99: NATIONAL SALES MANAGER. Established a short-term computer forecasting model for pricing and goal orientation that was adopted corporate wide.
- Reworked the representative relationship based on spot rate and share.
- Took national revenue share from less than rating share to greater than audience delivery.

1996-97: ACCOUNT EXECUTIVE. Began with a small client list, and achieved the status of Top Salesman each year; was the winner of every sales incentive contest.

1995-96: SALES ASSISTANT. KSOP-TV, Lexington, KY. Developed a large client list.

Other experience: **SALES ASSISTANT.** Fetter Productions, Lexington, KY (1993-1995). With a cable tv company, played a key role in growing the business from six to 40 employees.

EDUCATION   **B.A. in Media and Public Relations,** University of Louisville, Louisville, KY, 2003.

AFFILIATIONS   President and Founder, Kentucky State Endowment Foundation
Past Secretary/Treasurer of Trustees, The Louisville Club

Date

Exact Name of Person
Title or Position
Name of Company
Address (no., street)
Address (city, state, zip)

TELEVISION PRODUCER
for two television
broadcast shows

Dear Exact Name of Person: (or Dear Sir or Madam if answering a blind ad.)

I would appreciate an opportunity to talk with you soon about how I could contribute to your organization through my excellent communication and organizational skills as well as through my experience in television production, reporting, and broadcasting.

As you will see from my resume, I hold both a bachelor's degree and a master's degree in the broadcasting field. While earning my undergraduate degree from Hofstra University in New York, I worked for two years as a news reporter and television producer for a half-hour show which featured local news. I also worked at the student newspaper writing feature stories, editing copy, and designing page layout.

While earning my master's degree, I worked as an Assistant Professor for TV Production at the university where I received my degree, and I taught TV Production I and II as well as a Communications and the Law course given to seniors. After receiving my master's degree, I became a marketing manager and television producer/co-host for a cable network, where I was given credit for increasing ratings of the two shows I produced. I also contributed to the station's profitability through the innovative marketing strategies I implemented.

My organizational and management skills have been refined through experience. For example, I have worked as an Assistant Producer of a popular children's show broadcast to 23 countries. I am also comfortable on the air; in my most recent job I co-hosted a popular auction show, and I have worked as a model and actor in commercials for a prominent modeling agency.

I feel certain you would find me to be a warm professional who could contribute much to your organization through my strong organizational and management skills. I can provide strong personal and professional references.

I hope you will write or call me soon to suggest a time when we might meet to discuss your current and future needs and how I might serve them. Thank you in advance for your time.

Sincerely yours,

Marirosa N. Sartini

MARIROSA N. SARTINI

1110½ Hay Street, Fayetteville, NC 28305   •   preppub@aol.com   •   (910) 483-6611

OBJECTIVE

I want to contribute to an organization that can use a talented young professional with excellent communication and public relations skills along with experience in teaching, marketing, and television production/broadcasting.

EDUCATION

Master of Arts degree, Broadcasting in Journalism, Clarkson University, Potsdam, NY, 2003.
• Was involved in extracurricular activities which involved extensive public speaking.
Bachelor of Science degree with a major in Broadcasting, Hofstra University, Hempstead, NY, 2000. Was an active member of the Public Relations Club.

EXPERIENCE

TELEVISION PRODUCER and **CO-HOST**. WPIX-TV of Warner Brothers, New York, NY (2003-present). After earning my Master's degree in Broadcasting in Journalism, became marketing manager and producer of two shows: an auction show broadcast four hours a week which auctions a variety of products and a cultural magazine show three times a week.
• Increased overall earnings of the channel through innovative marketing, and also increased the ratings of the two shows I produce.

ASSISTANT PROFESSOR FOR TV PRODUCTION. Clarkson University, Potsdam, NY (2002-03). At this prominent university where I earned my Master's degree, taught TV Production I and II as well as a Communications and Law course given to seniors.
• Also worked in my spare time as a model and actor on TV commercials under contract with the Phillip Maxwell's Modeling Agency; appeared in commercials for Pepsi, Hersey Milk Chocolate, and the Gap; assisted in producing fashion shows. Equipped the university's television studio and editing rooms with cameras and Betacam systems.

ASSISTANT PRODUCER and **MARKETING ASSISTANT**. The Fun-Time Children's Show, Viacom Productions, Hempstead, NY (1999-02). Played a key role in producing this enormously popular four-hour children's show broadcast every weekend with footage from 23 countries in South and Central America; acted as video coordinator for shows in Peru, Chile, Argentina, Costa Rica, Venezuela, and the U.S.
• Produced different segments for guest artists from South America.
• Created a new way to market the television show by giving concert tours and promotional items which increased the popularity and earnings of the program and which also led to a PBS pilot show for the American version of Fun-Time.

NEWS REPORTER/TELEVISION PRODUCER. WGOL-TV, Napleston Broadcasting, Channel 15, Hempstead, NY (1997-99). Worked in this job while earning my Bachelor of Science in Broadcasting. Performed research, reporting, and production for a half-hour magazine.

NEWS REPORTER. Hempstead Herald, Hempstead, NY (1997). Wrote feature stories, edited copy, and designed page layout.

PRODUCTION ASSISTANT. WWGR-TV, Hempstead, NY (1996). Was recruited for a highly competitive internship at a major television studio. Worked as a news reporter/researcher for a live talk show program broadcast nightly. Edited copy for future shows.

PERSONAL

Achievements include winning the Hempstead golf championship during the last three years. Skilled in preparing TV, radio, and film scripts and advertising storyboards.

Date

Exact Name of Person
Title or Position
Name of Company
Address (no., street)
Address (city, state, zip)

**TELEVISION PRODUCTION
ASSISTANT**

for a Colorado television
station

Dear Exact Name of Person: (or Dear Sir or Madam if answering a blind ad.)

I would appreciate an opportunity to talk with you soon about how I could contribute to your organization through my excellent communication and organizational skills as well as through my experience in television production, reporting, broadcasting, and communication skills.

As you will see from my resume, I have just received a bachelor's degree in broadcasting and journalism from Metropolitan State College in Colorado. I completed courses in media studies, broadcast writing, and television and radio production. I have also completed two internships at WPDP 102.2 FM and Virtual Productions as a production assistant. I was given credit for increasing ratings of the two shows I produced. I also contributed to the station's profitability through the innovative marketing strategies that I implemented.

My organizational and management skills have been refined through my experience as a television production assistant at Metro Broadcasting Inc. I have had the opportunity to produce a studio recruitment video and I have edited reading scripts for popular daily shows such as Teen Mania, and Blues Clues.

I feel certain you would find me to be a motivated and enthusiastic professional who could contribute much to your organization through my strong organizational and management skills. I can provide strong personal and professional references.

I hope you will write or call me soon to suggest a time when we might meet to discuss your current and future needs and how I might serve them. Thank you in advance for your time.

Sincerely yours,

Harold G. Coleman

Alternate last paragraph:
I hope you will welcome my call soon to arrange a brief meeting at your convenience to discuss your current and future needs and how I might serve them. Thank you in advance for your time.

HAROLD G. COLEMAN

1110½ Hay Street, Fayetteville, NC 28305   •   preppub@aol.com   •   (910) 483-6611

OBJECTIVE   To obtain a challenging position in television production utilizing skills my excellent communication and organizational skills as well as my experience in television production, reporting, broadcasting, and communication skills.

EDUCATION   **B.A. in Broadcasting and Journalism,** Metropolitan State College, Denver, CO, 2003. Certificate, Commercial Broadcasting (FCC License), Community College of Denver, CO, 2001.

EXPERIENCE   **TELEVISION PRODUCTION ASSISTANT.** KCNC-TV of Metro Broadcasting, Inc., Colorado Springs, CO (2003-present). Produce a video clip used by the studio for recruiting purposes.
- Assist Senior Producer with contract negotiations. Personally oversee the processing, printing, and editing videos and reading scripts used for daily shows.

AUDIOVISUAL TECHNICIAN INTERNSHIP. Virtual Productions, Denver, CO (2003). Completed an internship as an Audio-Visual Technician for a locally-owned video technology company.
- Installed equipment for meetings, conferences, and small- to medium-sized events.
- Operated television cameras and associated equipment to shoot studio or remote scenes for production of programs or commercials.
- Assisted in stage lighting and assisted in the setup and tear down of equipment.
- Operated audio mixer console videotaping, slide projections, and other related equipment.

BROADCAST PRODUCTION INTERN. WPDP 102.2 FM of Axbury Broadcasting Network, Colorado Springs, CO (2002-03). Used my communication skills to increase ratings by 26%.
- Developed marketing plans and strategies to approach clients.
- Assisted the news director of this National Public Radio Station by rewriting local stories which had appeared the newsletter, *City News.*
- Played traditional and contemporary jazz music as well as announcing news which effected residents within the region.

BROADCAST PRODUCTION ASSISTANT. WEJR-AM, Humphries Broadcasting, Denver, CO (2000-02). Edited and announced scripts for daily community events.
- Supervised the performance of personnel in a radio communication department which provided support to the Directorate of Information Management.

RADIO ANNOUNCER. News Radio 85-KOA, Denver, CO (1998-2000). Performed on-air commercial readings and live broadcasting promotions; Participated all station projects.
- Raised money and collected food baskets for needy families through radio announcements for several community projects. Enhanced the station's public image through my charismatic motivational skills. Improved market share ratings by 19%.

PRODUCTION ASSISTANT. WCXV AM/FM 100, Denver, CO (1997-1998). Supervised the installation, operation, and maintenance on two-way radio-teletype systems.
- Selected sites, established training programs, and checked operational logs for accuracy and detail. Edited copy for radio comedy skits and broadcast promotions.

PERSONAL   Vice President of the Communication Club at Metropolitan State. Volunteer for the United Way of Denver since 1997. Outstanding references upon request.

Date

Exact Name of Person
Title or Position
Name of Company
Address (no., street)
Address (city, state, zip)

TRAFFIC MANAGER
for a television station's
traffic department

Dear Exact Name of Person: (or Dear Sir or Madam if answering a blind ad.)

I would appreciate an opportunity to talk with you in person to show you how my skills in broadcast traffic management could benefit you and your organization.

As you will see from my resume, I have recently excelled as a traffic manager in "turning around" an operation that was losing thousands of dollars a year due to traffic errors. I have used my planning, organizing, and administrative abilities to reduce errors to zero! I have established all programming files, on-line formats, traffic procedures, and inventory systems.

I hope you will welcome my call soon to arrange a brief meeting at your convenience to discuss your current and future needs and how I might serve them. Thank you in advance for your time.

Sincerely yours,

Kindrell D. Hartwell

Alternate last paragraph:
I hope you will call or write me soon to suggest a time convenient for us to meet and discuss your current and future needs and how I might serve them. Thank you in advance for your time.

KINDRELL D. HARTWELL

1110½ Hay Street, Fayetteville, NC 28305 • preppub@aol.com • (910) 483-6611

OBJECTIVE

To contribute to an organization that can use an experienced manager and communicator who offers a proven "track record" of improving operations and increasing overall profitability.

COMPUTER KNOWLEDGE

- Install, set up, configure, and maintain IBM System 34, 36, and other PCs.
- Have expertise with Microsoft Word, Excel, and PageMaker.
- Can operate/troubleshoot broadcasting hardware/software.

EXPERIENCE

TRAFFIC MANAGER. WKPO TV 15, Newark, NJ (2003-present). Took over the management of a traffic department losing thousands of dollars a year due to traffic errors, and reduced errors to zero while establishing all programming files, on-line formats, traffic procedures, and inventory systems.

- Supervise traffic personnel and operations; produce daily log; plan schedules; coordinate program information. Enter/maintain contracts and provide instruction for commercial, promotional, and public service announcements.
- Maintain the commercial inventory system. Am respected for my outstanding administrative abilities in organizing information and maintaining records.

DATA PROCESSING MANAGER. A & Q Industries, Newark, NJ (2001-2003). Supervised office personnel and managed computer operations related to accounts payable, accounts receivable, payroll, billing, and purchasing.

- Implemented all hardware/software changes. Hired, trained, and evaluated personnel.
- Made major contributions to the company's increased profitability: 2002 was the first profitable year in more than 10 years!
- Stepped into a job which had been vacant for some time and soon was credited with "bringing order out of chaos." Saved the company from numerous $50-an-hour repair calls through my technical ability to install hardware and software updates.

DATA PROCESSING OPERATIONS SUPERVISOR and **TRAINING MANAGER.** Sears and Roebuck, Newark, NJ (1998-2000). Supervised personnel operating a retail outlet installment plan including billing, reporting, and customer relations activities.

- Operated/maintained equipment including a printer and six terminals.
- Trained and supervised three clerical employees.
- Led my department to achieve the highest collection rates among all departments.

COMPUTER SYSTEMS OPERATOR. White & Hastings Enterprises, Blackwood, NJ (1997-1998). Monitored all inventory control activity while operating an IBM System 34 for 32 stores with 16 on-line terminals and six printers.

- Resolved user/system problems; processed and maintained files/reports.
- Audited inventory control and quality control data.
- Maintained an exceptionally high 96% data accuracy rate.
- Earned rapid promotion; became Merchandise Manager for 32 stores.

TRAINING & EDUCATION

- Completed IBM corporate training in System 36 management, Newark, NJ.
- Studied computer technology and accounting/business, Camden County College, Blackwood, NJ.

PERSONAL

Am a creative professional. Excel in managing operations/time/people.

PART THREE

APPLYING FOR FEDERAL GOVERNMENT POSITIONS
SAMPLE APPLICATION FOR PUBLIC AFFAIRS OFFICER

The OF 612

This section is intended to provide some guidance to those who seek jobs in the federal government. There are numerous websites which will help you identify "position vacancy announcements" pertaining to federal job openings, and those vacancy announcements usually give you optional ways to apply for the particular positions which interest you. One traditional application is the Optional Form (OF) 612, and a sample 612 is shown on the following pages. As you will see, the OF 612 is usually a multi-page document.

KSAs

As part of the application process for federal jobs, you are sometimes asked to submit written narrative statements pertaining to specific knowledge, skills, or abilities. These narrative statements are often referred to as "KSAs" (standing for "Knowledge, Skills, Abilities"), and those KSAs are often sought because it is important to assess your precise knowledge, skills, or abilities in key job performance areas in order to assess your competence for the particular federal vacancy. The 612 which is shown on the following pages is followed by sample KSAs. PREP's book "Government Job Applications & Federal Resumes" contains numerous samples of federal applications and KSAs.

SF 171

Sometimes you are invited to apply for federal jobs with another type of application called the Standard Form (SF) 171. The 171 is also a multi-page document, much like the 612. If you wish to see samples of the 171, please consult PREP's book entitled "Government Job Applications & Federal Resumes." It is outside the scope of this book to show multiple federal applications.

Resumix and federal resumes

Some position vacancy announcements give you an option of applying for the position with a federal resume, sometimes called a "Resumix." A federal resume or Resumix differs from the traditional "civilian" resume. On a federal resume, you are asked to provide information about your salary history and supervisors' names, addresses, and phone numbers in addition to other private information not requested by civilian employers at the resume stage. It is outside the scope of this book to show samples of the Resumix or federal resumes. However, a very useful book which shows federal resumes in detail is PREP's book "Resumix and Federal Resumes."

Job title in announcement: Public Affairs Officer

Grade(s) applied for: GS-1035-11/12

Announcement number: 00-65I

4. **Last Name**   **First and Middle Name**
   JARVIS   LOUISE

5. **Social Security Number**
   000-00-0000

6. **Mailing Address**
   1110 1/2 Hay Street

City	**State**	**Zip Code**
Fayetteville	NC	28305

7. **Phone Numbers (include area codes)**
   Home: (910) 483-6111
   Work: (910) 483-2439
   E-mail: PREPPub@aol.com

WORK EXPERIENCE

8. See attached continuation sheets.

PUBLIC AFFAIRS OFFICER

From: 2/03
To: Present
Salary: E7
Hours per week: 40+
Employer's Name and Address: Department of Defense, Oregon Division, 4874 Hollingdale Circle, Portland, OR 46464
Supervisor's Name and Phone Number: Gene Boden, phone: 910-483-6611

Overview of responsibilities:
Oversee day-to-day administrative support while handling all phases of short, medium, and long-range planning. Apply strong computer skills while preparing a wide range of written materials. Brief pilots and crew members.

Earning degree from University of Portland in my spare time:
In an attempt to advance my knowledge as well as my professional skills, I am taking courses in my leisure time which will lead to an M.A. in Government. This degree is intended to make me an even more astute executive within the federal government system.

Public Relations responsibilities:
In this 98-person unit, I am one of only three full-timers, so I am a key point of contact with the outside world, and I function as the organization's "voice and face" to the outside world as needed. For example, on July 27, 2004, our organization was mobilized during a prison guard strike, which was a highly visible statewide event. I was available for communication with outside organizations during this statewide emergency. The correctional officers went back to work on July 28 and we were proud that the Oregon Division Department of Defense could assist the public.

Skill in developing written materials:
My skills in developing concise and informative written materials is a major focus in assignment. I write a monthly column for the unit newsletter which is directed at both junior and senior personnel. Prepare memoranda on a daily basis which are disseminated to both higher echelon headquarters and to lower echelon units. Develop ideas for changes and improvement to unit training procedures and submit them to the commanding officer, training officer, and headquarters. Write and submit written requests for the use of training areas and which are then forwarded to a wide variety of personnel including civilians. Write After Action Review (AAR) reports at the conclusion of each mission.

Skill in analyzing conflicting data, drawing conclusions, and making recommendations:
Receive information simultaneously from various sources which include multiple aircraft and ground troops communicating by radio. Quickly analyze the situation and then make recommendations on the appropriate course of action to fit the circumstances. These recommendations may be made to the commanding officer or directly to the troops or air crews.

Verbal communication skills and ability to present briefings:
Brief passengers and air crews on mission requirements and objectives.

Skill in presenting points of view tailored to the audience:
Deal with senior and subordinates on a daily basis and these people range from junior enlisted personnel to senior military executives. As the single point of contact for the unit, I must tailor my responses to the individuals professional and educational background. Based on my ability to deal with such a wide range of people, I have quickly developed a reputation as a "consensus builder."

PUBLIC AFFAIRS SPECIALIST (Volunteer)
From: 11/02
To: 01/03
Salary: NA
Hours per week: 5 hours a week
Employer's Name and Address: NA
Supervisor's Name and Phone Number: NA

Overview of responsibilities:
On my own initiative, have taken the opportunity to participate in community and church organizations where my skills have been primarily in the area of public affairs. Through these volunteer and civic leadership positions, have greatly refined my skills related to public affairs and public relations.

As a **Candidate for State Representative** in 2003, wrote press releases, was interviewed by the press, and made numerous public speeches. Gained extensive public relations skills in the process. Wrote and distributed press releases. Was interviewed on the phone and in person by radio, tv, and print media. Prepared and delivered speeches ranging from a few minutes in length to 45 minutes in length. Gained experience in responding to negativity. For example, on one occasion while I was delivering a speech a retirement center, I responded with politeness and firmness and tact to an elderly lady who was shouting accusations. I was later commended for my poise by members of the audience. I delivered dozens of speeches throughout the Portland area.

As **Chairman of the Public Relations Committee** for my church, St. Peter's Cathedral in Portland in 2002, I applied my excellent communication and interpersonal skills. Assumed this position at a time when we had a new church building, and I wrote and submitted press releases to the media about the new church and related events included contests. Presided over meetings of a small committee, and trained committee members in various aspects of public relations.

As **Treasurer** of the local chapter of the Portland Waterfront Committee, I demonstrated my public relations skills in the process of providing leadership in establishing a new scholarship fund. The first $1,000 scholarship was awarded in 2002.

FLIGHT COORDINATOR/RELOCATION MANAGER

From: 2/99
To: 9/02
Salary: SFC/E-7
Hours per week: 40+
Employer's Name and Address: Lockheed Martin Support Systems, Inc., 4885 Ashbrook, Lane, Portland, OR, 46464
Supervisor's Name and Phone Number: Richard Pringle, 254-464-8179

Overview of responsibilities:
Duties include receiving, processing, and coordinating support for flight mission request for Lockheed Martin Support Systems. Process Logistics Flight Records (LFR) and update air craft status based on maintenance requirements and air crew availability. Additional responsibilities as unit supply and property book manager as well as safety manager.

Earlier with this unit as a Database Manager, handled basically the same duties except for preparing and submitting pay documents for all assigned personnel. Input accountable data into the Budget Accounting Database System.

Skill in developing written materials:
Applied written skills while processing Mission Assignment Reports in accordance with standard operating procedures.

Skill in analyzing conflicting data, drawing conclusions, and making recommendations:
Gained skill in analyzing conflicting data, making decisions, and advising others on recommended courses of action as a **dispatcher.** While directing air and ground traffic, I de-conflicted problems which often occurred due to the different policies and procedures of the various military services which might be participating in joint missions or exercises. Officially cited for my "excellent intuitive judgment," was highly regarded as a subject matter expert who could be counted on to be resourceful in ensuring success. Maintained complete and accurate records of equipment and accounts and was called on to analyze any problem areas in supply and logistics, safety, or administrative issues and make recommendations on improvements. Prepared Mission Assignment Reports which called for analyzing unit activities, developing conclusions as to the success or problems encountered on the mission, and presented recommendations based on my analysis of each situation.

Verbal communication skills and ability to present briefings:
Was highly regarded for my ability to motivate others and encourage them to follow my example of dedication to excellence in all areas of operations. Was known for my ability to share my knowledge with subordinates and peers and to effectively organize and present new material.

Ability to deal with a wide range of people and represent viewpoints through print and broadcast media:
During one temporary assignment when the organization was deployed to Korea and when the Public Affairs Officer was unavailable, **represented the Lockheed Support**

....PUBLIC AFFAIRS
OFFICER
CONTINUED

You can often apply for a federal government job with a 612, such as you see on these pages, or with a 171, or with a federal resume.

Systems as the Acting Public Affairs Officer. Applied my knowledge and expertise of the Lockheed Support Systems mission while meeting with two local TV crews (one CNN and one CBS affiliate) to brief media. Was the individual responsible for planning, developing implementing, and evaluating public affairs efforts if the need arose while I was Acting Public Affairs Officer. Became acquainted with the tasks involved in formulating long-range plans and developing policy aimed at enhancing public understanding, support , and acceptance of Lockheed Support Systems programs and activities. Played a role in developing and writing information materials designed to reach audiences through various media such as wire service, radio, television, and newspaper. Learned to target and service media markets with print, photographic, and electronic materials. Responded to media re quests for information of both a routine and controversial nature. Provided advice in support of polices and programs of interest to internal audiences. Analyzed, coordinated, and updated assigned personnel, Established and maintained close working relations with officials of various civic, media, veterans, and community groups as well as with state officials. Developed insight into the budget process utilized to insure that funding requirements were identified and adequate funds requested and available.

Knowledge of the Lockheed Martin Support Systems organization and mission:
In an administrative position, must be aware of the Lockheed's organization, mission, policies, and procedures in order to ensure mission support actions are carried out in a timely and thorough manner. This knowledge was most evident as I interacted with personnel from the general staff down to the individual enlisted members of the unit. I determined the appropriate type of airlift for each unit and for each mission based on my knowledge of government standards.

Knowledge of applicable of the Lockheed Martin Support Systems, Departments of the Airlift Support policies and directives:
As a Dispatcher with a wide range of support duties related to supply, logistics, safety, and administration, I am known for my competence and thorough knowledge. While maintaining flight, supply, and pay records for all assigned personnel, input data into the Budget Accounting Database System according to all high headquarters and governing agencies and organizations. I developed a reputation as somewhat of a "country lawyer" on Lockheed Martin and Department Of Defense polices, directives and regulations. Particularly in regard to Operational Support Airlift (OSA) and was often asked to act as a consultant and interpret my views of conflicting regulations and policies by the Operational Airlift Support Command.

Public Relations Duties During Air Shows:
Annually Lockheed Martin sponsors an air show during the summer at Deerfield Point, which is attended by approximately 100,000 people. I was involved in communicating with the public during the air show demonstrations, and I provide formal tours of aircraft to the public.

Honors and accomplishments earned during this period:
* Was described on official performance reports as "highly motivated, dedicated, and extremely competent" as well as for "integrity beyond reproach."
* Served as the Acting Public Affairs Officer during the deployment of an Army aviation unit to Korea. During "Operation Upward Bound," interacted with local television crews and reporters to present the Army's objectives and missions to the local media representatives.

TELECOMMUNICATIONS MANAGER
From: 5/96
To: 12/98
Salary: $38,000-42,000 annual
Hours per week: 40
Employer's Name and Address: Portland International Airport, 76445 Hanahan Blvd, Portland, OR 44794
Supervisor's Name and Phone Number: Veronica Miller, phone unknown

Overview of responsibilities:
Advanced to a supervisory role overseeing and personally performing the installation and operation of airfield telephones and wire communications systems, switchboards, small switching systems, FM radio, and associated COMSEC (communications security) equipment. Performed preventive and unit-level maintenance checks on assigned equipment as well as on assigned vehicles and power generation equipment. Assigned personnel to meet workload demands.

....PUBLIC AFFAIRS
OFFICER
CONTINUED

Skill in analyzing conflicting data, drawing conclusions, determining strategic options, and making recommendations:
On numerous occasions there were conflicting simultaneous nets promulgated by various radios, and I had to make decisions related to conflicting data. I advised executives of my findings after I analyzed conflicting data, drew conclusions, and made recommendations.

Verbal communication skills and ability to present briefings:
As a Supervisor, I was speaking routinely and frequently on the radio, and my voice was heard by between 50 to 300 people as I spoke about flight matters, weather, and situation reports. I greatly improved my verbal skills during this process and learned to clearly enunciate and articulate my point of view in a way that was understandable.

Knowledge of the Portland International Airport organization and mission:
Refined my knowledge of the Portland International Airport organization and mission.

Honors and accomplishments earned during this period:
* Was praised in an official performance evaluation as one who" establishes and enforces firm, sound management practices" and "a hard-working individual who takes charge and makes positive things happen."

RECOVERY OPERATIONS OFFICER (SSG)
From: 5/95
To: 3/96
Salary: 2 LT
Hours per week: 40
Employer's Name and Address: Delta Company Recovery Division, 359th Regiment, Ft. Stewart, GA 38116
Supervisor's Name and Phone Number: 2 LT Otis Nathaniel, phone unknown

Overview of responsibilities:
Managed the training and combat efficiency of the Rescue and Recovery Center and acted as Rescue Operations Officer (second in command) in his absence. Handled a wide range of tasks including overseeing training, dining facilities, and energy conservation activities.

Verbal communication skills and ability to present briefings:
As the resident manager for a technical training center, applied outstanding communication skills and presented numerous briefings on the status and capabilities of the center's systems.

Knowledge of the Delta Company Recovery Division organization and mission:
Gained knowledge of the organization and missions of the **Delta Company Recovery Division** through this experience as well as of all applicable military polices and directives.

BUSINESS MANAGER/LEASE MANAGER/SALES REPRESENTATIVE

From: 3/85

To: 2/95

Salary: $40,000 - $60,000

Hours per week: 40-60

Employer's Name and Address: Various automobile dealerships in Oregon

Supervisor's Name and Phone Number: NA

Overview of responsibilities:

Advanced to Business Manager at Coxx Chrysler-Plymouth, Eugene, OR; and Lease Manager at Rick Hendrix Jeep, Portland, OR; after earlier successes as a Sales Representative at Westside Ford, West Salem, OR; and Rick Hendrix Ford, Portland, OR.

While in sales, I negotiated extensively in making large deals for government contracts related to fleets of vehicles. Routinely addressed groups of various sizes, including town councils, who made decisions on expenditures and purchases. My strong public relations skills and communication skills were the keys on numerous occasions to establishing corporate and government accounts.

As Business Manager, functioned as Public Relations Manager for the dealership. Supervised sales staffs of up to 12 people. Oversaw advertising and the development of advertising materials for print, TV, and radio.

As a Salesman at Rick Hendrix Ford, I functioned as Air Show Coordinator for Lockheed Martin Support Systems, Inc. Handled public relations and promoted the air show through contests.

During my years in the car business, I was involved in numerous car shows. On many occasions, I demonstrated my resourcefulness while sponsoring contests, sponsoring raffles, and initiating numerous promotions.

9.   May we contact your current supervisor? **YES**

EDUCATION

10.   Highest level completed - **B.S.**
11.   Last High School or GED. Give the school's name, city, ZIP Code and year diploma or
        GED earned.
        Year received: 1981. Brennan High School, Portland, Oregon, 45528.
12.   Colleges and universities attended. Do not attach a copy of your transcript unless requested.

Name	Total Credits Earned	Major(s)	Degree	Year
Portland State University	130	Industrial Technology	B.S.	1999
University of Portland Division of Continuing Education	8	Government	Masters Anticipated	2005

OTHER QUALIFICATIONS

13.   **Job-related training** courses. **Job-related skills** (other languages, computer software/hardware, tools, machinery, typing, speed, etc.) **Job-related** certificates and licenses. Job-related honors, awards, and special accomplishments, publications, memberships in professional/honor societies, leadership activities, public speaking, and performance awards). Give dates, but do not send documents unless requested.

Graduate-level training:

Completed a Graduate level courses in Russian Foreign Policy and Post-Cold War Security Studies, University of Portland's Division of Continuing Education, Portland, OR, fall 1999.

Training related to Department of Defense organization and mission as well as Department of the Army policies and directives:
Completed the Advanced Non Commissioned Officer Course (ANCOC) and Basic Non Commissioned Officer Course (BNCOC) for Aviation Operations at Ft. Carson, CO. Completed the Aviation Safety Course at the Eastern Army Aviation Training Site (EAATS) at Ft. Eustis, VA. Completed the Battle Focused Instructor Training Course (BFITC) at Camp Macomb and received the "H" designator as a Army Instructor. Extensive on-the-job training through 2 years of full-time work experience with the Department of Defense.

Computer training:
Completed computer classes sponsored by the Oregon Division of the Department Of Defense for Microsoft Word, Excel, and Access.

Skills in public speaking:
As a candidate for State Representative in 2003, applied my written and verbal communication as well as my analytical skills writing press releases, being interviewed by members of the press, and making public speeches.

Served as the Chairman of the Public Relations Committee for my church, St. Peter's Cathedral in Portland, 2002.

Memberships and affiliations:
Member, Political Scientists Associate of Portland
St. Peter's Cathedral, Portland Oregon
Treasurer, local chapter of Portland Waterfront Committee, 2002-present
- Took the initiative in establishing a scholarship fund. The first $1,000 scholarship was awarded in 2002.

Computer skills:
Highly proficient in using the Microsoft Office Suite including Word, Excel, PowerPoint, Access.

GENERAL
14. Are you a U.S. citizen? **YES**
15. Do you claim veterans' preference? **NO**
16. Were you ever a Federal civilian employee? **NO**
17. Are you eligible for reinstatement based on career or career-conditional Federal status? **NO**

APPLICANT CERTIFICATION
18. I certify that, to the best of my knowledge and belief, all of the information on and attached to this application is true, correct, complete and made in good faith. I understand that false or fraudulent information on or attached to this application may be grounds for not hiring me or for firing me after I begin work, and may be punishable by a fine or imprisonment. I understand that any information I give may be investigated.

SIGNATURE

          DATE SIGNED

LOUISE JARVIS

QUALITY RANKING FACTOR #1: Skill in developing written materials to present concepts, ideas, or positions in a clear and logical manner to achieve an understanding by all types of audiences.

I am always seeking to refine my written communication skills and in my spare time I am pursuing a Master's degree from University of Portland Division of Continuing Education. The graduate courses I have taken require an exceptionally strong ability to communicate in writing through the preparation of insightful reports and papers designed to communicate ideas, concepts, and positions in a clear and logical manner..

As a **Public Affairs Officer** since 2/03, I oversee day-to-day administrative support while handling all phases of short, medium, and long-range planning. Apply strong computer skills while preparing a wide range of written materials. Brief pilots and crew members. My skills in developing concise and informative written materials is a major focus in assignment. I write a monthly column for the unit newsletter which is directed at both junior and senior personnel. Prepare memoranda on a daily basis which are disseminated to both higher echelon headquarters and to lower echelon units. Develop ideas for changes and improvement to unit training procedures and submit them to the commanding officer, training officer, and headquarters. Write and submit written requests for the use of training areas and which are then forwarded to a wide variety of personnel including civilians. Write After Action Review (AAR) reports at the conclusion of each mission.

In civilian volunteer activities as a **Public Affairs Specialist**, I have taken the opportunity to participate in community and church organizations where I refined my skill in developing written materials to present concepts, ideas, or positions in a clear and logical manner:
*   As a **candidate for State Representative** in 2003, I wrote press releases, was interviewed by the press, and made numerous public speeches. Gained extensive public relations skills in the process. Wrote and distributed press releases. Was interviewed on the phone and in person by radio, TV, and print media. Prepared and delivered speeches ranging from a few minutes in length to 45 minutes in length. Gained experience in responding to negativity. For example, on one occasion while I was delivering a speech at a retirement center, I responded with politeness and firmness and tact to an elderly lady who was shouting accusations. I was later commended for my poise by members of the audience. I delivered dozens of speeches throughout the Portland area.
*   As **Chairman of the Public Relations Committee** for my church, St. Peter's Cathedral in 2002, I applied my excellent communication and interpersonal skills. Assumed this position at a time when we had a new church building, and I wrote and submitted press releases to the media about the new church and related events included contests. Presided over meetings of a small committee, and trained committee members in various aspects of public relations.
*   As **Treasurer** of the local chapter of the Portland Waterfront Committee, I demonstrated my public relations skills in the process of providing leadership in establishing a new scholarship fund. The first $1,000 scholarship was awarded in 2002.

As a **Flight Coordinator/Relocation Manager** from 2/99 to 9/02, my duties included receiving, processing, and coordinating support for flight mission request for Lockheed Martin Support Systems. Process Logistics Flight Records (LFR) and update aircraft status based on maintenance requirements and air crew availability. Carry out additional responsibilities as unit supply and property book manager as well as safety manager. Earlier with this unit as a Database Manager, handled basically the same duties except for preparing and submitting pay documents for all assigned personnel. Input accountable data into the Budget Accounting Database System. Applied written skills while processing Mission Assignment Reports in accordance with standard operating procedures.

Education and Training related to this KSA:
Earned B.S. degree in Industrial Technology and pursuing M.A. in Government from the University of Portland.

QUALITY RANKING FACTOR #2: Skill in drawing appropriate conclusions from conflicting data to include determining the kinds of information that needed and developing new and specific ways of gathering and evaluating data for presenting conclusions and /or recommendations.

In my present position (since 2/03) as a **Public Relations Officer**, I receive information simultaneously from various sources which include multiple aircraft and ground troops communicating by radio. Quickly analyze the situation and then make recommendations on the appropriate course of action to fit the circumstances. These recommendations may be made to the commanding officer or directly to the troops or air crews.

In my previous assignment (2/99 to 9/02) as a **Flight Coordinator/Relocation Manager**, I displayed skill in analyzing conflicting data, making decisions, and advising others on recommended courses of action as a dispatcher. While directing air and ground traffic, I de-conflicted problems which often occurred due to the different policies and procedures of the various military services which might be participating in joint missions or exercises. Officially cited for my "excellent intuitive judgment," was highly regarded as a subject matter expert who could be counted on to be resourceful in ensuring success. Maintained complete and accurate records of equipment and accounts and was called on to analyze any problem areas in supply and logistics, safety, or administrative issues and make recommendations on improvements. Prepared Mission Assignment Reports which called for analyzing unit activities, developing conclusions as to the success or problems encountered on the mission, and presented recommendations based on my analysis of each situation.

As a **Telecommunications Manager** from 5/96 to 12/98, on numerous occasions there were conflicting simultaneous nets promulgated by various radios, and I had to make decisions related to conflicting data. I advised executives of my findings after I analyzed conflicting data, drew conclusions, and made recommendations. As a **Recovery Operations Officer with the Delta Company Recovery Division,** 1995, I continuously applied my ability to draw sound conclusions from conflicting data in an environment in which a wrong conclusion could potentially cost the loss of lives and assets.

Academic and volunteer experiences have also refined my skill in this area:
- In my spare time I am pursuing coursework leading to an M.A. in Government from University of Portland. This degree program is refining my ability to draw appropriate conclusions from conflicting data.
- As a **candidate for State Representative** in 2003, I demonstrated this skill as I wrote press releases, was interviewed by the press, and made numerous public speeches. Gained extensive public relations skills in the process. Wrote and distributed press releases. Was interviewed on the phone and in person by radio, TV, and print media. Prepared and delivered speeches ranging from a few minutes to 45 minutes in length.
- As **Chairman of the Public Relations Committee** for my church, St. Peter's Cathedral demonstrated my skill in drawing appropriate conclusions from conflicting data on and interpersonal skills. Presided over meetings of a small committee.

Education and Training related to this KSA:
Earned B.S. degree in Industrial Technology and pursuing M.A. in Government from the University of Portland.

ABOUT THE EDITOR

Anne McKinney holds an MBA from the Harvard Business School and a BA in English from the University of North Carolina at Chapel Hill. A noted public speaker, writer, and teacher, she is the senior editor for PREP's business and career imprint, which bears her name. Early titles in the Anne McKinney Career Series (now called the Real-Resumes Series) published by PREP include: *Resumes and Cover Letters That Have Worked, Resumes and Cover Letters That Have Worked for Military Professionals, Government Job Applications and Federal Resumes, Cover Letters That Blow Doors Open,* and *Letters for Special Situations.* Her career titles and how-to resume-and-cover-letter books are based on the expertise she has acquired in 20 years of working with job hunters. Her valuable career insights have appeared in publications of the "Wall Street Journal" and other prominent newspapers and magazines.

PREP Publishing Order Form

You may purchase any of our titles from your favorite bookseller! Or send a check or money order or your credit card number for the total amount*, plus $4.00 postage and handling, to PREP, 1110 1/2 Hay Street, Fayetteville, NC 28305. You may also order our titles on our website at www.prep-pub.com and feel free to e-mail us at preppub@aol.com or call 910-483-6611 with your questions or concerns.

Name: _____

Phone #:_____

Address: _____

E-mail address:_____

Payment Type: ☐ Check/Money Order   ☐ Visa   ☐ MasterCard

Credit Card Number: _____ Expiration Date: _____

Put a check beside the items you are ordering:

☐ Free—Packet describing PREP's professional writing and editing services

☐ $16.95—REAL-RESUMES FOR RESTAURANT, FOOD SERVICE & HOTEL JOBS. Anne McKinney, Editor

☐ $16.95—REAL-RESUMES FOR MEDIA, NEWSPAPER, BROADCASTING & PUBLIC AFFAIRS JOBS. Anne McKinney

☐ $16.95—REAL-RESUMES FOR RETAILING, MODELING, FASHION & BEAUTY JOBS. Anne McKinney, Editor

☐ $16.95—REAL-RESUMES FOR HUMAN RESOURCES & PERSONNEL JOBS. Anne McKinney, Editor

☐ $16.95—REAL-RESUMES FOR MANUFACTURING JOBS. Anne McKinney, Editor

☐ $16.95—REAL-RESUMES FOR AVIATION & TRAVEL JOBS. Anne McKinney, Editor

☐ $16.95—REAL-RESUMES FOR POLICE, LAW ENFORCEMENT & SECURITY JOBS. Anne McKinney, Editor

☐ $16.95—REAL-RESUMES FOR SOCIAL WORK & COUNSELING JOBS. Anne McKinney, Editor

☐ $16.95—REAL-RESUMES FOR CONSTRUCTION JOBS. Anne McKinney, Editor

☐ $16.95—REAL-RESUMES FOR FINANCIAL JOBS. Anne McKinney, Editor

☐ $16.95—REAL-RESUMES FOR COMPUTER JOBS. Anne McKinney, Editor

☐ $16.95—REAL-RESUMES FOR MEDICAL JOBS. Anne McKinney, Editor

☐ $16.95—REAL-RESUMES FOR TEACHERS. Anne McKinney, Editor

☐ $16.95—REAL-RESUMES FOR CAREER CHANGERS. Anne McKinney, Editor

☐ $16.95—REAL-RESUMES FOR STUDENTS. Anne McKinney, Editor

☐ $16.95—REAL-RESUMES FOR SALES. Anne McKinney, Editor

☐ $16.95—REAL ESSAYS FOR COLLEGE AND GRAD SCHOOL. Anne McKinney, Editor

☐ $25.00—RESUMES AND COVER LETTERS THAT HAVE WORKED. McKinney. Editor

☐ $25.00—RESUMES AND COVER LETTERS THAT HAVE WORKED FOR MILITARY PROFESSIONALS. McKinney, Ed.

☐ $25.00—RESUMES AND COVER LETTERS FOR MANAGERS. McKinney, Editor

☐ $25.00—GOVERNMENT JOB APPLICATIONS AND FEDERAL RESUMES: Federal Resumes, KSAs, Forms 171 and 612, and Postal Applications. McKinney, Editor

☐ $25.00—COVER LETTERS THAT BLOW DOORS OPEN. McKinney, Editor

☐ $25.00—LETTERS FOR SPECIAL SITUATIONS. McKinney, Editor

☐ $16.00—BACK IN TIME. Patty Sleem

☐ $17.00—(trade paperback) SECOND TIME AROUND. Patty Sleem

☐ $25.00—(hardcover) SECOND TIME AROUND. Patty Sleem

☐ $18.00—A GENTLE BREEZE FROM GOSSAMER WINGS. Gordon Beld

☐ $18.00—BIBLE STORIES FROM THE OLD TESTAMENT. Katherine Whaley

☐ $14.95—WHAT THE BIBLE SAYS ABOUT... *Words that can lead to success and happiness* (large print edition) Patty Sleem

_____ **TOTAL ORDERED**

_____ **(add $4.00 for shipping and handling)**

_____ **TOTAL INCLUDING SHIPPING**

PREP offers volume discounts on large orders. Call us at (910) 483-6611 for more information.

Would you like to explore the possibility of having PREP's writing
team create a resume for you similar to the ones in this book?

For a brief free consultation, call 910-483-6611
or send $4.00 to receive our Job Change Packet to
PREP, 1110 1/2 Hay Street, Fayetteville, NC 28305. Visit our
website to find valuable career resources: www.prep-pub.com!

QUESTIONS OR COMMENTS? E-MAIL US AT PREPPUB@AOL.COM

www.ingramcontent.com/pod-product-compliance
Lightning Source LLC
Chambersburg PA
CBHW081445170526
45166CB00008B/2317